DOVER · THRIFT · EDITIONS

Great Speeches of the Twentieth Century

Edited by
Bob Blaisdell

DOVER PUBLICATIONS, INC.
Mineola, New York

DOVER THRIFT EDITIONS

GENERAL EDITOR: MARY CAROLYN WALDREP
EDITOR OF THIS VOLUME: JANET BAINE KOPITO

Copyright

Bibliographical Note

Great Speeches of the Twentieth Century is a new compilation, first published by Dover Publications, Inc., in 2011. An Introduction has been written specially for the Dover edition by Bob Blaisdell, who has also prepared a note for each speech. Minor inconsistencies and other style vagaries derive from the original sources and have been retained for the sake of authenticity.

Library of Congress Cataloging-in-Publication Data

Great speeches of the twentieth century
    p. cm.
   "Great Speeches of the Twentieth Century is a new compilation, first published by Dover Publications, Inc., in 2011. An Introduction has been written specially for the Dover edition by Bob Blaisdell, who has also prepared a note for each speech."—T.p. verso.
  ISBN-13: 978-0-486-47467-0
  ISBN-10: 0-486-47467-4
 1. Speeches, addresses, etc.   I. Blaisdell, Robert.
  PN6121.G74 2011
  808.85—dc22

                                                 2011042826

Manufactured in the United States by Courier Corporation
47467404   2014
www.doverpublications.com

Introduction to the Dover Edition

These are speeches of politics and peace, commemoration and tolerance, calls for freedom of speech and cries for independence, with only an occasional rallying to arms. In these outpourings we can witness a shorthand history of the political movements, wars, and social progress of the twentieth century. While there are so many varieties of speeches with such varying purposes, the speakers are necessarily famous in themselves or as participants in burgeoning movements, historical events, or crises.

Early in the century, for instance, we hear president of the United States Theodore Roosevelt's ecstasy over the Grand Canyon and the treasures of nature ("In the Grand Canyon, Arizona has a natural wonder which, so far as I know, is, in kind, absolutely unparalleled throughout the rest of the world. I want to ask you to do one thing in connection with it, in your own interest and in the interest of the country—to keep this great wonder of nature as it now is").

In the 1920s, the persecuted women's rights advocate Margaret Sanger argues for a woman's right to birth control ("We claim that woman should have the right over her own body and to say if she shall or if she shall not be a mother, as she sees fit. We further claim that the first right of a child is to be desired. While the second right is that it should be conceived in love, and the third, that it should have a heritage of sound health"), and in the last decade of the twentieth century we hear, at President Clinton's National Prayer Breakfast, the Nobel Peace Prize winner Mother Teresa of Calcutta ruing the prevalence of abortion: "I feel that the greatest destroyer of peace today is abortion, because it is a war against the child—a direct killing of the innocent child—murder by the mother herself. And if we accept that a mother can kill her own child, how can we tell other people not to kill one another?"

What a contrast, what a historical revolution we see in the United States, when in 1906 the teacher and civil rights advocate Mary Church Terrell bemoans the entrenched racism in Washington, D.C. ("I might go on citing instance after instance to show the variety of ways in which our people are sacrificed on the altar of prejudice in the Capital of the United States and how almost insurmountable are the obstacles which block his path to success"), and a hundred years later Barack Obama responds to his voters' joy at his election as the forty-fourth president of the United States: "If there is anyone out there who still doubts that America is a place where all things are possible, who still wonders if the dream of our founders is alive in our time, who still questions the power of our democracy, tonight is your answer."

In war we meet national leaders, from David Lloyd George and Vladimir Lenin to Winston Churchill and Charles de Gaulle to John F. Kennedy; in grueling, confrontational politics we meet the Communist revolutionary Che Guevara lambasting United States foreign policy ("The Soviet Union and the People's Republic of China have given serious warning to the United States. Not only the peace of the world is in danger in this situation, but also the lives of millions of human beings in this part of Asia are being constantly threatened and subjected to the whim of the United States invader"); and at the Berlin Wall the U.S. President Ronald Reagan upstaging the U.S.S.R.'s general secretary: "We welcome change and openness; for we believe that freedom and security go together, that the advance of human liberty can only strengthen the cause of world peace. There is one sign the Soviets can make that would be unmistakable, that would advance dramatically the cause of freedom and peace. General Secretary Gorbachev, if you seek peace, if you seek prosperity for the Soviet Union and Eastern Europe, if you seek liberalization: Come here to this gate! Mr. Gorbachev, open this gate! Mr. Gorbachev, tear down this wall!"

What makes these speeches outstanding are that for the most part they moved their listeners into moral reflection and action. There is almost no end to the research and discovery possible about the background of the individual speakers and the influence and aftermath of the speeches, and there is also certainly no gainsaying that many more great speeches of the twentieth century are available and ready to be read, heard, and discussed. A good number of the texts in this volume come from the fourth edition of *The World's Great Speeches* edited by Lewis Copeland, Lawrence W. Lamm, and Stephen J. McKenna, and while their edition provides the heart of the speeches, they are not necessarily always complete or definitive. When the speeches have an identifying title in the source materials, that is the title given. I have provided a representative quotation as a subtitle for each selection. Finally, I would like to thank my friends Daniel Evan Weiss and Ann Braybrooks and my parents, Marilyn and Bill Blaisdell, for their suggestions of great and memorable speeches from their lifetimes.

—Bob Blaisdell
New York City 2011

CONTENTS

SOURCES

Roosevelt, Theodore. *A Compilation of the Messages and Speeches of Theodore Roosevelt, 1901–1905*. Edited by Alfred Henry Lewis. Bureau of National Literature and Art, 1906.

Terrell, Mary Church and Gerda Lerner. *Black Women in White America*. New York: Pantheon Books, 1972; http://www.americanrhetoric.com/speeches/marychurchterrellcolored.htm.

Goldman, Emma. Thelizlibrary.org

Montezuma, Carlos (Wassaja). *The Quarterly Journal of the Society of American Indians*. January–April, 1913. 50–55.

Pankhurst, Emmeline. *The World's Greatest Speeches. Fourth Enlarged Edition*. New York: Dover Publications, Inc., 1999. 196–198.

Lloyd George, David. *The World's Greatest Speeches. Fourth Enlarged Edition*. New York: Dover Publications, Inc., 1999. 200–204.

Lenin, Vladimir. *The World's Greatest Speeches. Fourth Enlarged Edition*. New York: Dover Publications, Inc., 1999. 141–143.

Gandhi, Mohandas K. *Mahatma Gandhi: His Life, Writings and Speeches*. Madras: Ganesh & Co., 1921), 403–409; also: *The Communist Manifesto and Other Revolutionary Documents*. New York: Dover Publications, Inc., 2003. 239–242.

Garvey, Marcus. *The Negro World*. September 10, 1921; also: *Selected Writings and Speeches of Marcus Garvey*. New York: Dover Publications, Inc., 2004.

Sanger, Margaret. http://www.nyu.edu/projects/sanger/webedition/app/documents/show.php.sangerDoc=238254.xml

Smith, Alfred E. *The World's Greatest Speeches. Fourth Enlarged Edition*. New York: Dover Publications, Inc., 1999. 408–410.

De Valera, Eamon. *The World's Greatest Speeches. Fourth Enlarged Edition*. New York: Dover Publications, Inc., 1999. 466–468.

Selassie, Haile. http://www.mtholyoke.edu/acad/intrel/selassie.htm

Edward VIII. *The World's Greatest Speeches. Fourth Enlarged Edition*. New York: Dover Publications, Inc., 1999. 732–733.

Churchill, Winston. *The World's Greatest Speeches. Fourth Enlarged Edition*. New York: Dover Publications, Inc., 1999. 431–433.

De Gaulle, Charles. Guardian.co.uk

Roosevelt, Franklin Delano. *The World's Greatest Speeches. Fourth Enlarged Edition*. New York: Dover Publications, Inc., 1999. 517–524.

Patton, Jr., George S. http://www.famous-speeches-and-speech-topics. info/famous-speeches/george-patton-invasion-of-normandy-speech. htm

Du Bois, W. E. B. *The World's Greatest Speeches. Fourth Enlarged Edition*. New York: Dover Publications, Inc., 1999. 818–822.

Nehru, Jawaharlal. *The World's Greatest Speeches. Fourth Enlarged Edition*. New York: Dover Publications, Inc., 1999. 619–620.

Robeson, Paul. *Paul Robeson Speaks: Writing, Speeches, Interviews, 1918–1974*. Edited by Philip S. Foner. New York: Brunner/Mazel Publishers, 1978.

Smith, Margaret Chase. www.mcslibrary.org/program/library/declaration. htm

Roosevelt, Eleanor. *The World's Greatest Speeches. Fourth Enlarged Edition*. New York: Dover Publications, Inc., 1999. 640–641.

Khrushchev, Nikita Sergeyevich. *The World's Greatest Speeches. Fourth Enlarged Edition*. New York: Dover Publications, Inc., 1999. 782–786.

MacArthur, Douglas A. http://americanrhetoric.com/speeches/douglas macarthurthayeraward.html; text version transcribed directly from audio."

Kennedy, John F. *The World's Greatest Speeches. Fourth Enlarged Edition*. New York: Dover Publications, Inc., 1999. 742–748.

King, Jr., Martin Luther. *The World's Greatest Speeches. Fourth Enlarged Edition*. New York: Dover Publications, Inc., 1999. 751–754.

Guevara, [Ernesto] Che. www.marxists.org/archive/guevara/1966/12/11. htm. Also: The Communist Manifesto and Other Revolutionary Writings. New York: Dover Publications, Inc., 2003.

Chavez, Cesar. http://www.americanrhetoric.com/speeches/cesarchavezsp eechmexicanamerican&church.htm

Johnson, Lyndon Baines. *The World's Greatest Speeches. Fourth Enlarged Edition*. New York: Dover Publications, Inc., 1999. 761–764.

Chisolm, Shirley. http://www.famous-speeches-and-speech-topics.info.fa mous-speeches-by-women/shirley-chisholm-speech.htm

Trudeau, Pierre. Privy Council Office (PCO).

Herzog, Chaim. http://www.thespeeches.com/other_greats3.html

Milk, Harvey. Randy Shilts. *The Mayor of Castro Street*. New York: St. Martin's Press, 1982. 359–363.

Le Guin, Ursula K. http://ursulakleguin.com/LeftHandMillsCollege.html

Nader, Ralph. *The Ralph Nader Reader*. New York: Seven Stories Press, 2000. 80–91.

Reagan, Ronald. http://www.americanrhetoric.com/speeches/ronald reaganbrandenburggate.htm

Mandela, Nelson. *The World's Greatest Speeches. Fourth Enlarged Edition*. New York: Dover Publications, Inc., 1999. 883–885.

Havel, Václav. *The World's Greatest Speeches. Fourth Enlarged Edition*. New York: Dover Publications, Inc., 1999. 886–893.

Mother Teresa. http://www.orthodoxytoday.org/articles4/MotherTeresa Abortion.shtml

Aung San Suu Kyi, Daw. *The World's Greatest Speeches. Fourth Enlarged Edition*. New York: Dover Publications, Inc., 1999. 898–902.

Bhutto, Benazir. http://www.famous-speeches-and-speech-topics.info/famous-speeches/benazir-bhutto-speech-male-domination-of-women.htm

Wiesel, Elie. http://www.famous-speeches-and-speech-topics.info/famous-speeches/elie-wiesel-speech-the-perils-of-indifference.htm

Giuliani, Rudolph. http://transcripts.cnn.com/TRANSCRIPTS/0109/11/bn.42.html

Obama, Barack. *The Washington Post*.

Great Speeches of the Twentieth Century

THEODORE ROOSEVELT
The Natural Wonder of the Grand Canyon
("Leave it as it is. You cannot improve upon it.")
Grand Canyon, Arizona Territory
May 6, 1903

As president of the United States (1901–1909), Theodore Roosevelt, a lifelong bird-lover and big-game hunter, created parkland in the United States the size of Western Europe. In the following speech, in the midst of his awe and appreciation of the Grand Canyon, the rough-riding hero of San Juan Hill in the Spanish-American War of 1898, greets some of his former soldiers who hailed from the area. In 1908, Roosevelt put into law the designation of the Grand Canyon as a National Monument. As noted in the speech, irrigation of the arid southwest was one of his other goals. No American president ever accomplished more for the environment.

Mr. Governor, and you, my fellow citizens:

I am glad to be in Arizona today. From Arizona many gallant men came into the regiment which I had the honor to command. Arizona sent men who won glory on fought fields, and men to whom came a glorious and an honorable death fighting for the flag of their country. As long as I live it will be to me an inspiration to have served with Bucky O'Neill. I have met so many comrades whom I prize, for whom I feel respect and admiration and affection, that I shall not particularize among them except to say that there is none for whom I feel all of respect and admiration and affection more than for your Governor.

I have never been in Arizona before. It is one of the regions from which I expect most development through the wise action of the National Congress in passing the irrigation act. The first and biggest experiment now in view under that act is the one that we are trying in Arizona. I look forward to the effects of irrigation partly as applied by and through the government, still more as applied by individuals, and especially by associations of individuals, profiting by the example

1

of the government, and possibly by help from it—I look forward to
the effects of irrigation as being of greater consequence to all this
region of country in the next fifty years than any other material
movement whatsoever.

In the Grand Canyon, Arizona has a natural wonder which, so far
as I know, is, in kind, absolutely unparalleled throughout the rest of
the world. I want to ask you to do one thing in connection with it, in
your own interest and in the interest of the country—to keep this
great wonder of nature as it now is. I was delighted to learn of the
wisdom of the Santa Fe railroad people in deciding not to build their
hotel on the brink of the canyon. I hope you will not have a building
of any kind, not a summer cottage, a hotel, or anything else, to mar
the wonderful grandeur, the sublimity, the great loneliness and beauty
of the canyon. Leave it as it is. You cannot improve on it. The ages
have been at work on it, and man can only mar it. What you can do
is to keep it for your children, your children's children and for all who
come after you, as one of the great sights which every American, if he
can travel at all, should see. We have gotten past the stage, my fellow-
citizens, when we are to be pardoned if we treat any part of our country as something to be skinned for two or three years for the use of the
present generation, whether it is the forest, the water, the scenery.
Whatever it is, handle it so that your children's children will get the
benefit of it. If you deal with irrigation, apply it under circumstances
that will make it of benefit, not to the speculator who hopes to get
profit out of it for two or three years, but handle it so that it will be
of use to the home-maker, to the man who comes to live here, and to
have his children stay after him. Keep the forests in the same way.
Preserve the forests by use; preserve them for the ranchman and the
stockman, for the people of the Territory, for the people of the region
round about. Preserve them for that use, but use them so that they will
not be squandered, that they will not be wasted, so that they will be
of benefit to the Arizona of 1953 as well as the Arizona of 1903.

To the Indians here I want to say a word of welcome. In my regiment I had a good many Indians. They were good enough to fight
and to die, and they are good enough to have me treat them exactly
as square as any white man. There are many problems in connection
with them. We must save them from corruption and from brutality;
and I regret to say that at times we must save them from unregulated
Eastern philanthropy. All I ask is a square deal for every man. Give
him a fair chance. Do not let him wrong any one, and do not let him
be wronged.

I believe in you. I am glad to see you. I wish you well with all my
heart, and I know that your future will justify all the hopes we have.

MARY CHURCH TERRELL

What It Means to Be Colored in the Capital of the United States
(". . . nowhere in the world do oppression and persecution
based solely on the color of the skin appear more hateful
and hideous than in the capital of the United States")
United Women's Club, Washington, D.C.
October 10, 1906

*A public school teacher and civil rights and suffrage activist, Terrell (1863–
1954) was born in Memphis, Tennessee, the daughter of slaves. She earned
her bachelor's and master's degrees from Oberlin College in Ohio, and was a
founding member of the National Association for the Advancement of Colored
People. Through her advocacy, she helped overturn segregation laws in Washington, D.C., in 1953.*

Washington, D.C., has been called "The Colored Man's Paradise."
Whether this sobriquet was given to the national capital in bitter
irony by a member of the handicapped race, as he reviewed some of
his own persecutions and rebuffs, or whether it was given immediately after the war by an ex-slaveholder who for the first time in his
life saw colored people walking about like free men, minus the over-
seer and his whip, history saith not. It is certain that it would be difficult to find a worse misnomer for Washington than "The Colored
Man's Paradise" if so prosaic a consideration as veracity is to determine the appropriateness of a name.

For fifteen years I have resided in Washington, and while it was far
from being a paradise for colored people when I first touched these
shores it has been doing its level best ever since to make conditions
for us intolerable. As a colored woman I might enter Washington any
night, a stranger in a strange land, and walk miles without finding a
place to lay my head. Unless I happened to know colored people who
live here or ran across a chance acquaintance who could recommend
a colored boarding-house to me, I should be obliged to spend the
entire night wandering about. Indians, Chinamen, Filipinos, Japanese

and representatives of any other dark race can find hotel accommodations, if they can pay for them. The colored man alone is thrust out of the hotels of the national capital like a leper.

As a colored woman I may walk from the Capitol to the White House, ravenously hungry and abundantly supplied with money with which to purchase a meal, without finding a single restaurant in which I would be permitted to take a morsel of food, if it was patronized by white people, unless I were willing to sit behind a screen. As a colored woman I cannot visit the tomb of the Father of this country, which owes its very existence to the love of freedom in the human heart and which stands for equal opportunity to all, without being forced to sit in the Jim Crow section of an electric car which starts form the very heart of the city—midway between the Capitol and the White House. If I refuse thus to be humiliated, I am cast into jail and forced to pay a fine for violating the Virginia laws. . . .

As a colored woman I may enter more than one white church in Washington without receiving that welcome which as a human being I have the right to expect in the sanctuary of God. . . .

Unless I am willing to engage in a few menial occupations, in which the pay for my services would be very poor, there is no way for me to earn an honest living, if I am not a trained nurse or a dressmaker or can secure a position as teacher in the public schools, which is exceedingly difficult to do. It matters not what my intellectual attainments may be or how great is the need of the services of a competent person, if I try to enter many of the numerous vocations in which my white sisters are allowed to engage, the door is shut in my face.

From one Washington theater I am excluded altogether. In the remainder certain seats are set aside for colored people, and it is almost impossible to secure others. . . .

With the exception of the Catholic University, there is not a single white college in the national capital to which colored people are admitted. . . . A few years ago the Columbian Law School admitted colored students, but in deference to the Southern white students the authorities have decided to exclude them altogether.

Some time ago a young woman who had already attracted some attention in the literary world by her volume of short stories answered an advertisement which appeared in a Washington newspaper, which called for the services of a skilled stenographer and expert typewriter. . . . The applicants were requested to send specimens of their work and answer certain questions concerning their experience and their speed before they called in person. In reply to her application the young colored woman . . . received a letter from the firm stating that her references and experience were the most satisfactory that had been sent and requesting her to call. When she presented herself there was some doubt in the mind of the man to whom she was directed concerning her racial pedigree, so he asked her point-blank whether she was colored or white. When she confessed the truth the merchant expressed . . . deep regret that he could not avail himself of the services of so competent a person, but frankly admitted that employing a colored woman in his establishment in any except a menial position was simply out of the question. . . .

Not only can colored women secure no employment in the Washington stores, department and otherwise, except as menials, and such positions, of course, are few, but even as customers they are not infrequently treated with discourtesy both by the clerks and the proprietor himself. . . .

Although white and colored teachers are under the same Board of Education and the system for the children of both races is said to be uniform, prejudice against the colored teachers in the public schools is manifested in a variety of ways. From 1870 to 1900 there was a colored superintendent at the head of the colored schools. During all that time the directors of the cooking, sewing, physical culture, manual training, music and art departments were colored people. Six years ago a change was inaugurated. The colored superintendent was legislated out of office and the directorships, without a single exception, were taken from colored teachers and given to the whites. . . .

Now, no matter how competent or superior the colored teachers in our public schools may be, they know that they can never rise to the height of a directorship, can never hope to be more than an assistant and receive the meager salary therefore, unless the present regime is radically changed. . . .

Strenuous efforts are being made to run Jim Crow cars in the national capital. . . . Representative Heflin, of Alabama, who introduced a bill providing for Jim Crow street cars in the District of Columbia last winter, has just received a letter from the president of the East Brookland Citizens' Association "indorsing the movement for separate street cars and sincerely hoping that you will be successful in getting this enacted into a law as soon as possible." Brookland is a suburb of Washington.

The colored laborer's path to a decent livelihood is by no means smooth. Into some of the trades unions here he is admitted, while from others he is excluded altogether. By the union men this is denied, although I am personally acquainted with skilled workmen who tell me they are not admitted into the unions because they are colored. But even when they are allowed to join the unions they frequently derive little benefit, owing to certain tricks of the trade. When the word passes round that help is needed and colored laborers apply, they are often told by the union officials that they have secured all the men they needed, because the places are reserved for white men, until they have been provided with jobs, and colored men must remain idle, unless the supply of white men is too small. . . .

And so I might go on citing instance after instance to show the variety of ways in which our people are sacrificed on the altar of prejudice in the capital of the United States and how almost insurmountable are the obstacles which block his path to success. . . .

It is impossible for any white person in the United States, no matter how sympathetic and broad, to realize what life would mean to him if his incentive to effort were suddenly snatched away. To the lack of incentive to effort, which is the awful shadow under which we live, may be traced the wreck and ruin of score of colored youth. And surely nowhere in the world do oppression and persecution based solely on the color of the skin appear more hateful and hideous than in the capital of the United States, because the chasm between the principles upon which this Government was founded, in which it still professes to believe, and those which are daily practiced under the protection of the flag, yawn so wide and deep.

EMMA GOLDMAN
What Is Patriotism?
("... patriotism is too narrow and limited a conception
to meet the necessities of our time")
San Francisco, California
May 1908

In the first two decades of the twentieth century, Emma Goldman (1869–1940), born in Russia, was one of the most famous and controversial speakers on socialism and women's rights. As a teenager, she was educated in Germany before she moved to the United States, where she became an anarchist and free-speech advocate. Immediately after this speech in the spring in San Francisco, an American war veteran complimented (or, as he would claim, simply greeted) her, and was consequently arrested for treason and sentenced to five years in prison. Goldman herself would serve two years in prison for encouraging resistance to the draft for World War I and was thereafter deported from the United States.

Men and Women:

What is patriotism? Is it love of one's birthplace, the place of childhood's recollections and hopes, dreams and aspirations? Is it the place where, in childlike naiveté, we would watch the passing clouds, and wonder why we, too, could not float so swiftly? The place where we would count the milliard glittering stars, terror-stricken lest each one "an eye should be," piercing the very depths of our little souls? Is it the place where we would listen to the music of the birds and long to have wings to fly, even as they, to distant lands? Or is it the place where we would sit on Mother's knee, enraptured by tales of great deeds and conquests? In short, is it love for the spot, every inch representing dear and precious recollections of a happy, joyous and playful childhood?

If that were patriotism, few American men of today would be called upon to be patriotic, since the place of play has been turned into factory, mill, and mine, while deepening sounds of machinery

7

have replaced the music of the birds. No longer can we hear the tales of great deeds, for the stories our mothers tell today are but those of sorrow, tears and grief.

What, then, is patriotism? "Patriotism, sir, is the last resort of scoundrels," said Dr. Samuel Johnson. Leo Tolstoy, the greatest anti-patriot of our time, defines patriotism as the principle that will justify the training of wholesale murderers; a trade that requires better equipment in the exercise of man-killing than the making of such necessities as shoes, clothing, and houses; a trade that guarantees better returns and greater glory than that of the honest workingman.

Indeed, conceit, arrogance and egotism are the essentials of patriotism. Let me illustrate. Patriotism assumes that our globe is divided into little spots, each one surrounded by an iron gate. Those who have had the fortune of being born on some particular spot consider themselves nobler, better, grander, more intelligent than those living beings inhabiting any other spot. It is, therefore, the duty of everyone living on that chosen spot to fight, kill and die in the attempt to impose his superiority upon all the others.

The inhabitants of the other spots reason in like manner, of course, with the result that from early infancy the mind of the child is provided with blood-curdling stories about the Germans, the French, the Italians, Russians, etc. When the child has reached manhood he is thoroughly saturated with the belief that he is chosen by the Lord himself to defend his country against the attack or invasion of any foreigner. It is for that purpose that we are clamoring for a greater army and navy, more battleships and ammunition.

An army and navy represent the people's toys. To make them more attractive and acceptable, hundreds and thousands of dollars are being spent for the display of toys. That was the purpose of the American government in equipping a fleet and sending it along the Pacific coast, that every American citizen should be made to feel the pride and glory of the United States.

The city of San Francisco spent one hundred thousand dollars for the entertainment of the fleet; Los Angeles, sixty thousand; Seattle and Tacoma, about one hundred thousand. Yes, two hundred and sixty thousand dollars were spent on fireworks, theater parties, and revelries, at a time when men, women, and children through the breadth and length of the country were starving in the streets; when thousands of unemployed were ready to sell their labor at any price.

What could not have been accomplished with such an enormous sum? But instead of bread and shelter, the children of those cities were taken to see the fleet, that it may remain, as one newspaper said, "a lasting memory for the child." A wonderful thing to remember, is it not? The implements of civilized slaughter. If the mind of the child is poisoned with such memories, what hope is there for a true realization of human brotherhood?

We Americans claim to be a peace-loving people. We hate bloodshed; we are opposed to violence. Yet we go into spasms of joy over the possibility of projecting dynamite bombs from flying machines upon helpless citizens. We are ready to hang, electrocute, or lynch anyone, who, from economic necessity, will risk his own life in the attempt upon that of some industrial magnate. Yet our hearts swell with pride at the thought that America is becoming the most powerful nation on earth, and that she will eventually plant her iron foot on the necks of all other nations.

Such is the logic of patriotism.

Thinking men and women the world over are beginning to realize that patriotism is too narrow and limited a conception to meet the necessities of our time. The centralization of power has brought into being an international feeling of solidarity among the oppressed nations of the world; a solidarity which represents a greater harmony of interests between the workingman of America and his brothers abroad than between the American miner and his exploiting compatriot; a solidarity which fears not foreign invasion, because it is bringing all the workers to the point when they will say to their masters, "Go and do your own killing. We have done it long enough for you." The proletariat of Europe has realized the great force of that solidarity and has, as a result, inaugurated a war against patriotism and its bloody specter, militarism. Thousands of men fill the prisons of France, Germany, Russia and the Scandinavian countries because they dared to defy the ancient superstition.

America will have to follow suit. The spirit of militarism has already permeated all walks of life. Indeed, I am convinced that militarism is a greater danger here than anywhere else, because of the many bribes capitalism holds out to those whom it wishes to destroy.

The beginning has already been made in the schools. Children are trained in military tactics, the glory of military achievements extolled in the curriculum, and the youthful mind perverted to suit the government. Further, the youth of the country is appealed to in glaring posters to join the Army and the Navy. "A fine chance to see the world!" cries the governmental huckster. Thus innocent boys are morally shanghaied into patriotism, and the military Moloch strides conquering through the nation.

When we have undermined the patriotic lie, we shall have cleared the path for the great structure where all shall be united into a universal brotherhood—a truly free society.

CARLOS MONTEZUMA (WASSAJA)
Light on the Indian Situation
("For four hundred years we have pleaded, begged—yes,
sacrificed our lives—to receive fair treatment")
Ohio State University
October 5, 1912

A doctor and long-time advocate for Native American rights and independence, Montezuma (c. 1867–1923) details his amazing life and education and some of the history of anti-Native Americanism for this meeting of the Society of American Indians.

Senator Smith of Arizona, when a member of the House of Representatives, said, "There is more hope of educating the rattlesnake, than of educating the Apaches." I am an Apache.

When I was ushered into civilization the warning among the palefaces was: "Look out! an Indian is an Indian. If you do not get the first drop on him, he will drop you."

Rounding up the Apaches by the soldiers and Indian scouts was worse than catching bears and rattlesnakes. The Apaches were destroyed in bunches while caged in caves and gulches. If they stampeded they were shot down like dogs. They were deceived into surrender and then killed. Indian scouts were paid for making midnight massacre raids on Apache camps and taking [as] prisoners their children who were sold into captivity.

In one of these midnight raids made by the Pimas in 1871 many Apaches were slaughtered, and I was captured. That dark memorable night with all its awful horrors of massacre is indelibly impressed upon my mind.

The next morning, as from a supernatural stupor I awoke in another world. Childlike, I cried as if my heart would break. I wanted to go to my mother and my father. Not so. Life had another mission for me.

Two days on horseback under the broiling sun brought us to the 'Pimas' homes, where I was kept for several days.

10

To celebrate their victory, about four hundred Pimas danced around me and then helped me onto a horse and carried me off to be sold.

I was purchased for the sum of $30 by Mr. Carlos Gentile, who was on his way east, at Adamsville, Arizona. He legally adopted me and cared for me as his own. In the east we traveled from place to place and within one year landed in Chicago.

Here I entered the public school before I could speak with much intelligence in English. I made rapid progress, because I was a lone Apache in school with English-speaking children. Very soon, unconsciously, I took on their ways. I could do nothing else. In school, in the streets and in whatever way I turned I was led to become like my schoolmates. I was carried by the current of my environment. I was lost in it and had to stick to it. In my earlier days I had become Apache in speech and habit because I had associated with those who spoke only the Apache Indian language.

My public school education was not only in Chicago but also in a little red country schoolhouse near Galesburg, Illinois, where I grasped the rudiments of farm life during a two years' stay.

I was taken to Brooklyn, New York. There I studied with the children of other races learning to become American citizens; and then came west to Urbana, Illinois, where I was tutored and prepared for the state university.

While a student at the university without money, to pay part of my expenses I helped around the house—gardened, took care of a horse, and worked at whatever I could find to do outside of my study hours. During vacations I worked on a farm. Graduating in the spring of 1884, I came back to Chicago.

Here, like all new comers, I experienced that even with a university degree it was not an easy task to convince the people that you can do anything. After many days of fruitless search I found a "job," not a "position," where I worked only for my meals and a place in the store to sleep.

Through kind friends my tuition was remitted to me at the Chicago Medical College. For five years alternately behind the counter and attending lectures I finally graduated in medicine and obtained my coveted license to practice medicine and surgery. After several months of private practice I entered the Indian service as physician and clerk at the Fort Stevenson Indian School in North Dakota. Here I saw an Indian school for the first time. One year later I was transferred to Western Shoshone Agency in Nevada as agency physician. There I saw in full what deterioration a reservation is for the Indians. I watched these Indians, cut off from civilized life, trying to become like Yankees with the aid of a few government employees. Because of my own experience I was now able to fully realize how their situation held them to their old Indian life, and often wondered why the government held them so arbitrarily to their tribal life, when better things were all around them.

After three years and a half of hard service in Nevada I was sent to the Colville Agency in Washington, where I had the honor of being physician to the Chief Moses band of Columbia River Indians and Chief Joseph's band of Nez Percés, these two chiefs being among the greatest in our history.

Though I longed to help these Indians, yet my heart yearned for civilization, and, as God would have it, I received without solicitation a call from the east—a call to become resident physician at the renowned Carlisle Indian School in Pennsylvania. Here I had the blessed privilege of working with those who had at heart the real uplift of my people.

Two and one-half years at this institution under the famous God-fearing man, General Pratt, was an inspiration. At that time this school was a lighthouse for all the Indians. It was a stepping stone to all its students helping them to go out into every avenue of civilized American life.

That I might better acquaint myself with all human kind by coming in contact with all races of all climes; that I might see with my own eyes the world's progress; and that I might exert the energies with which God blessed me and developed in me to the best interest of my fellow men, I resigned my position at Carlisle. Again coming back to Chicago I started at the bottom of my profession, equipped with a firm determination to learn and struggle on. After sixteen years of the steady and persistent practice of medicine, I believe that I am justified in feeling a merited pride in that I can refer with confidence of support to hundreds of the best physicians and surgeons in Chicago and elsewhere, who are my friends and know me, my work and my observance of its professional ethics.

To draw the *lesson* from this recital of my life, I wish you to note that I am not a Reservation Indian. I never was a Reservation Indian. The world was my sphere of action and not the limitations, nearly as binding as a prison, of a strictly Bureau-ruled reservation. It may have been cruel to have been forced away from paternal love, care and protection, but after all these years, to me it has proven the greatest blessing. I studied in public schools and not in Indian schools. I did not spend a few hours in a Reservation schoolroom and the rest of the time in Indian camps. At an early age I was compelled to earn my own way in life. The government never paid one cent for my education. I have no trouble with the Indian Bureau about my money, my property or my rights as a citizen. Indian Bureau care and restrictions are unknown to me. I obey the laws of the State and Nation under whose protection I live, and so have widest freedom.

Rather than go back to my people I stayed in the east. I had to make my civilized life good within one generation and not in thousands and thousands of years.

Such is the embodiment of my life and that is why I ask the same liberty for my noble race—the American Indians. In these forty years' absence from my people I have not forgotten them. They have been in my heart day and night. For them my pen and tongue have not been idle.

You cannot treat on Temperance without thinking of Frances Willard; on the Salvation Army without keeping in mind General Booth; nor can you grasp the Indian situation without bringing in Gen. R. H. Pratt. The ex-president "who can do no wrong" relieved the general from the Indian service; from the institution he founded, loved and to which he gave twenty-five years of the best of his life. The bard that had kept the best interests of the Indians intact, went down. At that moment the steering of the Indian ship was given into hands opposed to General Pratt's ideals and it has been heading wrong ever since. It is drifting and we only can help it to sail in the right direction and for the right port by dropping out these past eight years and beginning again where we then left off.

Colonization, segregation and reservation are the most damnable creations of men. They are the home, the very hothouse of personal slavery—and are no place for the free and the "home of the brave."

I do not desire to criticize the individuals composing the guiding power of the Indian Bureau of our government, but I am unalterably opposed to the system itself.

I firmly believe that the only true solution of the so-called "Indian problem" is the entire wiping out of the reservation system; of the absolute free association of the Indian race with the paleface. Let us have an opportunity of joining with them on the basis on which all other races have been placed. No race on earth has contended so long, so diligently, so persistently for "equal rights" as has ours. No race on earth has ever survived such handicaps, oppression and the denial of any basis of freedom as has ours. Look back in history and find if you can, any race that ever inhibited this earth, who have contended against a greater force than ours for a period of four hundred years; and we are still struggling and fighting for liberty and equal privilege. God only knows the trials, tribulations, slavery and oppressions to which the Indian race has been obliged to submit and yet is valiantly fighting to overcome. If it were not for the sturdiness, the physical and moral strength of our ancestors,—would it be possible for us here today—descendants of the greatest aboriginal race in the world—still to contend for liberty and freedom?

Years and years ago the Indian only knew that truth and righteousness governed all things. But a century and more of deceit and hypocrisy has naturally taught him to distrust the paleface, through their unfulfilled promises and double dealing.

Only as an exception has a paleface appeared who in truth and in fact was a friend. Yet with all our oppression, with all the deceit that has been practiced upon us, I challenge any paleface who can meet the fidelity "even unto death" that is today and has always existed in the heart of every Indian in this country.

All who understand the Indian as a man know that his possibilities, given half a chance, are limitless. They know that there is nothing in the world we can not master. For four hundred years we have pleaded, begged—yes, sacrificed our lives—to receive fair treatment. We knew little of murder, rape, assassination and other crimes until the paleface taught us these things in their most exquisite form. History records where we, time after time, have sought peaceful solution of our rights and interests and as many times and more have we been deceived, cheated and defrauded. Is it surprising that we fought? Will a rat forced into a corner die without a fight?

The Indian Bureau system is wrong. It must by virtue of its powers be oppressive. It is not human and therefore can not be just. If the good government as our guardian has failed to place us where we rightfully belong in this world, remember that the fault lies there and not with the Indian. Therefore, it behooves every member of this Society and all Indians throughout the country to compel the government to realize its injustice. We educated Indians must awaken and express ourselves.

How often have I looked unto Heaven and said: "Oh, Lord, how long, how long!" when it seemed as though there was no shadow of hope for my people and that even God had forsaken us. But not so, my brothers and sisters, God is near and will help us. The light that comes from an Indian's heart is not yet dead. We still have among us men and women with the spirit of Red Jacket, Logan and Pocahontas, and the dawn of a better day is here.

Cease not to pray that He will yet give us an administration that will legislate and administer the end of reservation prison life for our people and open as wide opportunities for them into American civilization as it gives to all other races, and then will we be free to work out our own salvation.

EMMELINE PANKHURST
Militant Suffragists
(". . . sympathy is a very unsatisfactory thing
if it is not practical sympathy")
Hartford, Connecticut
November 13, 1913

A native of Manchester, Pankhurst (1858–1928) headed a militant women's suffrage movement in England, where women over thirty won the right to vote in 1918. In the midst of her battles, she toured America, where she also rallied for women's right to vote; women gained the same voting rights as men in 1920 with the Nineteenth Amendment to the Constitution.

I do not come here as an advocate, because whatever position the suffrage movement may occupy in the United States of America, in England it has passed beyond the realm of advocacy and it has entered into the sphere of practical politics. It has become the subject of revolution and civil war, and so to-night I am not here to advocate woman suffrage. American suffragists can do that very well for themselves. I am here as a soldier who has temporarily left the field of battle in order to explain—it seems strange it should have to be explained—what civil war is like when civil war is waged by women. I am not only here as a soldier temporarily absent from the field of battle; I am here—and that, I think, is the strangest part of my coming—I am here as a person who, according to the law courts of my country, it has been decided, is of no value to the community at all; and I am adjudged because of my life to be a dangerous person, under sentence of penal servitude in a convict prison. So you see there is some special interest in hearing so unusual a person address you. I dare say, in the minds of many of you—you will perhaps forgive me this personal touch—that I do not look either very like a soldier or very like a convict, and yet I am both.

It would take too long to trace the course of militant methods as adopted by women, because it is about eight years since the word militant was first used to describe what we were doing; it is about eight years since the first militant action was taken by women. It was not militant at all, except that it provoked militancy on the part of those who were opposed to it. When women asked questions in political meetings and failed to get answers, they were not doing anything militant. To ask questions at political meetings is an acknowledged right of all people who attend public meetings; certainly in my country, men have always done it, and I hope they do it in America, because it seems to me that if you allow people to enter your legislatures without asking them any questions as to what they are going to do when they get there you are not exercising your citizen rights and your citizen duties as you ought. At any rate in Great Britain it is a custom, a time-honored one, to ask questions of candidates for Parliament and ask questions of members of the government. No man was ever put out of a public meeting for asking a question until Votes for Women came onto the political horizon. The first people who were put out of a political meeting for asking questions, were women; they were brutally ill-used; they found themselves in jail before twenty-four hours had expired. But instead of the newspapers, which are largely inspired by the politicians, putting militancy and the reproach of militancy, if reproach there is, on the people who had assaulted the women, they actually said it was the women who were militant and very much to blame.

It was not the speakers on the platform who would not answer them, who were to blame, or the ushers at the meeting; it was the poor women who had had their bruises and their knocks and scratches, and who were put into prison for doing precisely nothing but holding a protest meeting in the street after it was all over. However, we were called militant for doing that, and we were quite willing to accept the name, because militancy for us is time-honored; you have the church militant and in the sense of spiritual militancy we were very militant indeed. We were determined to press this question of the enfranchisement of the women to the point where we were no longer to be ignored by the politicians as had been the case for about fifty years, during which time women had patiently used every means open to them to win their political enfranchisement.

Experience will show you that if you really want to get anything done, it is not so much a matter of whether you alienate sympathy; sympathy is a very unsatisfactory thing if it is not practical sympathy. It does not matter to the practical suffragist whether she alienates sympathy that was never of any use to her. What she wants is to get something practical done, and whether it is done out of sympathy or whether it is done out of fear, or whether it is done because you want to be comfortable again and not be worried in this way, doesn't particularly matter so long as you get it. We have enough of sympathy for fifty years; it never brought us anything; and we would rather have an angry man going to the government and saying, my business is interfered with and I won't submit to its being interfered with any longer because you won't give women the vote, than to have a gentleman come onto our platforms year in and year out and talk about his ardent sympathy with woman suffrage.

"Put them in prison," they said; "that will stop it." But it didn't stop it. They put women in prison for long terms of imprisonment, for making a nuisance of themselves—that was the expression when they took petitions in their hands to the door of the House of Commons; and they thought that by sending them to prison, giving them a day's imprisonment, would cause them to all settle down again and there would be no further trouble. But it didn't happen so at all: instead of the women giving it up, more women did it, and more and more and more women did it until there were three hundred women at a time, who had not broken a single law, only "made a nuisance of themselves" as the politicians say.

The whole argument with the anti-suffragists, or even the critical suffragist man, is this: that you can govern human beings without their consent. They have said to us, "Government rests upon force; the women haven't force, so they must submit." Well, we are showing them that government does not rest upon force at all; it rests upon consent. As long as women consent to be unjustly governed, they can be; but directly women say: "We withhold our consent, we will not be governed any longer so long as that government is unjust," not by the forces of civil war can you govern the very weakest woman. You can kill that woman, but she escapes you then; you cannot govern her. And that is, I think, a most valuable demonstration we have been making to the world.

Now, I want to say to you who think women cannot succeed, we have brought the government of England to this position, that it has to face this alternative; either women are to be killed or women are to have the vote. I ask American men in this meeting, what would you say if in your State you were faced with that alternative, that you must either kill them or give them their citizenship,—women, many of whom you respect, women whom you know have lived useful lives, women whom you know, even if you do not know them personally, are animated with the highest motives, women who are in pursuit of liberty and the power to do useful public service? Well, there is only one answer to that alternative; there is only one way out of it, unless you are prepared to put back civilization two or three generations; you must give those women the vote. Now that is the outcome of our civil war.

You won your freedom in America when you had the Revolution, by bloodshed, by sacrificing human life. You won the Civil War by the sacrifice of human life when you decided to emancipate the negro. You have left it to the women in your land, the men of all civilized countries have left it to women, to work out their own salvation. That is the way in which we women of England are doing. Human life for us is sacred, but we say if any life is to be sacrificed it shall be ours; we won't do it ourselves, but we will put the enemy in the position where they will have to choose between giving us freedom or giving us death.

DAVID LLOYD GEORGE
An Appeal to the Nation
("They think we cannot beat them. It will not be easy.")
Queen's Hall, London
September 19, 1914

As Great Britain's commissioner of munitions, the Liberal Party member Lloyd George (1863–1945) rallied the nation for the World War. He became prime minister in December of 1916 and was credited with bringing the war to an end in 1918.

There is no man in this room who has always regarded the prospect of engaging in a great war with greater reluctance and with greater repugnance than I have done throughout the whole of my political life. ["Hear, hear!"] There is no man either inside or outside this room more convinced that we could not have avoided it without national dishonor. [Great applause.] I am fully alive to the fact that every nation that has ever engaged in war has always invoked the sacred name of honor. Many a crime has been committed in its name; there are some being committed now. All the same, national honor is a reality, and any nation that disregards it is doomed. ["Hear, hear!"] Why is our honor as a country involved in this war? Because, in the first instance, we are bound by honorable obligations to defend the independence, the liberty, the integrity, of a small neighbor that has always lived peaceably. [Applause.] She could not have compelled us; she was weak; but the man who declines to discharge his duty because his creditor is too poor to enforce it is a blackguard. [Loud applause.] We entered into a treaty—a solemn treaty—two treaties—to defend Belgium and her integrity. Our signatures are attached to the documents. Our signatures do not stand there alone; this country was not the only country that undertook to defend the integrity of Belgium. Russia, France, Austria, Prussia—they are all there. Why are Austria and Prussia not performing the obligations of their bond? It is suggested that when we quote this treaty it is purely an excuse on our part—it is our low craft and cunning to cloak our jealously of a superior civilization—[Laughter]—that we are attempting to destroy.

It is the interest of Prussia to break the treaty, and she has done it. [Hisses.] She avows it with cynical contempt for every principle of justice. She says "Treaties only bind you when your interest is to keep them." [Laughter.] "What is a treaty?" says the German Chancellor; "A scrap of paper." Have you any £5 notes about you? [Laughter and applause.] I am not calling for them. [Laughter.] Have you any of those neat little Treasury £1 notes? [Laughter.] If you have, burn them; they are only scraps of paper. [Laughter and applause.] What are they made of? Rags. [Laughter.] What are they worth? The whole credit of the British Empire. [Loud applause.] Scraps of paper! I have been dealing with scraps of paper within the last month. One suddenly found the commerce of the world coming to a standstill. The machine had stopped. Why? I will tell you. We discovered—many of us for the first time, for I do not pretend that I do not know much more about the machinery of commerce to-day than I did six weeks ago, and there are many others like me—we discovered that the machinery of commerce was moved by bills of exchange. I have seen some of them—[Laughter]—wretched, crinkled, scrawled over, blotched, frowsy, and yet those wretched little scraps of paper move great ships laden with thousands of tons of precious cargo from one end of the world to the other. [Applause.] What is the motive power behind them? The honor of commercial men. [Applause.] Treaties are the currency of International statesmanship. [Applause.] Let us be fair: German merchants, German traders, have the reputation of being as upright and straightforward as any traders in the world—["Hear, hear!"]—but if the currency of German commerce is to be debased to the level of that of her statesmanship, no trader from Shanghai to Valparaiso will ever look at a German signature again. [Loud applause.] This doctrine of the scrap of paper, this doctrine which is proclaimed by Bernhardi, that treaties only bind a nation as long as it is to its interest, goes under the root of all public law. It is the straight road to barbarism. ["Hear, hear!"] It is as if you were to remove the Magnetic Pole because it was in the way of a German cruiser. [Laughter.] The whole navigation of the seas would become dangerous, difficult, and impossible; and the whole machinery of civilization will break down if this doctrine wins in this way. ["Hear, hear!"] We are fighting against barbarism [Applause] and there is one way of putting it right. If there are nations that say they will only respect treaties when it is to their interest to do so, we must make it to their interest to do so for the future. [Applause.]

What is their defense? Consider the interview which took place between our Ambassador and the great German officials. When their attention was called to this treaty to which they were parties, they said, "We cannot help that. Rapidity of action is the great German asset." There is a greater asset for a nation than rapidity of action and that is honest dealing. [Loud applause.] What are Germany's excuses? She says Belgium was plotting against her; Belgium was engaged in a great conspiracy with Britain and France to attack her. Not merely is it not true, but Germany knows it is not true. ["Hear, hear!"] France offered Belgium five army corps to defend her if she was attacked. Belgium said, "I do not require them; I have the word of the Kaiser. Shall Cæsar send a lie?" [Laughter and applause.] All these tales about conspiracy have been vamped up since. A great nation ought to be ashamed to behave like a fraudulent bankrupt, perjuring its way through it obligations. ["Hear, hear!"] What she says is not true. She has deliberately broken this treaty, and we are in honor bound to stand by it. [Applause.]

Belgium has been treated brutally. ["Hear, hear!"] How brutally we shall not yet know. We already know too much. What had she done? Had she sent an ultimatum to Germany? Had she challenged Germany? Was she preparing to make war on Germany? Had she inflicted any wrong upon Germany which the Kaiser was bound to redress? She was one of the most unoffending little countries in Europe. ["Hear, hear!"] There she was—peaceable, industrious, thrifty, hard-working, giving offense to no one. And her cornfields have been trampled, her villages have been burnt, her art treasures have been destroyed, her men have been slaughtered—yea, and her women and children too. [Cries of "Shame."] Hundreds and thousands of her people, their neat comfortable little homes burnt to the dust, are wandering homeless in their own land. What was their crime? Their crime was that they trusted to the word of a Prussian King. [Applause.]

Have you read the Kaiser's speeches? If you have not a copy I advise you to buy one; they will soon be out of print, and you will not have many more of the same sort. [Laughter and applause.] They are full of the glitter and bluster of German militarism—"mailed fist," and "shining armor." Poor old mailed fist. Its knuckles are getting a little bruised. Poor shining armor! The shine is being knocked out of it. [Applause.] There is the same swagger and boastfulness running through the whole of the speeches.

Treaties? They tangle the feet of Germany in her advance. Cut them with the sword. Little nations? They hinder the advance of Germany. Trample them in the mire under the German heel! The

Russian Slav? He challenges the supremacy of Germany in Europe. Hurl your legions at him and massacre him! Christianity? Sickly sentimentalism about sacrifice for others! Poor pap for German digestion! We will have a new diet. We will force it upon the world. It will be made in Germany [Laughter and applause]—a diet of blood and iron. What remains? Treaties have gone. The honor of nations has gone. Liberty has gone. What is left? Germany! Germany is left!— *"Deutschland über Alles!"*

They think we cannot beat them. It will not be easy. It will be a long job; it will be a terrible war; but in the end we shall march through terror to triumph. [Applause.] We shall need all our qualities—every quality that Britain and its people possess—prudence in counsel, daring in action, tenacity in purpose, courage in defeat, moderation in victory; in all things faith. [Loud applause.]

VLADIMIR LENIN
The Dictatorship of the Proletariat
("Actual freedom and equality will exist only in the order
established by the Communists")
Communist International, First Congress
Moscow, Russia
March 4, 1919

Lenin (1870–1924), born Vladimir Ilyich Ulyanov in a city (renamed Ulyanovsk in his honor) on the Volga River, spent many years in European exile writing revolutionary socialist tracts before returning to his homeland in 1917. As the Marxist revolutionary who led the Bolsheviks in their takeover of Russia in 1917, he became the chairman and de facto ruler of the Soviet Union. In the midst of the subsequent Russian Civil War, he called for this Congress of the Communist International, to which members from Europe and Asia were invited, and where he delivered a multi-pointed organizational plan for the Communist International (or "Comintern"). The speech that follows contains excerpts from that plan. He died as a result of strokes.

The growth of the revolutionary movement of the proletariat in all countries has called forth convulsive efforts of the bourgeoisie and its agents in workmen's organizations, to find ideal political arguments in defense of the rule of the exploiters. Among these arguments stands out particularly condemnation of dictatorship and defense of democracy. The falseness and hypocrisy of such an argument, which has been repeated in thousands of forms in the capitalist press and at the conference of the yellow International in February, 1919, Berne, are evident to all who have not wished to betray the fundamental principle of socialism.

First of all, this argument is used with certain interpretations of "democracy in general" and "dictatorship in general" without raising the point as to which class one has in mind. Such a statement of the question, leaving out of consideration the question of class as though it were a general national matter, is direct mockery of the fundamental doctrine of socialism, namely, the doctrine of class struggle, which the socialists who have gone over to the side of the bourgeoisie recognize when they talk, but forget when they act. For in no civilized capitalist country does there exist "democracy in general," but there exists only bourgeois democracy, and one is speaking not of "dictatorship in general" but of dictatorship of the oppressed classes, that is, of the proletariat with respect to the oppressors and exploiters, that is, the bourgeoisie, in order to overcome the resistance which the exploiters make in their struggle to preserve their rule.

History teaches that no oppressed class has ever come into power and cannot come into power, without passing through a period of dictatorship, that is, the conquest of power and the forcible suppression of the most desperate and mad resistance which does not hesitate to resort to any crimes, such has always been shown by the exploiters. The bourgeoisie, whose rule is now defended by the socialists who speak against "dictatorship in general" and who espouse the cause of "democracy in general," has won power in the progressive countries at the price of a series of uprisings, civil wars, forcible suppression of kings, feudal lords, and slave owners, and of their attempts at restoration. The socialists of all countries in their books and pamphlets, in the resolutions of their congresses, in their propaganda speeches, have explained to the people thousands and millions of times the class character of these bourgeois revolutions, and of this bourgeois dictatorship. Therefore the present defense of bourgeois democracy in the form of speeches about "democracy in general," and the present wails and shouts against the dictatorship of the proletariat in the form of wails about "dictatorship in general," are a direct mockery of socialism, and represent in fact going over to the bourgeoisie and denying the right of the proletariat to its own proletariat revolution, and a defense of bourgeois reformism, precisely at the historic moment when bourgeois reformism is collapsing the world over, and when the war has created a revolutionary situation.

All socialists who explain the class character of bourgeois civilization, or bourgeois democracy, of bourgeois parliamentarism, express the thought which Marx and Engels expressed with the most scientific exactness when they said that the most democratic bourgeois republic is nothing more than a machine for the suppression of the working class by the bourgeoisie, for the suppression of the mass of the toilers by a handful of capitalists. There is not a single revolutionist, not a single Marxist of all those who are now shouting against dictatorship and for democracy, who would not have sworn before the workmen that he recognizes this fundamental truth of socialism. And now, when the revolutionary proletariat begins to act and move for the destruction of this machinery of oppression, and to win the proletarian dictatorship, these traitors to socialism report the situation as though the bourgeoisie were giving the laborers pure democracy, as though the bourgeoisie were abandoning resistance and were ready to submit to the majority of the toilers, as though there were no state machinery for the suppression of labor by capital in a democratic republic.

Workmen know very well that "freedom of meetings," even in the most democratic bourgeois republic is an empty phrase, for the rich have all the best public and private buildings at their disposal, and also sufficient leisure time for meetings and for protection of these meetings by the bourgeois apparatus of authority. The proletarians of the city and of the village, and the poor peasants, that is, the overwhelming majority of the population, have none of these three things. So long as the situation is such, "equality," that is, "pure democracy," is sheer fraud.

The capitalists have always called "freedom" the freedom to make money for the rich, and the freedom to die of hunger for workmen. The capitalists call "freedom" the freedom of the rich, freedom to buy up the press, to use wealth, to manufacture and support so-called public opinion. The defenders of "pure democracy" again in actual fact turn out to be the defenders of the most dirty and corrupt system of the rule of the rich over the means of education of the masses. They deceive the people by attractive, fine-sounding, beautiful but absolutely false phrases, trying to dissuade the masses from the concrete historic task of freeing the press from the capitalists who have gotten control of it. Actual freedom and equality will exist only in the order established by the Communists, in which it will be impossible to become rich at the expense of another, where it will be impossible either directly or indirectly to subject the press to the power of money, where there will be no obstacle to prevent any toiler from enjoying and actually realizing the equal right to the use of public printing presses and of the public fund of paper.

Dictatorship of the proletariat resembles dictatorship of the other classes in that it was called forth by the need to suppress the forcible resistance of a class that was losing its political rulership. But that which definitely distinguishes a dictatorship of the proletariat from a dictatorship of other classes, from a dictatorship of the bourgeoisie in all the civilized capitalist countries, is that the dictatorship of the landlords and of the bourgeoisie was the forcible suppression of the resistance of the overwhelming majority of the population, namely, the toilers. On the other hand, the dictatorship of the proletariat is the forcible suppression of the resistance of the exploiters, that is, of an insignificant minority of the population—of landlords and capitalists.

It therefore follows that a dictatorship of the proletariat must necessarily carry with it not only changes in the form and institutions of democracy, speaking in general terms, but specifically such a change as would secure an extension such as has never been seen in the history of the world of the actual use of democratism by the toiling classes.

MOHANDAS K. GANDHI
Ahmedabad
("For me life would not be worth living if Ahmedabad
continues to countenance violence in the name of truth")
Ahmedabad, India
April 14, 1919

*Born in western India in 1869, Mohandas Karamchand Gandhi ("Ma-
hatma," meaning "great-souled," was a title bestowed on him later by his
followers), was the greatest hero of peaceful revolution, inspiring among others
Martin Luther King, Jr. He earned his law degree in London in 1891 and
practiced in South Africa for twenty-one years before returning to India in
1914 as an advocate for satyagraha (usually translated as "passive resistance"
but literally "truth-force" or "soul-force"). On April 13, 1919, British troops
shot 1,500 nonviolent demonstrators for Indian independence, killing 400 of
them. After an outbreak of riots, Gandhi made this speech the next day to the
citizens of Ahmedabad in his ashram. The British authorities repeatedly jailed
Gandhi for his teachings. In spite of this, he led the nationalist movement in
India that resulted in independence in August 1947. On January 30, 1948,
a Hindu nationalist fanatic assassinated him.*

Brothers,—I mean to address myself mainly to you. Brothers, the
events that have happened in course of the last few days have been
most disgraceful to Ahmedabad, and as all these things have happened
in my name, I am ashamed of them, and those who have been responsible for them have thereby not honoured me but disgraced me.
A rapier run through my body could hardly have pained me more. I
have said times without number that Satyagraha admits of no violence, no pillage, no incendiarism; and still in the name of Satyagraha
we burnt down buildings, forcibly captured weapons, extorted
money, stopped trains, cut off telegraph wires, killed innocent people
and plundered shops and private houses. If deeds such as these could
save me from the prison house or the scaffold I should not like to be
so saved. I do wish to say in all earnestness that violence has not

secured my discharge. A most brutal rumour was set afloat that Anasuya Bai was arrested. The crowds were infuriated all the more, and disturbance increased. You have thereby disgraced Anasuya Bai and under the cloak of her arrest heinous deeds have been done.

These deeds have not benefited the people in any way. They have done nothing but harm. The buildings burnt down were public property and they will naturally be rebuilt at our expense. The loss due to the shops remaining closed is also our loss. The terrorism prevailing in the city due to Martial Law is also the result of this violence. It has been said that many innocent lives have been lost as a result of the operation of Martial Law. If this is a fact then for that too the deeds described above are responsible. It will thus be seen that the events that have happened have done nothing but harm to us. Moreover they have most seriously damaged the Satyagraha movement. Had an entirely peaceful agitation followed my arrest, the Rowlatt Act would have been out or on the point of being out of the Statute Book today. It should not be a matter for surprise if the withdrawal of the Act is now delayed. When I was released on Friday my plan was to start for Delhi again on Saturday to seek re-arrest, and that would have been an accession of strength to the movement. Now, instead of going to Delhi, it remains to me to offer Satyagraha against our own people, and as it is my determination to offer Satyagraha even unto death for securing the withdrawal of the Rowlatt legislation, I think the occasion has arrived when I should offer Satyagraha against ourselves for the violence that has occurred. And I shall do so at the sacrifice of my body, so long as we do not keep perfect peace and cease from violence to person and property. How can I seek imprisonment unless I have absolute confidence that we shall no longer be guilty of such errors? Those desirous of joining the Satyagraha movement or of helping it must entirely abstain from violence. They may not resort to violence even on my being rearrested or on some such events happening. Englishmen and women have been compelled to leave their homes and confine themselves to places of protection in Shahi Bag, because their trust in our harmlessness has received a rude shock. A little thinking should convince us that this is a matter of humiliation for us all. The sooner this state of things stops the better for us. They are our brethren and it is our duty to inspire them with the belief that their persons are as sacred to us as our own and this is what we call *Abhaydan,* the first requisite of true religion. Satyagraha without this is *Duxagraha.*

There are two distinct duties now before us. One is that we should firmly resolve upon refraining from all violence, and the other is that we should repent and do penance for our sins. So long as we don't repent and do not realise our errors and make an open confession of them, we shall not truly change our course. The first step is that those of us who have captured weapons should surrender them. To show that we are really penitent we will contribute each of us not less than eight annas towards helping the families of those who have been killed by our acts. Though no amount of money contribution can altogether undo the results of the furious deeds of the past few days, our contribution will be a slight token of our repentence. I hope and pray that no one will evade this contribution on the plea that he has had no part in those wicked acts. For if such as those who were no party to these deeds had all courageously and bravely gone forward to put down the lawlessness, the mob would have been checked in their career and would have immediately realised the wickedness of their doings. I venture to say that if instead of giving money to the mob out of fear we had rushed out to protect buildings and to save the innocent without fear of death we could have succeeded in so doing. Unless we have this sort of courage, mischief-makers will always try to intimidate us into participating in their misdeeds. Fear of death makes us devoid both of valour and religion. For want of valour is want of religious faith. And having done little to stop the violence we have been all participators in the sins that have been committed. And we ought, therefore, to contribute our mite as a mark of our repentence. Each group can collect its own contributions and send them on to me through its collectors. I would also advise, if it is possible for you, to observe a twenty-four hours fast in slight expiation of these sins. This fast should be observed in private and there is no need for crowds to go to the bathing ghats.

I have thus far drawn attention to what appears to be your duty. I must now consider my own. My responsibility is a million times greater than yours. I have placed Satyagraha before people for their acceptance, and I have lived in your midst for four years. I have also given some contribution to the special service of Ahmedabad. Its citizens are not quite unfamiliar with my views.

It is alleged that I have without proper consideration persuaded thousands to join the movement. That allegation is, I admit, true to a certain extent, but to a certain extent only. It is open to any body to say that but for the Satyagraha campaign there would not have been this violence. For this I have already done a penance, to my mind an unendurable one, namely, that I have had to postpone my visit to Delhi to seek rearrest and I have also been obliged to suggest a temporary restriction of Satyagraha to a limited field. This has been more painful to me than a wound but this penance is not enough, and I have therefore decided to fast for three days, *i.e.,* 72 hours. I hope my fast will pain no one. I believe a seventy-two hours fast is easier for me than a twenty-four hours' fast for you. And I have imposed on me a discipline which I can bear. If you really feel pity for the suffering that will be caused to me, I request that that pity should always restrain you from ever again being party to the criminal acts of which I have complained. Take it from me that we are not going to win Swarajya or benefit our country in the least by violence and terrorism. I am of opinion that if we have to wade through violence to obtain Swarajya and if a redress of grievances were to be only possible by means of ill will for and slaughter of English men I for one would do without that Swarajya and without a redress of those grievances. For me life would not be worth living if Ahmedabad continues to countenance violence in the name of truth. The poet has called Gujarat the "Garvi" (Great and Glorious) Gujarat. The Ahmedabad its capital is the residence of many religious Hindus and Muhammadans. Deeds of public violence in a city like this is like an ocean being on fire. Who can quench that fire? I can only offer myself as a sacrifice to be burnt in that fire, and I therefore ask you all to help in the attainment of the result that I desire out of my fast. May the love that lured you into unworthy acts awaken you to a sense of the reality, and if that love does continue to animate you, beware that I may not have to fast myself to death.

It seems that the deeds I have complained of have been done in an organised manner. There seems to be a definite design about them, and I am sure that there must be some educated and clever man or men behind them. They may be educated, but their education has not enlightened them. You have been misled into doing these deeds by such people. I advise you never to be so misguided, and I would ask them seriously to reconsider their views. To them and to you I commend my book "Hind Swarajya" which as I understand may be printed and published without infringing the law thereby.

Among the millhands the spinners have been on strike for some days. I advise them to resume work immediately and to ask for increase if they want any only after resuming work, and in a reasonable manner. To resort to the use of force to get any increase is suicidal. I would specially advise all millhands to altogether eschew violence. It is their interest to do so and I remind them of the promises made to Anasuya Bai and me that they would ever refrain from violence. I hope that all will now resume work.

MARCUS GARVEY
The Handwriting Is on the Wall
("No portion of humanity . . . [has] an eternal right
to oppress other sections or portions of humanity")
New York City
August 31, 1921

Garvey's newspaper, The Negro World, *describes how, at the Second International Convention of Negroes of the World, at Liberty Hall, in Harlem, New York City, he rose before a cheering crowd to give this speech, "smiling and bowing to the right and then to the left like a black Napoleon." Garvey (1887–1940) was the charismatic Jamaican who in the late 1910s and early 1920s concentrated and sparked the energy of hundreds of thousands of African-Americans with the dream of African redemption. After serving a prison term for mail fraud, he was deported, and his power faded. He died in England.*

We are assembled here tonight to bring to a close our great convention of thirty-one days and thirty-one nights. Before we separate ourselves and take our departure to the different parts of the world from which we came, I desire to give you a message; one that you will, I hope, take home and propagate among the scattered millions of Africa's sons and daughters.

We have been here, sent here by the good will of the 400,000,000 Negroes of the world to legislate in their interests, and in the time allotted to us we did our best to enact laws and to frame laws that in our judgment, we hope, will solve the great problem that confronts us universally. The Universal Negro Improvement Association seeks to emancipate the Negro everywhere, industrially, educationally, politically and religiously. It also seeks a free and redeemed Africa. It has a great struggle ahead; it has a gigantic task to face. Nevertheless, as representatives of the Negro people of the world we have undertaken the task of freeing the 400,000,000 of our race, and of freeing our bleeding Motherland, Africa. We counseled with each other during the thirty-one days; we debated with each other during the thirty-one days, and out of all we did, and out of all we said, we have come to the one conclusion—that speedily Africa must be redeemed! {*Applause.*} We have come to the conclusion that speedily there must be an emancipated Negro race everywhere {*applause*}; and on going back to our respective homes we go with our determination to lay down, if needs be, the last drop of our blood for the defense of Africa and for the emancipation of our race.

The handwriting is on the wall. You see it as plain as daylight; you see it coming out of India, the tribes of India rising in rebellion against their overlords. You see it coming out of Africa, our dear motherland, Africa; the Moors rising in rebellion against their overlords, and defeating them at every turn. {*Applause.*} According to the last report flashed to this country from Morocco by the Associated Press, the Moors have again conquered and subdued the Spanish hordes. The same Associated Press flashes to us the news that there is a serious uprising in India, and the English people are marshaling their troops to subdue the spirit of liberty, of freedom, which is now permeating India. The news has come to us, and I have a cable in my pocket that comes from Ireland that the Irish are determined to have liberty and nothing less than liberty. {*Applause.*}

The handwriting is on the wall, and as we go back to our respective homes we shall serve notice upon the world that we also are coming; coming with a united effort; coming with a united determination, a determination that Africa shall be free from coast to coast. {*Applause.*} I have before me the decision of the League of Nations. Immediately after the war a Council of the League of Nations was called, and at that council they decided that the territories wrested from Germany in West Africa, taken from her during the conflict, should be divided between France and England—608,000 square miles—without even asking the civilized Negroes of the world what disposition shall be made of their own homeland, of their own country. An insult was hurled at the civilized Negroes of the world when they thus took upon themselves the right to parcel out and apportion as they pleased 608,000 square miles of our own land; for we never gave it up; we never sold it. It is still ours. {*Cries of "Yes!"*} They parceled it out between these two nations—England and France— gave away our property without consulting us, and we are aggrieved, and we desire to serve notice on civilization and on the world that 400,000,000 Negroes are aggrieved. {*Cries of "Yes!" and applause.*}

And we are the more aggrieved because of the lynch rope, because of segregation, because of the Jim Crowism that is used, practiced and exercised here in this country, and in other parts of the world by the white nations of the earth, wherever Negroes happen accidentally or otherwise to find themselves. If there is no safety for Negroes in the white world, I cannot see what right they have to parcel out the homeland, the country of Negroes, without consulting Negroes and asking their permission to do so. Therefore, we are aggrieved. This question of prejudice will be the downfall of civilization {*Applause*}, and I warn the white race of this, and of their doom. I hope they will take heed, because the handwriting is on the wall. {*Applause.*} No portion of humanity, no group of humanity, has an abiding right, an everlasting right, an eternal right to oppress other sections or portions of humanity. God never gave them the right, and if there is such a right, man arrogated it to himself, and God in all ages has been displeased with the arrogance of man. I warn those nations which believe themselves above the law of God, above the commandments of God. I warn those nations that believe themselves above human justice. You cannot ignore the laws of God; you cannot long ignore the commandments of God; you cannot long ignore human justice, and exist. Your arrogance will destroy you, and I warn the races and the nations that have arrogated to themselves the right to oppress, the right to circumscribe, the right to keep down other races. I warn them that the hour is coming when the oppressed will rise in their might, in their majesty, and throw off the yoke of ages.

The world ought to understand that the Negro has come to life, possessed with a new conscience and a new soul. The old Negro is buried, and it is well the world knew it. It is not my purpose to deceive the world. I believe in righteousness; I believe in truth; I believe in honesty. That is why I warn a selfish world of the outcome of their actions towards the oppressed. There will come a day, Josephus Daniels wrote about it, a white statesman, and the world has talked about it, and I warn the world of it, that the day will come when the races of the world will marshal themselves in great conflict for the survival of the fittest. Men of the Universal Negro Improvement Association, I am asking you to prepare yourselves, and prepare your race the world over, because the conflict is coming, not because you will it, not because you desire it, because you will be forced into it. The conflict between the races is drawing nearer and nearer. You see it; I see it; I see it in the handwriting on the wall, as expressed in the uprising in India. You see the handwriting on the wall of Africa; you see it, the handwriting on the wall of Europe. It is coming; it is drawing nearer and nearer. Four hundred million Negroes of the world, I am asking you to prepare yourselves, so that you will not be found wanting when that day comes. Ah! what a sorry day it will be. I hope it will never come. But my hope, my wish, will not prevent its coming.

All that I can do is to warn humanity everywhere, so that humanity may change its tactics, and warn them of the danger. I repeat: I warn the white world against the prejudice they are practicing against Negroes; I warn them against the segregation and injustice they mete out to us, for the perpetuation of these things will mean the ultimate destruction of the present civilization, and the building up of a new civilization founded upon mercy, justice, and equality.

I know that we have good men in all races living at the present time. We have good men of the black race, we have good men of the white race, good men of the yellow race, who are endeavoring to do the best they can to ward off this coming conflict. White men who have the vision, go ye back and warn your people of this coming conflict! Black men of vision, go ye to the four corners of the earth, and warn your people of this coming conflict. Yellow men, go ye out and warn your people of this coming conflict, because it is drawing nearer and nearer; nearer and nearer. Oh! if the world will only listen to the heart-throbs, to the soul-beats of those who have the vision, those who have God's love in their hearts.

I see before me white men, black men and yellow men working assiduously for the peace of the world; for the bringing together of this thing called human brotherhood; I see them working through their organizations. They have been working during the last fifty years. Some worked to bring about the emancipation, because they saw the danger of perpetual slavery. They brought about the liberation of 4,000,000 black people. They passed away, and others started to work, but the opposition against them is too strong; the opposition against them is weighing them down. The world has gone mad; the world has become too material; the world has lost its spirit of kinship with God, and man can see nothing else but prejudice, avarice and greed. Avarice and greed will destroy the world, and I am appealing to white, black and yellow whose hearts, whose souls are touched with the true spirit of humanity, with the true feeling of human brotherhood, to preach the doctrine of human love, more, to preach it louder, to preach it longer, because there is great need for it in the world at this time. Ah! if they could but see the danger—the conflict between the races—races fighting against each other. What a destruction, what a holocaust it will be! Can you imagine it?

Just take your idea from the last bloody war, wherein a race was pitted against itself (for the whole white races united as one from a common origin), the members of which, on both sides, fought so tenaciously that they killed off each other in frightful, staggering numbers. If a race pitted against itself could fight so tenaciously to kill itself without mercy, can you imagine the fury, can you imagine the mercilessness, the terribleness of the war that will come when all the races of the world will be on the battlefield, engaged in deadly combat for the destruction or overthrow of the one or the other, when beneath it and as a cause of it lies prejudice and hatred? Truly, it will be an ocean of blood; that is all it will be. So that if I can sound a note of warning now that will echo and reverberate around the world and thus prevent such a conflict, God help me to do it; for Africa, like Europe, like Asia, is preparing for that day. { *Great applause.* }

You may ask yourselves if you believe Africa is still asleep. Africa has been slumbering; but she was slumbering for a purpose. Africa still possesses her hidden mysteries; Africa has unused talents, and we are unearthing them now for the coming conflict. { *Applause.* } Oh, I hope it will never come; therefore, I hope the white world will change its attitude towards the weaker races of the world, for we shall not be weak everlastingly. Ah, history teaches us of the rise and fall of nations, races and empires. Rome fell in her majesty; Greece fell in her triumph; Babylon, Assyria, Carthage, Prussia, the German Empire—all fell in their pomp and power; the French Empire fell from the sway of the great Napoleon, from the dominion of the indomitable Corsican soldier. As they fell in the past, so will nations fall in the present age, and so will they fall in the future ages to come, the result of their unrighteousness.

I repeat, I warn the world, and I trust you will receive this warning as you go into the four corners of the earth. The white race should teach humanity. Out there is selfishness in the world. Let the white race teach humanity first, because we have been following the cause of humanity for three hundred years, and we have suffered much. If a change must come, it must not come from Negroes; it must come from the white race, for they are the ones who have brought about this estrangement between the races. The Negro never hated; at no time within the last five hundred years can they point to one single instance of Negro hatred. The Negro has loved even under the severest punishment. In slavery the Negro loved his master; he protected his master; he safeguarded his master's home. "Greater love hath no man than that he should lay down his life for another." We gave not only our services, our unrequited labor; we gave also our souls, we gave our hearts, we gave our all, to our oppressors.

But, after all, we are living in a material world, even though it is partly spiritual, and since we have been very spiritual in the past, we are going to take a part of the material now, and will give others the opportunity to practice the spiritual side of life. Therefore, I am not telling you to lead in humanity; I am not telling you to lead in the bringing about of the turning of humanity, because you have been doing that for three hundred years, and you have lost. But the compromise must come from the dominant races. We are warning them. We are not preaching a doctrine of hatred, and I trust you will not go back to your respective homes and preach such a doctrine. We are preaching, rather, a doctrine of humanity, a doctrine of human love. But we say love begins at home; "charity begins at home."

We are aggrieved because of this partitioning of Africa, because it seeks to deprive Negroes of the chance of higher national development; no chance, no opportunity, is given us to prove our fitness to govern, to dominate in our own behalf. They impute so many bad things against Haiti and against Liberia, that they themselves circumvented Liberia so as to make it impossible for us to demonstrate our ability for self-government. Why not be honest? Why not be straightforward? Having desired the highest development, as they avowed and professed, of the Negro, why not give him a fair chance, an opportunity to prove his capacity for governing? What better opportunity ever presented itself than the present, when the territories of Germany in Africa were wrested from her control by the Allies in the last war—what better chance ever offered itself for trying out the higher ability of Negroes to govern themselves than to have given those territories to the civilized Negroes, and thus give them a trial to exercise themselves in a proper system of government? Because of their desire to keep us down, because of their desire to keep us apart, they refuse us a chance. The chance that they did give us is the chance that we are going to take. {*Great applause.*} Hence tonight, before I take my seat, I will move a resolution, and I think it is befitting at this time to pass such a resolution as I will move, so that the League of Nations and the Supreme Council of the Nations will understand that Negroes are not asleep; that Negroes are not false to themselves; that Negroes are wide awake, and that Negroes intend to take a serious part in the future government of this world; that God Almighty created him and placed him in it. This world owes us a place, and we are going to occupy that place.

We have a right to a large part in the political horizon, and I say to you that we are preparing to occupy that part.

Go back to your respective corners of the earth and preach the real doctrine of the Universal Negro Improvement Association—the doctrine of universal emancipation for Negroes, the doctrine of a free and a redeemed Africa!★

★The resolution protesting "against the distribution of the land of Africa by the Supreme Council and the League of Nations among the white nations of the world" followed and was carried "unanimously."

MARGARET SANGER
Morality of Birth Control
("If we cannot trust woman with the knowledge of her
own body, then I claim that two thousand years of
Christian teaching has proved a failure")
Park Theatre, New York City
November 18, 1921

A New York State native who had worked as a nurse, Sanger (1879–1966) was a women's rights activist who concerned herself with issues of women's health. Having organized the first American Birth Control Conference in New York City in 1921 (her American Birth Control League was a precursor to Planned Parenthood), Sanger was arrested at the closing meeting where she was to give this speech. After her release she gave the speech at another venue.

The meeting tonight is a postponement of one which was to have taken place at the Town Hall last Sunday evening. It was to be a culmination of a three day conference, two of which were held at the Hotel Plaza, in discussing the birth control subject in its various and manifold aspects.

The one issue upon which there seems to be most uncertainty and disagreement exists in the moral side of the subject of birth control. It seemed only natural for us to call together scientists, educators, members of the medical profession and the theologians of all denominations to ask their opinion upon this uncertain and important phase of the controversy. Letters were sent to the most eminent men and women in the world. We asked in this letter, the following questions:—

1. Is over-population a menace to the peace of the world?
2. Would the legal dissemination of scientific birth control information through the medium of clinics by the medical profession be the most logical method of checking the problem of over-population?
3. Would knowledge of birth control change the moral attitude of men and women toward the marriage bond or lower the moral standards of

the youth of the country? 4. Do you believe that knowledge which enables parents to limit the families will make for human happiness, and raise the moral, social and intellectual standards of population?

We sent such a letter not only to those who, we thought, might agree with us, but we sent it also to our known opponents. Most of these people answered. Everyone who answered did so with sincerity and courtesy, with the exception of one group whose reply to this important question as demonstrated at the Town Hall last Sunday evening was a disgrace to liberty-loving people, and to all traditions we hold dear in the United States. (Applause.) I believed that the discussion of the moral issue was one which did not solely belong to theologians and to scientists, but belonged to the people. (Applause.) And because I believed that the people of this country may and can discuss this subject with dignity and with intelligence I desired to bring them together, and to discuss it in the open.

When one speaks of moral, one refers to human conduct. This implies action of many kinds, which in turn depends upon the mind and the brain. So that in speaking of morals one must remember that there is a direct connection between morality and brain development. Conduct is said to be action in pursuit of ends, and if this is so, then we must hold the irresponsibility and recklessness in our action is immoral, while responsibility and forethought put into action for the benefit of the individual and the race becomes in the highest sense the finest kind of morality.

We know that every advance that woman has made in the last half century has been made with opposition, all of which has been based upon the grounds of immorality. When women fought for higher education, it was said that this would cause her to become immoral and she would lose her place in the sanctity of the home. When women asked for the franchise it was said that this would lower her standard of morals, that it was not fit that she should meet with and mix with the members of the opposite sex, but we notice that there was no objection to her meeting with the same members of the opposite sex when she went to church. The church has ever opposed the progress of woman on the ground that her freedom would lead to immorality. We ask the church to have more confidence in women. We ask the opponents of this movement to reverse the methods of the church, which aims to keep women moral by keeping them in fear and in ignorance, and to inculcate into them a higher and truer morality based upon knowledge. (Applause). And ours is the morality of knowledge. If we cannot trust woman with the knowledge of her own body, then I claim that two thousand years of Christian teaching has proved to be a failure. (Applause.)

We stand on the principle that birth control should be available to every adult man and woman. We believe that every adult man and woman should be taught the responsibility and the right use of knowledge. We claim that woman should have the right over her own body and to say if she shall or if she shall not be a mother, as she sees fit. (Applause.) We further claim that the first right of a child is to be desired. (Applause.) While the second right is that it should be conceived in love, and the third, that it should have a heritage of sound health.

Upon these principles the birth control movement in America stands.

When it comes to discussing the methods of birth control, that is far more difficult. There are laws in this country which forbid the imparting of practical information to the mothers of the land. We claim that every mother in this country, either sick or well, has the right to the best, the safest, the most scientific information. This information should be disseminated directly to the mothers through clinics by members of the medical profession, registered nurses and registered midwives. (Applause.)

Our first step is to have the backing of the medical profession so that our laws may be changed, so that motherhood may be the function of dignity and choice, rather than one of ignorance and chance. (Applause.) Conscious control of offspring is now becoming the ideal and the custom in all civilized countries.

Those who oppose it claim that however desirable it may be on economic or social grounds, it may be abused and the morals of the youth of the country may be lowered. Such people should be reminded that there are two points to be considered. First, that such control is the inevitable advance in civilization. Every civilization involves an increasing forethought for others, even for those yet unborn. (Applause.) The reckless abandonment of the impulse of the moment and the careless regard for the consequences, is not morality. (Applause). The selfish gratification of temporary desire at the expense of suffering to lives that will come may seem very beautiful to some, but it is not our conception of civilization, or is it our concept of morality. (Applause.)

In the second place, it is not only inevitable, but it is right to control the size of the family for by this control and adjustment we can raise the level and the standards of the human race. While Nature's way of reducing her numbers is controlled by disease, famine and war, primitive man has achieved the same results by infanticide, exposure of infants, the abandonment of children, and by abortion. But such ways of controlling population is no longer possible for us. We have attained high standards of life, and along the lines of science must we conduct such control. We must begin farther back and control the beginnings of life. We must control conception. This is a better method, it is a more civilized method, for it involves not only greater forethought for others, but finally a higher sanction for the value of life itself.

Society is divided into three groups. Those intelligent and wealthy members of the upper classes who have obtained knowledge of birth control and exercise it in regulating the size of their families. They have already benefited by this knowledge, and are today considered the most respectable and moral members of the community. They have only children when they desire and all society points to them as types that should perpetuate their kind.

The second group is equally intelligent and responsible. They desire to control the size of their families, but are unable to obtain knowledge or to put such available knowledge into practice.

The third are those irresponsible and reckless ones having little regard for the consequence of their acts, or whose religious scruples prevent their exercising control over their numbers. Many of this group are diseased, feeble-minded, and are of the pauper element dependent entirely upon the normal and fit members of society for their support. There is no doubt in the minds of all thinking people that the procreation of this group should be stopped. (Applause.) For if they are not able to support and care for themselves, they should certainly not be allowed to bring offspring into this world for others to look after. (Applause.) We do not believe that filling the earth with misery, poverty and disease is moral. And it is our desire and intention to carry on our crusade until the perpetuation of such conditions has ceased.

We desire to stop at its source the disease, poverty and feeble-mindedness and insanity which exist today, for these lower the standards of civilization and make for race deterioration. We know that the masses of people are growing wiser and are using their own minds to decide their individual conduct. The more people of this kind we have, the less immorality shall exist. For the more responsible people grow, the higher do they and shall they attain real morality. (Applause.)

ALFRED E. SMITH
Religious Prejudice and Politics
(". . . there is no greater mockery in this world today
than the burning of the Cross, the emblem
of faith, the emblem of salvation")
Oklahoma City, Oklahoma
September 20, 1928

As the Democratic nominee for the presidency of the United States, Smith (1873–1944), the governor of New York State, campaigned across the country. He was the first Roman Catholic nominee from a major party for the presidency, and he directly addressed this as an issue in the radio broadcast speech that follows. Herbert Hoover defeated him in the election on November 6.

"I feel that I owe it to the Democratic party to talk out plainly. If I had listened to the counselors that advised political expediency I would probably keep quiet, but I'm not by nature a quiet man. (Laughter and applause.)

"I never keep anything to myself. I talk it out. And I feel I owe it, not only to the party, but I sincerely believe that I owe it to the country itself to drag this un-American propaganda out into the open.

"Because this country, to my way of thinking, cannot be successful if it ever divides on sectarian lines. (Applause.) If there are any considerable number of our people that are going to listen to appeals to their passion and to their prejudice, if bigotry and intolerance and their sister vices are going to succeed, it is dangerous for the future life of the Republic, and the best way to kill anything un-American is to drag it out into the open; because anything un-American cannot live in the sunlight. (Applause.)

"Where does all this propaganda come from? Who is paying for its distribution? One of the women leaders of North Carolina was talking to me in the executive chamber in Albany about two weeks ago, and she said: 'Governor, I have some notion about the cost of distributing election material. The amount of it that has come into our state could not be printed and distributed for less than $1,000,000.'

"Where is the money coming from? I think we got the answer the other day when a woman went into the national committee in Washington and meekly walked up to the man in charge and said: 'I want some literature on Governor Smith; I want the non-political kind.' And he brought her down stairs, put her in an automobile and took her over to an office where a paper is published called 'The Fellowship Forum,' which, for a number of years, has been engaged in this senseless, foolish, stupid attack upon the Catholic Church and the members of the faith. (Applause.)

"Prior to the convention the grand dragon of the Realm of Arkansas wrote to one of the delegates from Arkansas, and in the letter he advised the delegate that he not vote for me in the national convention, and he put it on the ground of upholding American ideals against institutions as established by our forefathers. Now, can you think of any man or any group of men banded together in what they call the Ku-Klux Klan, who profess to be 100 per cent Americans, and forget the great principle that Jefferson stood for, the equality of man, and forget that our forefathers in their wisdom, foreseeing probably such a sight as we look at today, wrote into the fundamental law of the country that at no time was religion to be regarded as a qualification for public office.

"Just think of a man breathing the spirit of hatred against millions of his fellow citizens, proclaiming and subscribing at the same time to the doctrine of Jefferson, of Lincoln, of Roosevelt and of Wilson. Why, there is no greater mockery in this world today than the burning of the Cross, the emblem of faith, the emblem of salvation, the place upon which Christ Himself made the great sacrifice for all of mankind, by these people who are spreading this propaganda, while the Christ they are supposed to adore, love and venerate, during all of His lifetime on earth, taught the holy, sacred writ of brotherly love.

"So much for him. (A voice: "That is plenty.")

"Now we know there is another lie, or series of lies, being carefully put out around the country, and it is surprising to find the number of people who seem to believe it. I would have refrained from talking about this if it were not for the avalanche of letters that have poured into the national committee and have poured into my own office in the executive department at Albany asking for the facts. And that is the lie that has been spread around: that since I have been Governor of the State of New York nobody has ever been appointed to office but Catholics. (Loud noises.)

"We are losing time on the radio. Please wait.

"The cabinet of the governorship is made up of fourteen men. Three of them are Catholics, ten of them are Protestants and one of them is a Jew. (Applause.) Outside of the cabinet members, the Governor appoints two boards and commissions under the cabinet of twenty-six people. Twelve of them are Catholics, fourteen of them are Protestants. Aside from that of his boards and commissions, the Governor appoints 157. Thirty-five of them are Catholics, 106 of them are Protestants, twelve of them are Jews, and four I was unable to find out anything about. (Laughter and applause.)

"Judicial appointments, county appointments, and all positions in the various judicial and country districts of the state not directly related to the Executive Department, although appointed by the Governor to fill vacancies: Total number of appointments, 175; 64 Catholics, 90 Protestants, and 12 that we don't know anything about. (Laughter and applause.)

"Now just another word and I am going to finish. Here is the meanest thing that I have seen in the whole campaign. This is the product of the lowest and most cunning mind that could train itself to do something mean and dirty. This was sent to me by a member of the Masonic order, a personal friend of mine. It purports to be a circular sent out under Catholic auspices to Catholic voters and tells how 'We have control in New York, stick together and we'll get control of the country.' And designedly it said to the roster of the Masonic order in my state, because so many of that order are friends of mine and have been voting for me for the last ten years, 'Stand together.'

"Now, I disown that circular, the Democratic party disowns it, and I have no right to talk for the Catholic Church, but I'll take a chance and say that nobody inside of the Catholic Church has been stupid enough to do a thing like that. (Applause.)

"Let me make myself perfectly clear. I do not want any Catholic in the United States of America to vote for me on the 6th of November because I am a Catholic (applause). If any Catholic in this country believes that the welfare, the well-being, the prosperity, the growth and the expansion of the United States is best conserved and best promoted by the election of Hoover, I want him to vote for Hoover and not for me (applause).

"But, on the other hand, I have the right to say that any citizen of this country that believes I can promote its welfare, that I am capable of steering the ship of state safely through the next four years and then votes against me because of my religion, he is not a real, pure, genuine American. (Applause.)

EAMON DE VALERA
Ireland among the Nations
("... what Ireland has done in the past
she can do in the future")
Moydrum, Athlone, Ireland
February 6, 1933

In his broadcast on Radio Athlone, de Valera (1882–1975) discussed Ireland's history and its potential. Born in New York City, he grew up in his mother's homeland, Ireland, where he went to college and became a mathematics professor. As an Irish patriot, he fought for the country in the 1916 rising. He went to prison for his participation in that rising, but in 1920 became president of the Irish Republic. Through decades of tumultuous politics, de Valera remained in the spotlight, becoming the first prime minister of Ireland in 1938.

Ireland has much to seek from the rest of the world, and much to give back in return, much that she alone can give. Her gifts are the fruit of special qualities of mind and heart, developed by centuries of eventful history. Alone among the countries of Western Europe, she never came under the sway of Imperial Rome. When all her neighbours were in tutelage, she was independent, building up her own civilisation undisturbed. When Christianity was brought to her shores it was received with a joy and eagerness, and held with a tenacity of which there is hardly such another example.

Since the period of her missionary greatness, Ireland has suffered a persecution to which for cruelty, ingenuity and persistence there is no parallel. It did not break—it strengthened—the spirit and devotion of her people and prepared them for the renewal of their mission at a time when it is of no less vital importance to the world than was the mission of the Irish saints of the seventh and eighth centuries to the world of their day.

Next to her services to religion, Ireland's greatest contribution to the welfare of humanity has been the example of devotion to freedom which she has given throughout seven hundred years. The invaders who came to Ireland in the twelfth century belonged to a race that had already subjugated England and a great part of Western Europe. Like the Norsemen before them, it was in Ireland that they met the most serious resistance—a resistance which was continued generation after generation against the successors of the first invaders until our own time, a resistance which will inevitably continue until the last sod of Irish soil is finally freed.

The Irish language is one of the oldest, and, from the point of view of the philologist, one of the most interesting in Europe. It is a member of the Indo-European family, principal of the Celtic group, of which the other two dialects are ancient Gaulish, which has come down to us only in inscriptions, and Brythonic, represented to-day by Welsh and Breton. Irish is closely related to Greek and Sanscrit, and still more closely to Latin.

The tradition of Irish learning—the creation of the monastic and bardic schools—was not wholly lost even during the darkest period of the English occupation. So far as the law could do it, education was made impossible for the Catholic population at home, but Irish scholarship was kept alive in the colleges for Irish ecclesiastics in Louvain, Rome, Salamanca, Paris and elsewhere on the Continent. In Ireland itself the schools of poetry survived in some places until the beginning of the eighteenth century, maintaining to the end their rigorous discipline. The "hedge schools," taught by wandering scholars, frustrated in a measure the design to reduce the people to illiteracy, and kept the flame of knowledge alight, however feebly, throughout the island.

Anglo-Irish literature, though far less characteristic of the nation than that produced in the Irish language, includes much that is of lasting worth. Ireland has produced in Dean Swift perhaps the greatest satirist in the English language; in Edmund Burke probably the greatest writer on politics; in William Carleton a novelist of the first rank; in Oliver Goldsmith a poet of rare merit. Henry Grattan was one of the most eloquent orators of his time—the golden age of oratory in the English language. Theobald Wolfe Tone has left us one of the most delightful autobiographies in literature. Several recent or still living Irish novelists and poets have produced work which is likely to stand the test of time. The Irish theatre movement has given us the finest school of acting of the present day, and some plays of high quality.

Ireland's music is of a singular beauty. Based on pentatonic scale its melodies reach back to a period anterior to the dawn of musical history. It stands pre-eminent amongst the music of the Celtic nations.

It is characterised by perfection of form and variety of melodic content. It is particularly rich in tunes that imply exquisite sensitiveness. The strange fitfulness of the lamentations and love songs, the transition from gladness to pathos, have thrilled the experts, and made them proclaim our music the most varied and the most poetical in the world. Equal in rhythmic variety are our dance tunes—spirited and energetic in keeping with the temperament of our people.

I have spoken at some length of Ireland's history and her contributions to European culture, because I wish to emphasize that what Ireland has done in the past she can do in the future. The Irish genius has always stressed spiritual and intellectual rather than material values. That is the characteristic that fits the Irish people in a special manner for the task, now a vital one, of helping to save Western civilisation. The great material progress of recent times, coming in a world where false philosophies already reigned, has distorted men's sense of proportion; the material has usurped the sovereignty that is the right of the spiritual. Everywhere today the consequences of this perversion of the natural order are to be seen. Spirit and mind have ceased to rule. The riches which the world sought, and to which it sacrificed all else, have become a curse by their very abundance.

In this day, if Ireland is faithful to her mission, and, please God, she will be, if as of old she recalls men to forgotten truths, if she places before them the ideals of justice, of order, of freedom rightly used, of Christian brotherhood—then, indeed, she can do the world a service as great as that which she rendered in the time of Columcille and Columbanus, because the need of our time is in no wise less.

You sometimes hear Ireland charged with a narrow and intolerant Nationalism, but Ireland to-day has no dearer hope than this; that, true to her own holiest traditions, she may humbly serve the truth and help by truth to save the world.

HAILE SELASSIE
Address to the League of Nations
("Should it happen that a strong government finds it may with impunity destroy a weak people, then the hour strikes for that weak people to appeal to the League of Nations")
Geneva, Switzerland
June 30, 1936

Haile Selassie I (c. 1890–1975) was the emperor of Ethiopia, which had successfully fought off colonization by Italy at the end of the nineteenth century. Italy had invaded the African country and used chemical weapons on non-combatants. Selassie went to Europe to appeal to the European community. The League of Nations offered little help, and Selassie spent the next five years in exile in England before resuming the throne.

I, Haile Selassie I, Emperor of Ethiopia, am here today to claim that justice which is due to my people, and the assistance promised to it eight months ago, when fifty nations asserted that aggression had been committed in violation of international treaties.

There is no precedent for a head of state himself speaking in this assembly. But there is also no precedent for a people being victim of such injustice and being at present threatened by abandonment to its aggressor. Also, there has never before been an example of any government proceeding to the systematic extermination of a nation by barbarous means, in violation of the most solemn promises made by the nations of the earth that there should not be used against innocent human beings the terrible poison of harmful gases. It is to defend a people struggling for its age-old independence that the head of the Ethiopian Empire has come to Geneva to fulfill this supreme duty, after having himself fought at the head of his armies.

I pray to Almighty God that He may spare nations the terrible sufferings that have just been inflicted on my people, and of which the chiefs who accompany me here have been the horrified witnesses.

It is my duty to inform the governments assembled in Geneva, responsible as they are for the lives of millions of men, women and children, of the deadly peril which threatens them, by describing to them the fate which has been suffered by Ethiopia. It is not only upon warriors that the Italian Government has made war. It has above all attacked populations far removed from hostilities, in order to terrorize and exterminate them.

At the beginning, towards the end of 1935, Italian aircraft hurled upon my armies bombs of tear-gas. Their effects were but slight. The soldiers learned to scatter, waiting until the wind had rapidly dispersed the poisonous gases. The Italian aircraft then resorted to mustard gas. Barrels of liquid were hurled upon armed groups. But this means also was not effective; the liquid affected only a few soldiers, and barrels upon the ground were themselves a warning to troops and to the population of the danger.

It was at the time when the operations for the encircling of Makalle were taking place that the Italian command, fearing a rout, followed the procedure which it is now my duty to denounce to the world. Special sprayers were installed on board aircraft so that they could vaporize, over vast areas of territory, a fine, death-dealing rain. Groups of nine, fifteen, eighteen aircraft followed one another so that the fog issuing from them formed a continuous sheet. It was thus that, as from the end of January 1936, soldiers, women, children, cattle, rivers, lakes and pastures were drenched continually with this deadly rain. In order to kill off systematically all living creatures, in order more surely to poison waters and pastures, the Italian command made its aircraft pass over and over again. That was its chief method of warfare.

The very refinement of barbarism consisted in carrying ravage and terror into the most densely populated parts of the territory, the points farthest removed from the scene of hostilities. The object was to scatter fear and death over a great part of the Ethiopian territory. These fearful tactics succeeded. Men and animals succumbed. The deadly rain that fell from the aircraft made all those whom it touched fly shrieking with pain. All those who drank the poisoned water or ate the infected food also succumbed in dreadful suffering. In tens of thousands, the victims of the Italian mustard gas fell. It is in order to denounce to the civilized world the tortures inflicted upon the Ethio-pian people that I resolved to come to Geneva. None other than myself and my brave companions in arms could bring the League of Nations the undeniable proof. The appeals of my delegates addressed to the League of Nations had remained without any answer; my del-egates had not been witnesses. That is why I decided to come myself to bear witness against the crime perpetrated against my people and give Europe a warning of the doom that awaits it, if it should bow before the accomplished fact.

Is it necessary to remind the assembly of the various stages of the Ethiopian drama? For twenty years past, either as Heir Apparent, Regent of the Empire, or as Emperor, I have never ceased to use all my efforts to bring my country the benefits of civilization, and in particular to establish relations of good neighborliness with adjacent powers. In particular I succeeded in concluding with Italy the Treaty of Friendship of 1928, which absolutely prohibited the resort, under any pretext whatsoever, to force of arms, substituting for force and pressure the conciliation and arbitration on which civilized nations have based international order.

In its report of October 5, 1935, the Committee of Thirteen recognized my effort and the results that I had achieved. The governments thought that the entry of Ethiopia into the League, whilst giving that country a new guarantee for the maintenance of her territorial integrity and independence, would help her to reach a higher level of civilization. It does not seem that in Ethiopia today there is more disorder and insecurity than in 1923. On the contrary, the country is more united and the central power is better obeyed.

I should have procured still greater results for my people if obstacles of every kind had not been put in the way by the Italian government, the government which stirred up revolt and armed the rebels. Indeed the Rome government, as it has today openly proclaimed, has never ceased to prepare for the conquest of Ethiopia. The Treaties of Friendship it signed with me were not sincere; their only object was to hide its real intention from me. The Italian government asserts that for fourteen years it has been preparing for its present conquest. It therefore recognizes today that when it supported the admission of Ethiopia to the League of Nations in 1923, when it concluded the Treaty of Friendship in 1928, when it signed the Pact of Paris outlawing war, it was deceiving the whole world. The Ethiopian government was, in these solemn treaties, given additional guarantees of security which would enable it to achieve further progress along the specific path of reform on which it had set its feet, and to which it was devoting all its strength and all its heart.

The Wal–Wal incident, in December 1934, came as a thunderbolt to me. The Italian provocation was obvious and I did not hesitate to appeal to the League of Nations. I invoked the provisions of the treaty of 1928, the principles of the covenant; I urged the procedure of conciliation and arbitration. Unhappily for Ethiopia this was the time when a certain government considered that the European situation made it imperative at all costs to obtain the friendship of Italy. The price paid was the abandonment of Ethiopian independence to the greed of the Italian government. This secret agreement, contrary to the obligations of the covenant, has exerted a great influence over the course of events. Ethiopia and the whole world have suffered and are still suffering today its disastrous consequences.

This first violation of the covenant was followed by many others. Feeling itself encouraged in its policy against Ethiopia, the Rome government feverishly made war preparations, thinking that the concerted pressure which was beginning to be exerted on the Ethiopian government, might perhaps not overcome the resistance of my people to Italian domination. The time had to come, thus all sorts of difficulties were placed in the way with a view to breaking up the procedure; of conciliation and arbitration. All kinds of obstacles were placed in the way of that procedure. Governments tried to prevent the Ethiopian government from finding arbitrators amongst their nationals: when once the arbitral tribunal was set up pressure was exercised so that an award favorable to Italy should be given.

All this was in vain: the arbitrators, two of whom were Italian officials, were forced to recognize unanimously that in the Wal–Wal incident, as in the subsequent incidents, no international responsibility was to be attributed to Ethiopia.

Following on this award, the Ethiopian government sincerely thought that an era of friendly relations might be opened with Italy. I loyally offered my hand to the Roman government. The assembly was informed by the report of the Committee of Thirteen, dated October 5, 1935, of the details of the events which occurred after the month of December 1934, and up to October 3, 1935.

It will be sufficient if I quote a few of the conclusions of that report Nos. 24, 25 and 26:

The Italian memorandum (containing the complaints made by Italy) was laid on the Council table on September 4, 1935, whereas Ethiopia's first appeal to the Council had been made on December 14, 1934. In the interval between these two dates, the Italian government opposed the consideration of the question by the Council on the ground that the only appropriate procedure was that provided for in the Italo-Ethiopian Treaty of 1928. Throughout the whole of that period, moreover, the dispatch of Italian troops to East Africa was proceeding. These shipments of troops were represented to the Council by the Italian Government as necessary for the defense of its colonies menaced by Ethiopia's preparations. Ethiopia, on the contrary, drew attention to the official pronouncements made in Italy which, in its opinion, left no doubt "as to the hostile intentions of the Italian Government."

From the outset of the dispute, the Ethiopian Government has sought a settlement by peaceful means. It has appealed to the procedures of the covenant. The Italian government desiring to keep strictly to the procedures of the Italo-Ethiopian Treaty of 1928, the Ethiopian government assented. It invariably stated that it would faithfully carry out the arbitral award even if the decision went against it. It agreed that the question of the ownership of Wal-Wal should not be dealt with by the arbitrators, because the Italian government would not agree to such a course. It asked the council to dispatch neutral observers and offered to lend itself to any enquiries upon which the council might decide.

Once the Wal-Wal dispute had been settled by arbitration, however, the Italian government submitted its detailed memorandum to the Council in support of its claim to liberty of action. It asserted that a case like that of Ethiopia cannot be settled by the means provided by the Covenant. It stated that, "since this question affects vital interest and is of primary importance to Italian security and civilization" it "would be failing in its most elementary duty, did it not cease once and for all to place any confidence in Ethiopia, reserving full liberty to adopt any measures that may become necessary to ensure the safety of its colonies and to safeguard its own interests."

Those are the terms of the report of the Committee of Thirteen. The council and the assembly unanimously adopted the conclusion that the Italian government had violated the covenant and was in a state of aggression. I did not hesitate to declare that I did not wish for war, that it was imposed upon me, and I should struggle solely for the independence and integrity of my people, and that in that struggle I was the defender of the cause of all small states exposed to the greed of a powerful neighbor.

In October 1935, the fifty-two nations who are listening to me today gave me an assurance that the aggressor would not triumph, that the resources of the covenant would be employed in order to ensure the reign of right and the failure of violence.

I ask the fifty-two nations not to forget today the policy upon which they embarked eight months ago, and on faith of which I directed the resistance of my people against the aggressor whom they had denounced to the world. Despite the inferiority of my weapons, the complete lack of aircraft, artillery, munitions, hospital services, my confidence in the League was absolute. I thought it to be impossible that fifty-two nations, including the most powerful in the world, should be successfully opposed by a single aggressor. Counting on the faith due to treaties, I had made no preparation for war, and that is the case with certain small countries in Europe.

When the danger became more urgent, being aware of my responsibilities towards my people, during the first six months of 1935 I tried to acquire armaments. Many governments proclaimed an embargo to prevent my doing so, whereas the Italian government through the Suez Canal, was given all facilities for transporting without cessation and without protest, troops, arms, and munitions.

On October 3, 1935, the Italian troops invaded my territory. A few hours later only I decreed general mobilization. In my desire to maintain peace I had, following the example of a great country in Europe on the eve of the Great War, caused my troops to withdraw thirty kilometers so as to remove any pretext of provocation.

War then took place in the atrocious conditions which I have laid before the assembly. In that unequal struggle between a government commanding more than forty-two million inhabitants, having at its disposal financial, industrial and technical means which enabled it to create unlimited quantities of the most death-dealing weapons, and, on the other hand, a small people of twelve million inhabitants, without arms, without resources having on its side only the justice of its own cause and the promise of the League of Nations. What real assistance was given to Ethiopia by the fifty-two nations who had declared the Rome government guilty of a breach of the covenant and had undertaken to prevent the triumph of the aggressor? Has each of the states' members, as it was its duty to do in virtue of its signature appended to Article 15 of the covenant, considered the aggressor as having committed an act of war personally directed against itself? I had placed all my hopes in the execution of these undertakings. My confidence had been confirmed by the repeated declarations made in the council to the effect that aggression must not be rewarded, and that force would end by being compelled to bow before right.

In December 1935, the council made it quite clear that its feelings were in harmony with those of hundreds of millions of people who, in, all parts of the world, had protested against the proposal to dismember Ethiopia. It was constantly repeated that there was not merely a conflict between the Italian Government and the League of Nations, and that is why I personally refused all proposals to my personal advantage made to me by the Italian government, if only I would betray my people and the covenant of the League of Nations. I was defending the cause of all small peoples who are threatened with aggression.

What have become of the promises made to me as long ago as October 1935? I noted with grief, but without surprise that three powers considered their undertakings under the covenant as absolutely of no value. Their connections with Italy impelled them to refuse to take any measures whatsoever in order to stop Italian aggression. On the contrary, it was a profound disappointment to me to learn the attitude of a certain government which, whilst ever protesting its scrupulous attachment to the covenant, has tirelessly used all its efforts to prevent its observance. As soon as any measure which was likely to be rapidly effective was proposed, various pretexts were devised in order to postpone even consideration of the measure. Did the secret agreements of January 1935 provide for this tireless obstruction?

The Ethiopian government never expected other governments to shed their soldiers' blood to defend the covenant when their own immediately personal interests were not at stake. Ethiopian warriors asked only for means to defend themselves. On many occasions I have asked for financial assistance for the purchase of arms. That assistance has been constantly refused me. What, then, in practice, is the meaning of Article 16 of the covenant and of collective security?

The Ethiopian government's use of the railway from Djibouti to Addis Ababa was in practice a hazardous regards transport of arms intended for the Ethiopian forces. At the present moment this is the chief if not the only means of supply of the Italian armies of occupation. The rules of neutrality should have prohibited transports intended for Italian forces, but there is not even neutrality since Article 16 lays upon every state member of the League the duty not to remain a neutral but to come to the aid not of the aggressor but of the victim of aggression. Has the covenant been respected? Is it today being respected?

Finally a statement has just been made in their parliaments by the governments of certain powers, amongst them the most influential members of the League of Nations, that since the aggressor has succeeded in occupying a large part of Ethiopian territory they propose not to continue the application of any economic and financial measures that may have been decided upon against the Italian government. These are the circumstances in which at the request of the Argentine government, the Assembly of the League of Nations meets to consider the situation created by Italian aggression. I assert that the problem submitted to the assembly today is a much wider one. It is not merely a question of the settlement of Italian aggression.

It is collective security: it is the very existence of the League of Nations. It is the confidence that each state is to place in international treaties. It is the value of promises made to small states that their integrity and their independence shall be respected and ensured. It is the principle of the equality of states on the one hand, or otherwise the obligation laid upon small powers to accept the bonds of vassalship. In a word, it is international morality that is at stake. Have the signatures appended to a treaty value only in so far as the signatory powers have a personal, direct and immediate interest involved?

No subtlety can change the problem or shift the grounds of the discussion. It is in all sincerity that I submit these considerations to the assembly. At a time when my people are threatened with extermination, when the support of the league may ward off the final blow, may I be allowed to speak with complete frankness, without reticence, in all directness such as is demanded by the rule of equality as between all states members of the League?

Apart from the Kingdom of the Lord there is not on this earth any nation that is superior to any other. Should it happen that a strong government finds it may with impunity destroy a weak people, then the hour strikes for that weak people to appeal to the League of Nations to give its judgment in all freedom. God and history will remember your judgment.

I have heard it asserted that the inadequate sanctions already applied have not achieved their object. At no time, and under no circumstances could sanctions that were intentionally inadequate, intentionally badly applied, stop an aggressor. This is not a case of the impossibility of stopping an aggressor but of the refusal to stop an aggressor. When Ethiopia requested and requests that she should be given financial assistance, was that a measure which it was impossible to apply whereas financial assistance of the League has been granted, even in times of peace, to two countries and exactly to two countries who have refused to apply sanctions against the aggressor?

Faced by numerous violations by the Italian government of all international treaties that prohibit resort to arms, and the use of barbarous methods of warfare, it is my painful duty to note that the initiative has today been taken with a view to raising sanctions. Does this initiative not mean in practice the abandonment of Ethiopia to the aggressor? On the very eve of the day when I was about to attempt a supreme effort in the defense of my people before this assembly does not this initiative deprive Ethiopia of one of her last chances to succeed in obtaining the support and guarantee of states members? Is that the guidance the League of Nations and each of the states members are entitled to expect from the great powers when they assert their right and their duty to guide the action of the League? Placed by the aggressor face to face with the accomplished fact, are states going to set up the terrible precedent of bowing before force?

Your assembly will doubtless have laid before it proposals for the reform of the covenant and for rendering more effective the guarantee of collective security. Is it the covenant that needs reform? What undertakings can have any value if the will to keep them is lacking? It is international morality which is at stake and not the articles of the covenant. On behalf of the Ethiopian people, a member of the League of Nations, I request the assembly to take all measures proper to ensure respect for the covenant. I renew my protest against the violations of treaties of which the Ethiopian people has been the victim. I declare in the face of the whole world that the Emperor, the government and the people of Ethiopia will not bow before force; that they maintain their claims that they will use all means in their power to ensure the triumph of right and the respect of the covenant.

I ask the fifty-two nations, who have given the Ethiopian people a promise to help them in their resistance to the aggressor, what are they willing to do for Ethiopia? And the great powers who have promised the guarantee of collective security to small states on whom weighs the threat that they may one day suffer the fate of Ethiopia, I ask what measures do you intend to take?

Representatives of the world, I have come to Geneva to discharge in your midst the most painful of the duties of the head of a state. What reply shall I have to take back to my people?

EDWARD VIII
Farewell Address
("I now quit altogether public affairs and
I lay down my burden")
Radio broadcast
December 11, 1936

*On the day before this broadcast, the king of England (1894–1972) abdi-
cated his throne in order to be able to marry Mrs. Wallis Simpson, an American divorcée. Edward's brother Albert became King George VI. Edward and
Simpson married in 1937.*

At long last I am able to say a few words of my own. I have never
wanted to withhold anything, but until now it has not been constitu-
tionally possible for me to speak.

A few hours ago I discharged my last duty as King and Emperor,
and now that I have been succeeded by my brother, the Duke of
York, my first words must be to declare my allegiance to him. This I
do with all my heart.

You all know the reasons which have impelled me to renounce the
throne. But I want you to understand that in making up my mind I
did not forget the country or the empire, which, as Prince of Wales
and lately as King, I have for twenty-five years tried to serve.

But you must believe me when I tell you that I have found it impossible to carry the heavy burden of responsibility and to discharge
my duties as King as I would wish to do without the help and support
of the woman I love.

And I want you to know that the decision I have made has been
mine and mine alone. This was a thing I had to judge entirely for
myself. The other person most nearly concerned has tried up to the
last to persuade me to take a different course.

I have made this, the most serious decision of my life, only upon
the single thought of what would, in the end, be best for all.

This decision has been made less difficult to me by the sure knowledge that my brother, with his long training in the public affairs of this country and with his fine qualities, will be able to take my place forthwith without interruption or injury to the life and progress of the empire. And he has one matchless blessing, enjoyed by so many of you, and not bestowed on me—a happy home with his wife and children.

During these hard days I have been comforted by her majesty my mother and by my family. The ministers of the crown, and in particular, Mr. Baldwin, the Prime Minister, have always treated me with full consideration. There has never been any constitutional difference between me and them, and between me and Parliament. Bred in the constitutional tradition by my father, I should never have allowed any such issue to arise.

Ever since I was Prince of Wales, and later on when I occupied the throne, I have been treated with the greatest kindness by all classes of the people wherever I have lived or journeyed throughout the empire. For that I am very grateful.

I now quit altogether public affairs and I lay down my burden. It may be some time before I return to my native land, but I shall always follow the fortunes of the British race and empire with profound interest, and if at any time in the future I can be found of service to his majesty in a private station, I shall not fail.

And now, we all have a new King. I wish him and you, his people, happiness and prosperity with all my heart. God bless you all! God save the King!

WINSTON CHURCHILL
Blood, Sweat and Tears
("I have nothing to offer but blood, toil, tears, and sweat")
London, England
May 13, 1940

One of the finest orators of the century and the prime minister of Great Britain from 1940 to 1945, Churchill (1874–1965) helped create the feeling that England could and would survive World War II and defeat Germany. Churchill replaced Neville Chamberlain, whose policy as prime minister had been to appease Hitler and the Nazis. This short radio message was Churchill's first speech as prime minister before Parliament.

On Friday evening last I received from His Majesty the mission to form a new administration.

It was the evident will of Parliament and the nation that this should be conceived on the broadest possible basis and that it should include all parties.

I have already completed the most important part of this task. A war cabinet has been formed of five members, representing, with the Labor, Opposition and Liberals, the unity of the nation.

It was necessary that this should be done in one single day on account of the extreme urgency and rigor of events. Other key positions were filled yesterday. I am submitting a further list to the King tonight. I hope to complete the appointment of principal Ministers during tomorrow.

The appointment of other Ministers usually takes a little longer. I trust when Parliament meets again this part of my task will be completed and that the administration will be complete in all respects.

I considered it in the public interest to suggest to the Speaker that the House should be summoned today. At the end of today's proceedings, the adjournment of the House will be proposed until May 21 with provision for earlier meeting if need be. Business for that will be notified to M. P.'s at the earliest opportunity.

I now invite the House by a resolution to record its approval of the steps taken and declare its confidence in the new government. The resolution:

"That this House welcomes the formation of a government representing the united and inflexible resolve of the nation to prosecute the war with Germany to a victorious conclusion."

To form an administration of this scale and complexity is a serious undertaking in itself. But we are in the preliminary phase of one of the greatest battles in history. We are in action at many other points—in Norway and in Holland—and we have to be prepared in the Mediterranean. The air battle is continuing, and many preparations have to be made here at home.

In this crisis I think I may be pardoned if I do not address the House at any length today, and I hope that any of my friends and colleagues or former colleagues who are affected by the political reconstruction will make all allowances for any lack of ceremony with which it has been necessary to act.

I say to the House as I said to Ministers who have joined this government, I have nothing to offer but blood, toil, tears and sweat. We have before us an ordeal of the most grievous kind. We have before us many, many months of struggle and suffering.

You ask, what is our policy? I say it is to wage war by land, sea and air. War with all our might and with all the strength God has given us, and to wage war against a monstrous tyranny never surpassed in the dark and lamentable catalogue of human crime. That is our policy.

You ask, what is our aim? I can answer in one word. It is victory. Victory at all costs—victory in spite of all terrors—victory, however long and hard the road may be, for without victory there is no survival.

Let that be realized. No survival for the British Empire, no survival for all that the British Empire has stood for, no survival for the urge, the impulse of the ages, that mankind shall move forward toward his goal.

I take up my task in buoyancy and hope. I feel sure that our cause will not be suffered to fail among men.

I feel entitled at this juncture, at this time, to claim the aid of all and to say, "Come then, let us go forward together with our united strength."

CHARLES DE GAULLE
The Flame of French Resistance
(". . . all free Frenchmen, wherever they be, should
continue the fight as best they may")
London, England, BBC radio broadcast
June 22, 1940

Charles de Gaulle (1890–1970) was the French general who led the resistance to the Nazi invasion during World War II. In early June of 1940, a new French prime minister, Henri-Philippe Petain, sought an armistice with Germany, which prompted de Gaulle's move to England and broadcasting BBC radio messages to the "free French." He became the recognized leader of the military resistance, became co-president in 1943 of the French Committee of National Liberation, and returned triumphant to France in 1944.

The French government, after having asked for an armistice, now knows the conditions dictated by the enemy.

The result of these conditions would be the complete demobilization of the French land, sea, and air forces, the surrender of our weapons and the total occupation of French territory. The French government would come under German and Italian tutelage.

It may therefore be said that this armistice would not only be a capitulation, but that it would also reduce the country to slavery. Now, a great many Frenchmen refuse to accept either capitulation or slavery, for reasons which are called: honor, common sense, and the higher interests of the country.

I say honor, for France has undertaken not to lay down arms save in agreement with her allies. As long as the allies continue the war, her government has no right to surrender to the enemy. The Polish, Norwegian, Belgian, Netherlands, and Luxemburg governments, though driven from their territories, have thus interpreted their duty. I say common sense, for it is absurd to consider the struggle as lost. True, we have suffered a major defeat. We lost the battle of France through a faulty military system, mistakes in the conduct of operations, and the defeatist spirit shown by the government during recent battles. But we still have a vast empire, our fleet is intact, and we possess large sums in gold. We still have the gigantic potentialities of American industry. The same war conditions which caused us to be beaten by 5,000 planes and 6,000 tanks can tomorrow bring victory by means of 20,000 tanks and 20,000 planes.

I say the higher interests of the country, for this is not a Franco-German war to be decided by a single battle. This is a world war. No one can foresee whether the neutral countries of today will not be at war tomorrow, or whether Germany's allies will always remain her allies. If the powers of freedom ultimately triumph over those of servitude, what will be the fate of a France which has submitted to the enemy?

Honor, common sense, and the interests of the country require that all free Frenchmen, wherever they be, should continue the fight as best they may.

It is therefore necessary to group the largest possible French force wherever this can be done. Everything which can be collected by way of French military elements and potentialities for armaments production must be organized wherever such elements exist.

I, General de Gaulle, am undertaking this national task here in England.

I call upon all French servicemen of the land, sea, and air forces; I call upon French engineers and skilled armaments workers who are on British soil, or have the means of getting here, to come and join me.

I call upon the leaders, together with all soldiers, sailors, and airmen of the French land, sea, and air forces, wherever they may now be, to get in touch with me.

I call upon all Frenchmen who want to remain free to listen to my voice and follow me.

Long live free France in honor and independence!

FRANKLIN DELANO ROOSEVELT
The Arsenal of Democracy
("If Great Britain goes down, the Axis powers will control
the continents of Europe, Asia, Africa, Australasia,
and the high seas")
Washington, D.C.
December 29, 1940

As president of the United States, Roosevelt (1882–1945) was steering the country out of the Great Depression, but had not yet convinced Congress to declare war. He spoke here in a national broadcast to American citizens to rally aid and support for the European countries fighting the Nazis and the Axis powers.

My friends:

This is not a fireside chat on war. It is a talk on national security; because the nub of the whole purpose of your President is to keep you now, and your children later, and your grandchildren much later, out of a last-ditch war for the preservation of American independence and all of the things that American independence means to you and to me and to ours.

Tonight, in the presence of a world crisis, my mind goes back eight years to a night in the midst of a domestic crisis. It was a time when the wheels of American industry were grinding to a full stop, when the whole banking system of our country had ceased to function.

I well remember that while I sat in my study in the White House, preparing to talk with the people of the United States, I had before my eyes the picture of all those Americans with whom I was talking. I saw the workmen in the mills, the mines, the factories; the girl behind the counter; the small shopkeeper; the farmer doing his spring plowing; the widows and the old men wondering about their life's savings.

I tried to convey to the great mass of American people what the banking crisis meant to them in their daily lives.

Tonight I want to do the same thing, with the same people, in this new crisis which faces America.

We met the issue of 1933 with courage and realism. We face this new crisis—this new threat to the security of our nation—with the same courage and realism.

Never before since Jamestown and Plymouth Rock has our American civilization been in such danger as now.

For on September 27th, 1940—this year—by an agreement signed in Berlin, three powerful nations, two in Europe and one in Asia, joined themselves together in the threat that if the United States of America interfered with or blocked the expansion program of these three nations—a program aimed at world control—they would unite in ultimate action against the United States.

The Nazi masters of Germany have made it clear that they intend not only to dominate all life and thought in their own country, but also to enslave the whole of Europe, and then to use the resources of Europe to dominate the rest of the world.

It was only three weeks ago that their leader stated this: "There are two worlds that stand opposed to each other." And then in defiant reply to his opponents he said this: "Others are correct when they say: 'With this world we cannot ever reconcile ourselves.' I can beat any other power in the world." So said the leader of the Nazis.

In other words, the Axis not merely admits but the Axis proclaims that there can be no ultimate peace between their philosophy—their philosophy of government—and our philosophy of government.

In view of the nature of this undeniable threat, it can be asserted, properly and categorically, that the United States has no right or reason to encourage talk of peace until the day shall come when there is a clear intention on the part of the aggressor nations to abandon all thought of dominating or conquering the world.

At this moment the forces of the States that are leagued against all peoples who live in freedom are being held away from our shores. The Germans and the Italians are being blocked on the other side of the Atlantic by the British and by the Greeks, and by thousands of soldiers and sailors who were able to escape from subjugated countries. In Asia the Japanese are being engaged by the Chinese nation in another great defense.

In the Pacific Ocean is our fleet.

Some of our people like to believe that wars in Europe and in Asia are of no concern to us. But it is a matter of most vital concern to us that European and Asiatic war-makers should not gain control of the oceans which lead to this hemisphere.

One hundred and seventeen years ago the Monroe Doctrine was conceived by our government as a measure of defense in the face of a threat against this hemisphere by an alliance in Continental Europe. Thereafter, we stood guard in the Atlantic, with the British as neighbors. There was no treaty. There was no "unwritten agreement."

And yet there was the feeling, proven correct by history, that we as neighbors could settle any disputes in peaceful fashion. And the fact is that during the whole of this time the Western Hemisphere has remained free from aggression from Europe or from Asia.

Does any one seriously believe that we need to fear attack anywhere in the Americas while a free Britain remains our most powerful naval neighbor in the Atlantic? And does any one seriously believe, on the other hand, that we could rest easy if the Axis powers were our neighbors there?

If Great Britain goes down, the Axis powers will control the Continents of Europe, Asia, Africa, Australasia, and the high seas—and they will be in a position to bring enormous military and naval resources against this hemisphere. It is no exaggeration to say that all of us in all the Americas would be living at the point of a gun—a gun loaded with explosive bullets, economic as well as military.

We should enter upon a new and terrible era in which the whole world, our hemisphere included, would be run by threats of brute force. And to survive in such a world, we would have to convert ourselves permanently into a militaristic power on the basis of war economy.

Some of us like to believe that even if Britain falls, we are still safe, because of the broad expanse of the Atlantic and of the Pacific.

But the width of those oceans is not what it was in the days of clipper ships. At one point between Africa and Brazil the distance is less than it is from Washington to Denver, Colorado, five hours for the latest type of bomber. And at the north end of the Pacific Ocean, America and Asia almost touch each other.

Why, even today we have planes that could fly from the British Isles to New England and back again without refueling. And remember that the range of the modern bomber is ever being increased.

During the past week many people in all parts of the nation have told me what they wanted to say tonight. Almost all of them expressed a courageous desire to hear the plain truth about the gravity of the situation. One telegram, however, expressed the attitude of the small minority who want to see no evil and hear no evil, even though they know in their hearts that evil exists. That telegram begged me not to tell again of the ease with which our American cities could be bombed by any hostile power which had gained bases in this Western Hemisphere. The gist of that telegram was: "Please, Mr. President, don't frighten us by telling us the facts."

Frankly and definitely there is danger ahead—danger against which we must prepare. But we well know that we cannot escape danger, or the fear of danger, by crawling into bed and pulling the covers over our heads.

Some nations of Europe were bound by solemn non-intervention pacts with Germany. Other nations were assured by Germany that they need never fear invasion. Non-intervention pact or not, the fact remains that they were attacked, overrun, thrown into modern slavery at an hour's notice or even without any notice at all.

As an exiled leader of one of these nations said to me the other day, "The notice was a minus quantity. It was given to my government two hours after German troops had poured into my country in a hundred places." The fate of these nations tells us what it means to live at the point of a Nazi gun.

The Nazis have justified such actions by various pious frauds. One of these frauds is the claim that they are occupying a nation for the purpose of "restoring order." Another is that they are occupying or controlling a nation on the excuse that they are "protecting it" against the aggression of somebody else.

For example, Germany has said that she was occupying Belgium to save the Belgians from the British. Would she then hesitate to say to any South American country: "We are occupying you to protect you from aggression by the United States"?

Belgium today is being used as an invasion base against Britain, now fighting for its life. And any South American country, in Nazi hands, would always constitute a jumping off place for German attack on any one of the other republics of this hemisphere.

Analyze for yourselves the future of two other places even nearer to Germany if the Nazis won. Could Ireland hold out? Would Irish freedom be permitted as an amazing pet exception in an unfree world? Or the islands of the Azores, which still fly the flag of Portugal after five centuries? You and I think of Hawaii as an outpost of defense in the Pacific. And yet the Azores are closer to our shores in the Atlantic than Hawaii is on the other side.

There are those who say that the Axis powers would never have any desire to attack the Western Hemisphere. That is the same dangerous form of wishful thinking which has destroyed the powers of resistance of so many conquered peoples. The plain facts are that the Nazis have proclaimed, time and again, that all other races are their inferiors and therefore subject to their orders. And most important of all, the vast resources and wealth of this American hemisphere constitute the most tempting loot in all of the round world.

Let us no longer blind ourselves to the undeniable fact that the evil forces which have crushed and undermined and corrupted so many others are already within our own gates. Your government knows much about them and every day is ferreting them out.

Their secret emissaries are active in our own and in neighboring countries. They seek to stir up suspicion and dissension, to cause internal strife. They try to turn capital against labor, and vice versa. They try to reawaken long slumbering racial and religious enmities which should have no place in this country. They are active in every group that promotes intolerance. They exploit for their own ends our own natural abhorrence of war.

These trouble-breeders have but one purpose. It is to divide our people, to divide them into hostile groups and to destroy our unity and shatter our will to defend ourselves.

There are also American citizens, many of them in high places, who, unwittingly in most cases, are aiding and abetting the work of these agents. I do not charge these American citizens with being foreign agents. But I do charge them with doing exactly the kind of work that the dictators want done in the United States.

These people not only believe that we can save our own skins by shutting our eyes to the fate of other nations. Some of them go much further than that. They say that we can and should become the friends and even the partners of the Axis powers. Some of them even suggest that we should imitate the methods of the dictatorships. But Americans never can and never will do that.

The experience of the past two years has proven beyond doubt that no nation can appease the Nazis. No man can tame a tiger into a kitten by stroking it. There can be no appeasement with ruthlessness. There can be no reasoning with an incendiary bomb. We know now that a nation can have peace with the Nazis only at the price of total surrender.

Even the people of Italy have been forced to become accomplices of the Nazis; but at this moment they do not know how soon they will be embraced to death by their allies.

The American appeasers ignore the warning to be found in the fate of Austria, Czecho-Slovakia, Poland, Norway, Belgium, the Netherlands, Denmark, and France. They tell you that the Axis powers are going to win anyway; that all of this bloodshed in the world could be saved, that the United States might just as well throw its influence into the scale of a dictated peace and get the best out of it that we can.

They call it a "negotiated peace." Nonsense! Is it a negotiated peace if a gang of outlaws surrounds your community and on threat of extermination makes you pay tribute to save your own skins?

Such a dictated peace would be no peace at all. It would be only another armistice, leading to the most gigantic armament race and the most devastating trade wars in all history. And in these contests the Americas would offer the only real resistance to the Axis powers. With all their vaunted efficiency, with all their parade of pious purpose in this war, there are still in their background the concentration camp and the servants of God in chains.

The history of recent years proves that the shootings and the chains and the concentration camps are not simply the transient tools but the very altars of modern dictatorships. They may talk of a "new order" in the world, but what they have in mind is only a revival of the oldest and the worst tyranny. In that there is no liberty, no religion, no hope.

The proposed "new order" is the very opposite of a United States of Europe or a United States of Asia. It is not a government based upon the consent of the governed. It is not a union of ordinary, self-respecting men and women to protect themselves and their freedom and their dignity from oppression. It is an unholy alliance of power and pelf to dominate and to enslave the human race.

The British people and their allies today are conducting an active war against this unholy alliance. Our own future security is greatly dependent on the outcome of that fight. Our ability to "keep out of war" is going to be affected by that outcome.

Thinking in terms of today and tomorrow, I make the direct statement to the American people that there is far less chance of the United States getting into war if we do all we can now to support the nations defending themselves against attack by the Axis than if we acquiesce in their defeat, submit tamely to an Axis victory, and wait our turn to be the object of attack in another war later on.

If we are to be completely honest with ourselves, we must admit that there is risk in any course we may take. But I deeply believe that the great majority of our people agree that the course that I advocate involves the least risk now and the greatest hope for world peace in the future.

The people of Europe who are defending themselves do not ask us to do their fighting. They ask us for the implements of war, the planes, the tanks, the guns, the freighters which will enable them to fight for their liberty and for our security. Emphatically, we must get these weapons to them, get them to them in sufficient volume and quickly enough so that we and our children will be saved the agony and suffering of war which others have had to endure.

Let not the defeatists tell us that it is too late. It will never be earlier. Tomorrow will be later than today.

Certain facts are self-evident.

In a military sense Great Britain and the British Empire are today the spearhead of resistance to world conquest. And they are putting up a fight which will live forever in the story of human gallantry.

There is no demand for sending an American expeditionary force outside our own borders. There is no intention by any member of your government to send such a force. You can therefore, nail, nail any talk about sending armies to Europe as deliberate untruth.

Our national policy is not directed toward war. Its sole purpose is to keep war away from our country and away from our people.

Democracy's fight against world conquest is being greatly aided, and must be more greatly aided, by the rearmament of the United States and by sending every ounce and every ton of munitions and supplies that we can possibly spare to help the defenders who are in the front lines. And it is no more unneutral for us to do that than it is for Sweden, Russia, and other nations near Germany to send steel and ore and oil and other war materials into Germany every day in the week.

We are planning our own defense with the utmost urgency, and in its vast scale we must integrate the war needs of Britain and the other free nations which are resisting aggression.

This is not a matter of sentiment or of controversial personal opinion. It is a matter of realistic, practical military policy, based on the advice of our military experts who are in close touch with existing warfare. These military and naval experts and the members of the Congress and the Administration have a single-minded purpose—the defense of the United States.

This nation is making a great effort to produce everything that is necessary in this emergency—and with all possible speed. And this great effort requires great sacrifice.

I would ask no one to defend a democracy which in turn would not defend every one in the nation against want and privation. The strength of this nation shall not be diluted by the failure of the government to protect the economic well-being of its citizens.

If our capacity to produce is limited by machines, it must ever be remembered that these machines are operated by the skill and the stamina of the workers. As the government is determined to protect the rights of the workers, so the nation has a right to expect that the men who man the machines will discharge their full responsibilities to the urgent needs of defense.

The worker possesses the same human dignity and is entitled to the same security of position as the engineer or the manager or the owner. For the workers provide the human power that turns out the destroyers, and the planes and the tanks.

The nation expects our defense industries to continue operation without interruption by strikes or lockouts. It expects and insists that management and workers will reconcile their differences by voluntary or legal means, to continue to produce the supplies that are so sorely needed.

And on the economic side of our great defense program, we are, as you know, bending every effort to maintain stability of prices and with that the stability of the cost of living.

Nine days ago I announced the setting up of a more effective organization to direct our gigantic efforts to increase the production of munitions. The appropriation of vast sums of money and a well-coordinated executive direction of our defense efforts are not in themselves enough. Guns, planes, ships and many other things have to be built in the factories and the arsenals of America. They have to be produced by workers and managers and engineers with the aid of machines which in turn have to be built by hundreds of thousands of workers throughout the land.

In this great work there has been splendid cooperation between the government and industry and labor. And I am very thankful.

American industrial genius, unmatched throughout all the world in the solution of production problems, has been called upon to bring its resources and its talents into action. Manufacturers of watches, of farm implements, of linotypes and cash registers and automobiles, and sewing machines and lawn mowers and locomotives, are now making fuses and bomb packing crates and telescope mounts and shells and pistols and tanks.

But all of our present efforts are not enough. We must have more ships, more guns, more planes—more of everything. And this can be accomplished only if we discard the notion of "business as usual." This job cannot be done merely by superimposing on the existing productive facilities the added requirements of the nation for defense.

Our defense efforts must not be blocked by those who fear the future consequences of surplus plant capacity. The possible consequences of failure of our defense efforts now are much more to be feared.

And after the present needs of our defense are past, a proper handling of the country's peacetime needs will require all of the new productive capacity, if not still more.

No pessimistic policy about the future of America shall delay the immediate expansion of those industries essential to defense. We need them.

I want to make it clear that it is the purpose of the nation to build now with all possible speed every machine, every arsenal, every factory that we need to manufacture our defense material. We have the men—the skill—the wealth—and above all, the will.

I am confident that if and when production of consumer or luxury goods in certain industries requires the use of machines and raw materials that are essential for defense purposes, then such production must yield, and will gladly yield, to our primary and compelling purpose.

So I appeal to the owners of plants—to the managers—to the workers—to our own government employees—to put every ounce of effort into producing these munitions swiftly and without stint. With this appeal I give you the pledge that all of us who are officers of your government will devote ourselves to the same whole-hearted extent to the great task that lies ahead.

As planes and ships and guns and shells are produced, your government, with its defense experts, can then determine how best to use them to defend this hemisphere. The decision as to how much shall be sent abroad and how much shall remain at home must be made on the basis of our over-all military necessities.

We must be the great arsenal of democracy. For us this is an emergency as serious as war itself. We must apply ourselves to our task with the same resolution, the same sense of urgency, the same spirit of patriotism and sacrifice as we would show were we at war.

We have furnished the British great material support and we will furnish far more in the future.

There will be no "bottlenecks" in our determination to aid Great Britain. No dictator, no combination of dictators, will weaken that determination by threats of how they will construe that determination.

The British have received invaluable military support from the heroic Greek Army and from the forces of all the governments in exile. Their strength is growing. It is the strength of men and women who value their freedom more highly than they value their lives.

I believe that the Axis powers are not going to win this war. I base that belief on the latest and best of information.

We have no excuse for defeatism. We have every good reason for hope—hope for peace, yes, and hope for the defense of our civilization and for the building of a better civilization in the future.

I have the profound conviction that the American people are now determined to put forth a mightier effort than they have ever yet made to increase our production of all the implements of defense, to meet the threat to our democratic faith.

As President of the United States, I call for that national effort. I call for it in the name of this nation which we love and honor and which we are privileged and proud to serve. I call upon our people with absolute confidence that our common cause will greatly succeed.

GEORGE S. PATTON, JR.
The Invasion of Normandy
("The shortest road home is through Berlin and Tokyo!")
England
May 17, 1944

The fiery general of the U.S. Third Army, George S. Patton, Jr. (1885–1945), prepared his men for D-Day, the Allied onslaught that would help defeat the Nazi forces in France. Because of an altercation with a soldier, Patton himself was held out of the action until August.

Men, this stuff some sources sling around about America wanting to stay out of the war and not wanting to fight is a lot of baloney! Americans love to fight, traditionally. All real Americans love the sting and clash of battle. America loves a winner. America will not tolerate a loser. Americans despise a coward; Americans play to win. That's why America has never lost and never will lose a war.

You are not all going to die. Only two percent of you, right here today, would be killed in a major battle. Death must not be feared. Death, in time, comes to all of us. And every man is scared in his first action. If he says he's not, he's a goddamn liar. Some men are cowards, yes, but they fight just the same, or get the hell slammed out of them.

The real hero is the man who fights even though he's scared. Some get over their fright in a minute, under fire; others take an hour; for some it takes days; but a real man will never let the fear of death overpower his honor, his sense of duty, to his country and to his manhood.

All through your Army careers, you've been bitching about what you call "chicken-shit drills." That, like everything else in the Army, has a definite purpose. That purpose is instant obedience to orders and to create and maintain constant alertness! This must be bred into every soldier. A man must be alert all the time if he expects to stay alive. If not, some German son-of-a-bitch will sneak up behind him with a

71

sock full of shit! There are four hundred neatly marked graves somewhere in Sicily, all because one man went to sleep on his job—but
they are German graves, because we caught the bastards asleep!

An Army is a team, lives, sleeps, fights, and eats as a team. This
individual hero stuff is a lot of horseshit! The bilious bastards who
write that kind of stuff for the *Saturday Evening Post* don't know any
more about real fighting under fire than they know about fucking!
Every single man in the Army plays a vital role. Every man has his job
to do and must do it. What if every truck driver decided that he
didn't like the whine of a shell overhead, turned yellow and jumped
headlong into a ditch? What if every man thought, "They won't miss
me, just one in millions?" Where in Hell would we be now? Where
would our country, our loved ones, our homes, even the world, be?

No, thank God, Americans don't think like that. Every man does
his job, serves the whole. Ordnance men supply and maintain the
guns and vast machinery of this war, to keep us rolling. Quartermas-
ters bring up clothes and food, for where we're going, there isn't a
hell of a lot to steal. Every last man on K.P. has a job to do, even the
guy who boils the water to keep us from getting the G.I. shits!

Remember, men, you don't know I'm here. No mention of that
is to be made in any letters. The U.S.A. is supposed to be wondering
what the hell has happened to me. I'm not supposed to be commanding this Army, I'm not supposed even to be in England. Let the first
bastards to find out be the goddamn Germans. I want them to look
up and howl, "Ach, it's the goddamn Third Army and that son-of-a-
bitch Patton again!"

We want to get this thing over and get the hell out of here, and
get at those purple-pissin' Japs! The shortest road home is through
Berlin and Tokyo! We'll win this war, but we'll win it only by showing the enemy we have more guts than they have or ever will have!

There's one great thing you men can say when it's all over and
you're home once more. You can thank God that twenty years from
now, when you're sitting around the fireside with your grandson on
your knee and he asks you what you did in the war, you won't have
to shift him to the other knee, cough, and say, "I shoveled shit in
Louisiana."

W. E. B. DU BOIS
Behold the Land
(". . . the working people of the South, white and black,
must come to remember that their emancipation depends
upon their mutual cooperation")
Southern Youth Legislature
Southern Negro Youth Congress
October 20, 1946

*Du Bois (1868–1963) was a scholar, author, civil rights activist, and in
1909 one of the founders of the National Association for the Advancement of
Colored People. Over his long life he went through many changes of philosophy about the pressing social problems facing African-Americans.*

The future of American Negroes is in the South. Here three hundred
and twenty-seven years ago, they began to enter what is now the
United States of America; here they have made their greatest contribution to American culture; and here they have suffered the domination of slavery, the frustration of reconstruction and the lynching of
emancipation. I trust then that an organization like yours is going to
regard the South as the battle-ground of a great crusade. Here is the
magnificent climate; here is the fruitful earth under the beauty of the
southern sun; and here, if anywhere on earth, is the need of the
thinker, the worker and the dreamer. This is the firing line not simply
for the emancipation of the American Negro but for the emancipation of the African Negro and the Negroes of the West Indies; for the
emancipation of the colored races; and for the emancipation of the
white slaves of modern capitalistic monopoly.

Remember here, too, that you do not stand alone. It may seem like
a failing fight when the newspapers ignore you; when every effort is
made by white people in the South to count you out of citizenship
and to act as though you did not exist as human beings while all the
time they are profiting by your labor; gleaning wealth from your
sacrifices and trying to build a nation and a civilization upon your

73

degradation. You must remember that despite all this, you have allies and allies even in the white South. First and greatest of these possible allies are the white working classes about you. The poor whites whom you have been taught to despise and who in turn have learned to fear and hate you. This must not deter you from efforts to make them understand, because in the past in their ignorance and suffering they have been led foolishly to look upon you as the cause of most of their distress. You must remember that this attitude is hereditary from slavery and that it has been deliberately cultivated ever since emancipation.

Slowly but surely the working people of the South, white and black, must come to remember that their emancipation depends upon their mutual cooperation; upon their acquaintanceship with each other; upon their friendship; upon their social intermingling. Unless this happens each is going to be made the football to break the heads and hearts of the other.

White youth in the South is peculiarly frustrated. There is not a single great ideal which they can express or aspire to, that does not bring them into flat contradiction with the Negro problem. The more they try to escape it, the more they land into hypocrisy, lying and double-dealing; the more they become, what they least wish to become, the oppressors and despisers of human beings. Some of them, in larger and larger numbers, are bound to turn toward the truth and to recognize you as brothers and sisters, as fellow travelers toward the dawn.

There has always been in the South that intellectual elite who saw the Negro problem clearly. They have always lacked and some still lack the courage to stand up for what they know is right. Nevertheless they can be depended on in the long run to follow their own clear thinking and their own decent choice. Finally even the politicians must eventually recognize the trend in the world, in this country, and in the South. James Byrnes, that favorite son of this commonwealth, and Secretary of State of the United States, is today occupying an indefensible and impossible position; and if he survives in the memory of men, he must begin to help establish in his own South Carolina something of that democracy which he has been recently so loudly preaching to Russia. He is the end of a long series of men whose eternal damnation is the fact that they looked *truth* in the face and did not see it; John C. Calhoun, Wade Hampton, Ben Tillman are men whose names must ever be besmirched by the fact that they fought against freedom and democracy in a land which was founded upon democracy and freedom.

Eventually this class of men must yield to the writing in the stars. That great hypocrite, Jan Smuts, who today is talking of humanity and standing beside Byrnes for a United Nations, is at the same time oppressing the black people of Africa to an extent which makes their two countries, South Africa and the American South, the most reactionary peoples on earth. Peoples whose exploitation of the poor and helpless reaches the last degree of shame. They must in the long run yield to the forward march of civilization or die.

If now you young people, instead of running away from the battle here in Carolina, George, Alabama, Louisiana and Mississippi, instead of seeking freedom and opportunity in Chicago and New York—which do spell opportunity—nevertheless grit your teeth and make up your minds to fight it out right here if it takes every day of your lives and the lives of your children's children; if you do this, you must in meetings like this ask yourselves what does the fight mean? How can it be carried on? What are the best tools, arms, and methods? And where does it lead?

I should be the last to insist that the uplift of mankind never calls for force and death. There are times, as both you and I know, when

> Tho' love repine and reason chafe,
> There came a voice without reply,
> 'Tis man's perdition to be safe
> When for truth he ought to die.

At the same time and even more clearly in a day like this, after the millions of mass murders that have been done in the world since 1914, we ought to be the last to believe that force is ever the final word. We cannot escape the clear fact that what is going to win in this world is reason if this ever becomes a reasonable world. The careful reasoning of the human mind backed by the facts of science is the one salvation of man. The world, if it resumes its march toward civilization, cannot ignore reason. This has been the tragedy of the South in the past; it is still its awful and unforgivable sin that it has set its face against reason and against the fact. It tried to build slavery upon freedom; it tried to build tyranny upon democracy; it tried to build mob violence on law and law on lynching and in all that despicable endeavor, the state of South Carolina has led the South for a century. It began not the Civil War—not the War between the States—but the War to Preserve Slavery; it began mob violence and lynching and today it stands in the front rank of those defying the Supreme Court on disfranchisement.

Nevertheless reason can and will prevail; but of course it can only prevail with publicity—pitiless, blatant publicity. You have got to make the people of the United States and of the world know what is going on in the South. You have got to use every field of publicity to force the truth into their ears, and before their eyes. You have got to make it impossible for any human being to live in the South and not realize the barbarities that prevail here. You may be condemned for flamboyant methods; for calling a congress like this; for waving your grievances under the noses and in the faces of men. That makes no difference; it is your duty to do it. It is your duty to do more of this sort of thing than you have done in the past. As a result of this you are going to be called upon for sacrifice. It is no easy thing for a young black man or a young black woman to live in the South today and to plan to continue to live here; to marry and raise children; to establish a home. They are in the midst of legal caste and customary insults; they are in continuous danger of mob violence; they are mistreated by the officers of the law and they have no hearing before the courts and the churches and public opinion commensurate with the attention which they ought to receive. But that sacrifice is only the beginning of battle, you must re-build this South.

There are enormous opportunities here for a new nation, a new economy, a new culture in a South really new and not a mere renewal of an old South of slavery, monopoly and race hate. There is a chance for a new cooperative agriculture on renewed land owned by the state with capital furnished by the state, mechanized and coordinated with city life. There is chance for strong, virile trade unions without race discrimination, with high wage, closed shop and decent conditions of work, to beat back and hold in check the swarm of landlords, monopolists and profiteers who are today sucking the blood out of this land. There is chance for cooperative industry, built on the cheap power of T.V.A. and its future extensions. There is opportunity to organize and mechanize domestic service with decent hours, and high wage and dignified training.

There is a vast field for consumers cooperation, building business on public service and not on private profit as the main-spring of industry. There is chance for a broad, sunny, healthy home life, shorn of the fear of mobs and liquor, and rescued from lying, stealing politicians, who build their delivery on race prejudice.

Here in this South is the gateway to the colored millions of the West Indies, Central and South America. Here is the straight path to Africa, the Indies, China and the South Seas. Here is the path to the greater, freer, truer world. It would be shame and cowardice to surrender this glorious land and its opportunities for civilization and humanity to the thugs and lynchers, the mobs and profiteers, the monopolists and gamblers who today choke its soul and steal its resources. The oil and sulphur; the coal and iron; the cotton and corn; the lumber and cattle belong to you the workers, black and white, and not to the thieves who hold them and use them to enslave you. They can be rescued and restored to the people if you have the guts to strive for the real right to vote, the right to real education, the right to happiness and health and the total abolition of the father of these scourges of mankind, *poverty*.

"Behold the beautiful land which the Lord thy God hath given thee." Behold the land, the rich and resourceful land, from which for a hundred years its best elements have been running away, its youth and hope, black and white, scurrying North because they are afraid of each other, and dare not face a future of equal, independent, upstanding human beings, in a real and not a sham democracy.

To rescue this land, in this way, calls for the *Great Sacrifice*. This is the thing that you are called upon to do because it is the right thing to do. Because you are embarked upon a great and holy crusade, the emancipation of mankind, black and white; the upbuilding of democracy; the breaking down, particularly here in the South, of forces of evil represented by race prejudice in South Carolina; by lynching in Georgia; by disfranchisement in Mississippi; by ignorance in Louisiana and by all these and monopoly of wealth in the whole South.

There could be no more splendid vocation beckoning to the youth of the twentieth century, after the flat failures of white civilization, after the flamboyant establishment of an industrial system which creates poverty and the children of poverty which are ignorance and disease and crime; after the crazy boasting of a white culture that finally ended in wars which ruined civilization in the whole world; in the midst of allied peoples who have yelled about democracy and never practiced it either in the British Empire or in the American Commonwealth or in South Carolina.

Here is the chance for young women and young men of devotion to lift again the banner of humanity and to walk toward a civilization which will be free and intelligent; which will be healthy and unafraid; and build in the world a culture led by black folk and joined by peoples of all colors and all races—without poverty, ignorance and disease!

Once, a great German poet cried: "Selig der den Er in Sieges Glanze findet."

"Happy man whom Death shall find in Victory's splendor."

But I know a happier one: he who fights in despair and in defeat still fights. Singing with Arna Bontemps the quiet, determined philosophy of undefeatable men:

> I thought I saw an angel flying low,
> I thought I saw the flicker of a wing
> Above the mulberry trees; but not again,
> Bethesda sleeps. This ancient pool that healed
> A Host of bearded Jews does not awake.
> This pool that once the angels troubled does not move.
> No angel stirs it now, no Saviour comes
> With healing in His hands to raise the sick
> And bid the lame man leap upon the ground.
>
> The golden days are gone. Why do we wait
> So long upon the marble steps, blood
> Falling from our open wounds? and why
> Do our black faces search the empty sky?
> Is there something we have forgotten? Some precious thing
> We have lost, wandering in strange lands?
>
> There was a day, I remember now,
> I beat my breast and cried, "Wash me God,"
> Wash me with a wave of wind upon
> The barley; O quiet one, draw near, draw near!
> Walk upon the hills with lovely feet
> And in the waterfall stand and speak!

JAWAHARLAL NEHRU
A Glory Has Departed
(". . . if we praise him, our words seem rather small")
Constituent Assembly
New Delhi, India
February 2, 1948

Nehru (1889–1964) was the first prime minister of India. In this speech he pays tribute to the great Mahatma Gandhi, assassinated three days before.

We praise people in well-chosen words and we have some kind of a measure for greatness. How shall we praise him and how shall we measure him, because he was not of the common clay that all of us are made of? He came, lived a fairly long span of life and has passed away. No words of praise of ours in this House are needed, for he has had greater praise in his life than any living man in history. And during these two or three days since his death he has had the homage of the world; what can we add to that? How can we praise him, how can we who have been children of his, and perhaps more intimately his children than the children of his body, for we have all been in some greater or smaller measure the children of his spirit, unworthy as we were?

A glory has departed and the sun that warmed and brightened our lives has set and we shiver in the cold and dark. Yet, he would not have us feel this way. After all, that glory that we saw for all these years, that man with the divine fire, changed us also—and such as we are, we have been moulded by him during these years; and out of that divine fire many of us also took a small spark which strengthened and made us work to some extent on the lines that he fashioned. And so if we praise him, our words seem rather small and if we praise him, to some extent we also praise ourselves. Great men and eminent men have monuments in bronze and marble set up for them, but this man of divine fire managed in his life-time to become enshrined in millions and millions of hearts so that all of us became somewhat of the stuff that he was made of, though to an infinitely lesser degree. He spread out in this way all over India not in palaces only, or in select places or in assemblies but in every hamlet and hut of the lowly and those who suffer. He lives in the hearts of millions and he will live for immemorial ages.

What then can we say about him except to feel humble on this occasion? To praise him we are not worthy—to praise him whom we could not follow adequately and sufficiently. It is almost doing him an injustice just to pass him by with words when he demanded work and labour and sacrifice from us; in a large measure he made this country, during the last thirty years or more, attain to heights of sacrifice which in that particular domain have never been equalled elsewhere. He succeeded in that. Yet ultimately things happened which no doubt made him suffer tremendously though his tender face never lost its smile and he never spoke a harsh word to anyone. Yet, he must have suffered—suffered for the failing of this generation whom he had trained, suffered because we went away from the path that he had shown us. And ultimately the hand of a child of his—for he after all is as much a child of his as any other Indian—a hand of the child of his struck him down.

Long ages afterwards history will judge of this period that we have passed through. It will judge of the successes and the failures—we are too near it to be proper judges and to understand what has happened and what has not happened. All we know is that there was a glory and that it is no more; all we know is that for the moment there is darkness, not so dark certainly because when we look into our hearts we still find the living flame which he lighted there. And if those living flames exist, there will not be darkness in this land and we shall be able, with our effort, remembering him and following his path, to illumine this land again, small as we are, but still with the fire that he instilled into us.

He was perhaps the greatest symbol of the India of the past, and may I say, of the India of the future, that we could have had. We stand on this perilous edge of the present between that past and the future to be and we face all manner of perils and the greatest peril is sometimes the lack of faith which comes to us, the sense of frustration that comes to us, the sinking of the heart and of the spirit that comes to us when we see ideals go overboard, when we see the great things that we talked about somehow pass into empty words and life taking a different course. Yet, I do believe that perhaps this period will pass soon enough.

He has gone, and all over India there is a feeling of having been left desolate and forlorn. All of us sense that feeling, and I do not know when we shall be able to get rid of it, and yet together with that feeling there is also a feeling of proud thankfulness that it has been given to us of this generation to be associated with this mighty person. In ages to come, centuries and maybe millenia after us, people will think of this generation when this man of God trod on earth and will think of us who, however small, could also follow his path and tread the holy ground where his feet had been. Let us be worthy of him.

PAUL ROBESON
For Freedom and Peace
("I am born and bred in this America of ours.
I want to love it. I love a part of it.")
New York City
June 19, 1949

Robeson (1898–1976) was one of the most multi-talented men of the century: an athlete, a scholar, an actor, singer, and political activist. In the following speech at the Rockland Palace in Harlem, he tells the story of his amazing life and the racism in America that led him into socialism and his admiration of the Soviet Union.

Thanks for the welcome home. I have traveled many lands and I have sung and talked to many peoples. Wherever I appeared, whether in professional concert, at peace meetings, in the factories, at trade union gatherings, at the mining pits, at assemblies of representative colonial students from all over the world, always the greeting came: "Take back our affection, our love, our strength to the Negro people and to the members of the progressive movement of America."

It is especially moving to be here in this particular auditorium in Harlem. Way back in 1918, I came here to this very hall from a football game at the Polo Grounds between Rutgers and Syracuse. There was a basketball game between St. Christopher and Alpha. Later I played here for St. Christopher against the Alphas, against the Spartans, and the Brooklyn YMCA, time and time again. This was a home of mine. It is still my home.

I was then, through my athletics and my university record, trying to hold up the prestige of my people; trying in the only way I knew to ease the path for future Negro boys and girls. And I am still in there slugging, yes, at another level, and you can bet your life that I shall battle every step of the way until conditions around these corners change and conditions change for the Negro people all up and down this land.

The road has been long. The road has been hard. It began about as tough as I ever had it—in Princeton, New Jersey, a college town of Southern aristocrats, who from Revolutionary time transferred Georgia to New Jersey. My brothers couldn't go to high school in Princeton. They had to go to Trenton, ten miles away. That's right—Trenton, of the "Trenton Six." My brother or I could have been one of the "Trenton Six."

Almost every Negro in Princeton lived off the college and accepted the social status that went with it. We lived for all intents and purposes on a Southern plantation. And with no more dignity than that suggests—all the bowing and scraping to the drunken rich, all the vile names, all the Uncle Tomming to earn enough to lead miserable lives.

My father was of slave origin. He reached as honorable a position as a Negro could under these circumstances, but soon after I was born he lost his church and poverty was my beginning. Relatives from my father's North Carolina family took me in, a motherless orphan, while my father went to new fields to begin again in a corner grocery store. I slept four in a bed, ate the nourishing greens and cornbread. I was and am forever thankful to my honest, intelligent, courageous, generous aunts, uncles and cousins, not long divorced from the cotton and tobacco fields of eastern North Carolina.

During the Wallace campaign, I stood on the very soil on which my father was a slave, where some of my cousins are sharecroppers and unemployed tobacco workers. I reflected upon the wealth bled from my near relatives alone, and of the very basic wealth of all this America, beaten out of millions of the Negro people, enslaved, freed, newly enslaved until this very day.

And I defied—and today I defy—any part of an insolent, dominating America, however powerful; I defy any errand boys, Uncle Toms of the Negro people, to challenge my Americanism, because by word and deed I challenge this vicious system to the death; because I refuse to let my personal success, as part of a fraction of one per cent of the Negro people, explain away the injustices to fourteen million of my people; because with all the energy at my command, I fight for the right of the Negro people and other oppressed labor-driven Americans to have decent homes, decent jobs, and the dignity that belongs to every human being!

Somewhere in my childhood these feelings were planted. Perhaps when I resented being pushed off the sidewalk, when I saw my women being insulted, and especially when I saw my elder brother answer each insult with blows that sent would-be slave masters crashing to the stone sidewalks, even though jail was his constant reward.

He never said it, but he told me day after day: "Listen to me, kid." (He loved me very dearly.) "Don't you ever take it, as long as you live."

I realized years after how grateful I was for that example. I've *never* accepted any inferior role because of my race or color. *And, by God, I never will!*

That explains my life. I'm looking for freedom, *full freedom,* not an inferior brand. That explains my attitude to different people, to Africa, the continent from which we came. I know much about Africa, and I'm not ashamed of my African origin. I'm *proud* of it. The rich culture of that continent, its magnificent potential, gives me plenty of cause for pride. This was true of the deep stirrings that took place within me when I visited the West Indies in January. This explains my feeling toward the Soviet Union, where in 1934 I for the first time walked this earth in complete human dignity, a dignity denied me at the Columbia University of Medina, denied me everywhere in my native land, despite all the protestations about freedom, equality, constitutional rights, and the sanctity of the individual.

And I say to the New York *Times* that personal success can be no answer. It can no longer be a question of an Anderson, a Carver, a Robinson, a Jackson, or a Robeson. It must be a question of the well-being and opportunities not of a few but for *all* of this great Negro people of which I am a part.

There, in my childhood, I saw my father choose allies. To him, it was the Taylor Pines' of the Wall Street millionaires. They helped the church. They spread around a little manna now and then—that was an age of philanthropy. But I recall that my father could never think of attacking these men for the conditions of those times. Always one had to bend and bow.

That was forty years ago. These present-day sycophants of big business, these supposed champions of Negro rights, can't grow up to the knowledge that the world has gone forward. Millions and millions of people have wrung their freedom from these same Taylor Pines', these same Wall Street operators, these traders in the lives of millions for their greedy profits. There is no more Eastern Europe to bleed; no more Russia, one-sixth of the earth's surface, to enslave; no more China at their disposal.

They can't imagine that our people, the Negro people,—forty millions in the Caribbean and Latin America, one hundred and fifty millions in Africa, and fourteen million here, today, up and down this America of ours,—are also determined to stop being industrial and agricultural serfs. They do not understand that a new reconstruction is here, and that this time we will not be betrayed by any coalition of

Northern big finance barons and Southern bourbon plantation owners. They do not realize that the Negro people, with their allies, other
oppressed groups, the progressive sections of labor, millions of the
Jewish and foreign-born of former white indentured labor, north,
south, east and west, in this day and time of ours are determined to
see some basic change.

Roosevelt foreshadowed it. We are going to realize it! We were
fooled in 1948. We aren't going to be fooled in 1949, 1950, and '51
and '52. We are going to fight for jobs and security at home, and we
are going to join the forces of friendship and cooperation with advanced peoples and move on to build a decent world.

And you stooges try to do the work of your white bourbon masters, work they have not the courage to do. You try to play the role
of cowardly labor leaders who are attempting to do the same job in
the ranks of labor. Try it, but the Negro people will give you your
answer! They'll drive you from public life! The Negro people know
when they're being sold down the river. They've been watching a
long, long time. It's good the challenge has come. Keep on, and
you'll have no magazines in which to publish your viciousness. You'll
not have many more opportunities to sell into a new slavery our
cousins in Liberia, our relatives in South Africa, our brothers in the
West Indies. You'll get your answer—and soon! The Negro people
are smoldering. They're not afraid of their radicals who point out the
awful, indefensible truth of our degradation and exploitation.

What a travesty is this supposed leadership of a great people! And
in this historic time, when their people need them most. How So-
journer Truth, Harriet Tubman, Fred Douglas[s] must be turning in
their graves at this spectacle of a craven, fawning, despicable leadership, able to be naught but errand boys, and—at the lowest level—
stooges and cowardly renegades, a disgrace to the Negro people and
to the real and true America of which they so glibly talk. Let them
get their crumbs from their Wall Street masters. Let them snatch their
bit of cheese and go scampering rat-like into their holes, where, by
heaven, the Negro people will keep them, left to their dirty consciences, if any they have.

Now, let's get out the record. In 1946, I declared in St. Louis on
the picket line against segregation of Negro people that I would give
up my professional career, then at its height, to devote my time and
energy to the struggle for the liberation of the Negro people. I appeared everywhere, north, south, east, and west, for Negro colleges,
churches, organizations.

I led an anti-lynch crusade to Washington. There I heard our
President declare that it was not politically expedient to take any

federal action against lynching. You may remember that I said that perhaps the Negro people would have to do something about it themselves. But a committee stepped in—one of those committees to stop the militant Negro struggle. And lynch law is still in committee, while Negroes continue being lynched.

I entered the struggle for peace and freedom with Wallace in 1948, talking at street corner meetings four and five times a day. Without that struggle of the Progressive Party the issues before the people would not have been clarified, and we might now be at war. Wallace made a tremendous contribution time and again to the cause of peace, to Negro freedom, and to American freedom. He said peace was the issue. *Peace was, and is, the issue.* He said a war economy was an economy of scarcity and unemployment. *That it was, and is.* He said it meant the loss of civil liberties, the loss of the freedom of European countries. *It has meant just that.* He said it meant slavery for colonial people. *That it is fast becoming.* He said it meant domestic fascism. *That is just around the corner.*

Negroes rallied to Wallace's banner, the banner of their freedom. Then their trusted leaders stepped in to confuse and to frighten them. They sold them a hollow bill of goods in the Democratic Party, and a nominee that even these leaders did not trust. Remember, they wanted Eisenhower. But they were afraid of any militant struggle for our people. Where is the civil rights program? Are we still subject to terror? Ask Mrs. Mallard, ask the boys in Virginia, ask the Trenton Six: "Where are our liberties?"

As a consequence of my activities for Negro freedom, I had 86 concerts cancelled out of 86. Of course, these were very special concerts. I don't blame auto barons in Detroit for not wanting to pay to hear me when I was in Cadillac Square fighting for the auto workers. I don't blame the iron-ore owners of the Michigan and Minnesota iron-ore ranges for not wanting to hear me when I was on picket lines for the steel workers in these regions. And so with the packing-house owners of Chicago, or the ship-owners of the east and west coasts, or the sugar plantation owners of Hawaii.

Well, they can have their concerts! I'll go back to their cities to sing for the people whom I love, for the Negro and white workers whose freedom will insure my freedom. I'll help, together with many other progressive artists, whenever I can get the time from freedom's struggle, to show how culture can be brought back to the people. We created it in the first place, and it's about time it came back to us!

Today the fight is still on for peace and freedom. Concerts must wait. There is a fierce political struggle which must be won. However, I decided to go to Europe to resume my professional concerts for a very short period, in order to make it perfectly clear that the world is wide and no few pressures could stop my career. Let's go to the record: Albert Hall (London) with its 8,000 seats sold out twice with a five dollar top; 10,000 in the Harringay Arena; thousands turned away all over Europe—the most successful concert tour of my career.

Why? Because I came to the English people from *progressive* America, from the America of Wallace and the Progressive Party, from the America of the twelve great Communist leaders who are on trial for their devotion to the Negro people and to the American working class; because I came from Negro America whose struggle had become known to the English during the war when a folk saying grew up: "We love those American soldiers, the black and the brown ones."

I finished my professional tour at its height and announced that never again would I sing at a five dollar top, that I would sing at prices so that workers could come in comfort and dignity. I did this because I belonged to working people. I struggled as a boy in the brick-yards, on the docks, in the hotels to get a living and an education. Ninety-five per cent of the Negro people are workers. So I said that my talents would henceforth belong to my people in their struggle. And I acted on this. Thousands and thousands came. That's my answer to the bourbons who think they can end my career!

Later I toured England in peace meetings for British-Soviet friendship, did a series of meetings on the issues of freedom for the peoples of Africa and the West Indies, and on the question of the right of colored seamen and colored technicians to get jobs in a land for which they had risked their lives. Ten thousand people turned out to a meeting in Liverpool on this latter issue.

I stood at the coal pits in Scotland and saw miners contribute from their earnings $1,500 to $2,000 for the benefit of African workers. I helped build up a substantial fund in England to help the cause of African freedom, saw this whole question of the relation of English and colonial peoples raised to a new level as English workers came to understand that if cheap labor could be obtained in Africa or the West Indies or in Southeast Asia, their living standards in England would suffer accordingly. This is a lesson white workers in America must increasingly learn. For the tentacles of American imperialism are stretched far and wide into colonial countries: Cuba, Haiti, Puerto Rico, Hawaii, Trinidad, Panama; down through Latin America; in the Philippines and some parts of the East; and all over the continent of Africa. White workers in America must be aware of this and watch it closely.

Then I moved into Scandinavia. Through a stroke of circumstance, I was booked through *Politiken*. This was an old liberal newspaper in years gone by, but the pressures of present-day American imperialism, exerted mainly through the Marshall Plan, had caused all pretense of liberalism to vanish. I read an editorial of *Politiken* in England supporting the Atlantic Pact, attacking the Eastern Democracies and the Soviet Union. I immediately asked that my contracts be cancelled. I explained to the press that it was unthinkable that I could appear under the sponsorship of a paper which had allied itself with an imperialism which had enslaved my father and forefathers and was in the process of enslaving my brothers and sisters in Africa, Latin America, the West and East Indies, and which was trying to work up a war against the greatest champion of the rights of colonial and exploited peoples,—the Union of Soviet Republics.

The contracts cancelled, I sang for the newspapers of the progressive and Communist forces of Scandinavia (papers like the *Daily Worker*). All the other press had gone the way of the Reuthers, Murrays, Careys, Townsends, et al, who have betrayed American workers and the Negro people to American, British, Dutch, French, Belgian and Japanese imperialists.

Thousands upon thousands in the Scandinavian countries turned out in support of peace and against the Atlantic Pact. These countries of Scandinavia had been freed by Soviet armies, had erected monuments to Soviet heroes. It was unthinkable that they would join the fascist elements of Western Germany and Vichy France against their natural friend and ally. It was clear from the meetings that the great majority of Scandinavian people did not support their governments. I am sure American imperialism is aware of this.

My role was in no sense personal. I represented to these people Progressive America, fighting for peace and freedom, and I bring back to you their love and affection, their promise of their strength to aid us, and their gratefulness for our struggles here. They beg us to send more progressive Americans—Wallace, Marcantonio, trade unionists, Negro and white. And they all sent special messages to the Negro people, assuring them of their support of the liberation of Negro peoples everywhere.

Our allies stretch far and wide and they beg us for information and for collective united action. If the originators of the vicious Atlantic Pact can get in a huddle to plot joint action against us, one by one, let us get together to see that nobody can ever take us one by one, that they will have to engage us as a strong, unbending, united force for the peace and freedom of all oppressed peoples.

Why did I take this stand on the Atlantic Pact—the Arms Pact—and its forerunner, the Marshall Plan? Let us examine the results of the Marshall Plan. We don't need to guess and theorize. Western European countries have completely lost their freedom. This was honestly acknowledged everywhere. American big business tells all of Western Europe what to do, what it can produce, where it must buy, with whom it can trade. And finally, with the Atlantic Pact, the western Europeans are told that they must be ready to die to the last man in order to defend American Big Business.

The Eisler case illustrated the European people's revolt against American domination. For the English people decided this was too much. They still have some respect for their judicial law, extending from Magna Charta days,—different from us as yet here in America with our Foley Square travesties. The English people move from below—it was a mass movement which forced their government to retreat on Eisler and tell the United States, "Nothing doing." And the Communists of Great Britain started the defense which soon involved great sections of the British people—another important lesson for us. For British people knew that if Eisler was not freed, no longer could they themselves be protected under British law and the whole structure of British freedom would be in danger.

That is just as true here. If the twelve Communists are not freed, all Americans can say goodbye to their civil liberties. *Especially* will we Negro people be forced to say goodbye to any attempts to add to the few civil liberties we as yet have. Just as a mass movement in a few days won this tremendous victory for peace and freedom in London—I was there at the time—so we here in New York and America can do the same if we act with speed and courage in the cause of *our* freedoms, not just those of the "Twelve."

But beyond this strangling of Western Europe, the real meaning of the Marshall Plan is the complete enslavement of the colonies. For how can British, French and other Western European bankers repay Wall Street? Only in raw materials—in gold, copper, cocoa, rubber, uranium, manganese, iron ore, ground nuts, oils, fats, sugar, bananas. From where? Why, from South Africa, Nigeria, East Africa, French Africa, Belgian Congo, Trinidad, Jamaica, Cuba, Honduras, Guatemala, Viet Nam, Malaya. The Marshall Plan means enslavement of our people all over the earth, including here in the United States on the cotton and sugar plantations and in the mines of the North and South.

And the Atlantic Pact means legal sanction for sending guns and troops to the colonies to insure the enslavement and terrorization of our people. They will shout our people down in Africa just as they lynch us in Mississippi. That's the other side of the same coin.

For who owns plantations in the South? Metropolitan Life—yes, the same Metropolitan Life Insurance Company that owns and won't let you live in the Stuyvesant Town flats in New York. It is such giant financial interests that are getting millions from the Marshall Plan. They enslave us, they enslave Western Europe, they enslave the colonies.

Many of our Negro leaders know this. But some of these so-called distinguished leaders are doing the dirty work for Stettinius, aiding his scheme for the exploitation of Liberia and its people, or are serving as errand boys for Forrestal's cartel interests, even though the chief has now departed. And there are a few other of these so-called Negro leaders who are too low and contemptible to give the courtesy of mention.

Are these financial big boys America? No! They are the former enemies of Roosevelt. They were the ones who were glad when Roosevelt died. They are the same ones who Roosevelt said were the core of American fascism. They are the allies of the remains of the Hitler entourage, that Hitler who burned up eight million of a great Jewish people and said he would like to burn up fourteen million of us. They are the friends of Franco, the living representatives of the Spanish Conquistadores who enslaved us and still enslave us in Latin America. They are the ones who hate American democracy as did the enemies of Jefferson and Lincoln before them. *They are no part of America!* They are the would-be preservers of world fascism and the enemies of progressive America!

And they are in the government, too,—you saw them deny your civil rights on the floors of Congress; you saw them throw our promised civil rights right into our teeth, while our supposed chief defender enjoyed the sun down in Florida, a state that is the symbol, of course, of the freedom and equality of the Negro people.

And now this greedy section of democratic America, by corrupting our leaders, by shooting us as we attempt to vote, by terrorizing us as in the case of the "Trenton Six," has the gall to try to lure us into a war against countries where the freedoms that we so deeply desire are being realized, together with a rich and abundant life, the kind of life that should be ours also, because so much of America's wealth is realized from our blood and from our labor.

My last weeks abroad were spent in these countries to the East, Czechoslovakia, Poland, and finally the Soviet Union. Here thousands of people—men, women, children—cried to me to thank progressive America for sending one of its representatives, begged me so to take back their love, their heart-felt understanding of the suffering of their Negro brothers and sisters, that I wept time and time again. Whole nations of people gave me a welcome I can never forget—a welcome not for me, Paul Robeson, but in your name, the name of the Negro people of America, of the colonies; in the name of the progressive America of Wallace and the Progressive Party; and in the name of the twelve Communist leaders. Outstanding people in the government treated me with the greatest respect and dignity because I represented *you* (but there were no calls from the American embassies).

Here in these countries are *the people;* their spokesmen are in the forefront of our struggle for liberation—on the floor of the United Nations, in the highest councils of world diplomacy. Here in the Soviet Union, in Czechoslovakia, in battered but gallant Warsaw with its brave saga of the ghetto, are the nations leading the battle for peace and freedom. They were busy building, reconstructing; and the very mention of war caused one to look at you as if you were insane.

I was in Stalingrad. I saw a letter from President Roosevelt,—no equivocation there. It said that in Stalingrad came the turning point in the battle for civilization. I stood in the little rectangle where the heroic people of Stalingrad fought with their backs to the mighty Volga—and saved us—saved you and me from Hitler's wrath. We loved them then. What has happened to us? For they are the same, only braver. Midst their ruins, they sing and laugh and dance. Their factories are restored—fifty per cent above prewar. I sang at their tractor factory and saw a tractor—*not a tank*—coming off the line every fifteen minutes. It was a factory built by Soviet hands, Soviet brains, Soviet know-how.

They want peace and an abundant life. Freedom is already theirs. The children cried, "Take back our love to the Negro children and the working class children." And they clasped and embraced me literally and symbolically for you. I love them.

Here is a whole one-sixth of the earth's surface, including millions of brown, yellow and black people who would be Negroes here in America and subject to the same awful race prejudice that haunts us. In this Soviet Union, the very term "backward country" is an insult, for in one generation former colonial peoples have been raised to unbelievable industrial and social levels. It is, indeed, a vast new concept of democracy. And these achievements make completely absurd the solemn pronouncements that it will take several generations, maybe hundreds of years, before we Negro people in the West Indies, Africa and America can have any real control over our own destiny.

Here is a whole nation which is now doing honor to our poet Pushkin—one of the greatest poets in history—the Soviet people's and our proud world possession. Could I find a monument to Pushkin in a public square of Birmingham or Atlanta or Memphis, as one stands in the center of Moscow? No. One perhaps to Goethe, but not to the dark-skinned Pushkin.

Yes, I love this Soviet people more than any other nation, because of their suffering and sacrifices for us, the Negro people, the progressive people, the people of the future in this world.

At the Paris Peace Conference I said it was unthinkable that the Negro people of America or elsewhere in the world could be drawn into war with the Soviet Union. I repeat it with hundred-fold emphasis. THEY WILL NOT.

And don't ask a few intellectuals who are jealous of their comfort. Ask the sugar workers whom I saw starving in Louisiana, the workers in the cotton lands and the tobacco belts in the South. Ask the sugar workers in Jamaica. Ask the Africans in Malan's South Africa. Ask *them* if they will struggle for peace and friendship with the Soviet people, with the peoples of China and the new democracies, or if they will help their imperialist oppressors to return them to an even worse slavery. The answer lies there in the millions of my struggling people, not only the 14 million in America, but the 40 million in the Caribbean and Latin America and the 150 million in Africa. No wonder all the excitement! For one day this mighty mass will strike for freedom, and a new strength like that of gallant China will add its decisive weight to insuring a world where all men can be free and equal.

I am born and bred in this America of ours. I want to love it. I love a part of it. But it's up to the rest of America when I shall love it with the same intensity that I love the Negro people from whom I spring,—in the way that I love progressives in the Caribbean, the black and Indian peoples of South and Central America, the peoples of China and Southeast Asia, yes suffering people the world over,—and in the way that I deeply and intensely love the Soviet Union. That burden of proof rests upon America.

Now these peoples of the Soviet Union, of the new Eastern Democracies, of progressive Western Europe, and the representatives of the Chinese people whom I met in Prague and Moscow, were in great part Communists. They were the first to die for our freedom and for the freedom of all mankind. So I'm not afraid of Communists; no, far from that. I will defend them as they defended us, the Negro people. And I stand firm and immovable by the side of that great leader who has given his whole life to the struggle of the American working class, Bill Foster; by the side of Gene Dennis; by the side of my friend, Ben Davis; Johnny Gates, Henry Winston, Gus Hall, Gil Green, Jack Stachel, Carl Winter, Irving Potash, Bob Thompson, Johnny Williamson,—twelve brave fighters for my freedom. Their struggle is *our* struggle.

But to fulfill our responsibilities as Americans, we must unite, especially we Negro people. We must know our strength. We are the decisive force. That's why they terrorize us. That's why they fear us. And if we unite in all our might, this world can fast be changed. Let us create that unity now. And this important, historic role of the Negro people our white allies here must fully comprehend. This means increasing understanding of the Negro, his tremendous struggle, his great contributions, his potential for leadership at all levels in the common task of liberation. It means courage to stand by our side whatever the consequences, as we the Negro people fulfill our historic duty in Freedom's struggle.

If we unite, we'll get our law against lynching, our right to vote and to labor. Let us march on Washington, representing 14,000,000 strong. Let us push aside the sycophants who tell us to be quiet.

The so-called western democracies—including our own, which so fiercely exploits us and daily denies us our simple constitutional guarantees—can find no answer before the bar of world justice for their treatment of the Negro people. Democracy, indeed! We must have the courage to shout at the top of our voices about our injustices and we must lay the blame where it belongs and where it has belonged for over 300 years of slavery and misery: right here on our own doorstep,—not in any far away place. This is the very time when we can win our struggle.

And we cannot win it by being lured into any kind of war with our closest friends and allies throughout the world. For any kind of decent life we need, we want, and *we demand* our constitutional rights—RIGHT HERE IN AMERICA. We do not want to die in vain any more on foreign battlefields for Wall Street and the greedy supporters of domestic fascism. If we must die, let it be in Mississippi or Georgia! Let it be wherever we are lynched and deprived of our rights as human beings!

Let this be a final answer to the warmongers. Let them know that we will not help to enslave our brothers and sisters and eventually ourselves. Rather, we will help to insure peace in our time—the freedom and liberation of the Negro and other struggling peoples, and the building of a world where we can all walk in full equality and full human dignity.

MARGARET CHASE SMITH
Declaration of Conscience
(". . . I don't want to see the Republican Party ride to
political victory on the Four Horsemen of Calumny—
Fear, Ignorance, Bigotry, and Smear")
United States Senate, Washington, D.C.
June 1, 1950

*A career politician from Maine, Smith (1897–1995) distinguished herself in
the era of the Red Scare by bravely rising to challenge her fellow senators for
their political persecution of innocent and patriotic Americans.*

I would like to speak briefly and simply about a serious national condition. It is a national feeling of fear and frustration that could result in national suicide and the end of everything that we Americans hold dear. It is a condition that comes from the lack of effective leadership in either the Legislative Branch or the Executive Branch of our Government.

That leadership is so lacking that serious and responsible proposals are being made that national advisory commissions be appointed to provide such critically needed leadership.

I speak as briefly as possible because too much harm has already been done with irresponsible words of bitterness and selfish political opportunism. I speak as simply as possible because the issue is too great to be obscured by eloquence. I speak simply and briefly in the hope that my words will be taken to heart.

I speak as a Republican. I speak as a woman. I speak as a United States Senator. I speak as an American.

The United States Senate has long enjoyed worldwide respect as the greatest deliberative body in the world. But recently that deliberative character has too often been debased to the level of a forum of hate and character assassination sheltered by the shield of congressional immunity.

94

It is ironical that we Senators can in debate in the Senate directly or indirectly, by any form of words, impute to any American who is not a Senator any conduct or motive unworthy or unbecoming an American—and without that non-Senator American having any legal redress against us—yet if we say the same thing in the Senate about our colleagues we can be stopped on the grounds of being out of order.

It is strange that we can verbally attack anyone else without restraint and with full protection and yet we hold ourselves above the same type of criticism here on the Senate Floor. Surely the United States Senate is big enough to take self-criticism and self-appraisal. Surely we should be able to take the same kind of character attacks that we "dish out" to outsiders.

I think that it is high time for the United States Senate and its members to do some soul-searching—for us to weigh our consciences—on the manner in which we are performing our duty to the people of America—on the manner in which we are using or abusing our individual powers and privileges.

I think that it is high time that we remembered that we have sworn to uphold and defend the Constitution. I think that it is high time that we remembered that the Constitution, as amended, speaks not only of the freedom of speech but also of trial by jury instead of trial by accusation.

Whether it be a criminal prosecution in court or a character prosecution in the Senate, there is little practical distinction when the life of a person has been ruined.

Those of us who shout the loudest about Americanism in making character assassinations are all too frequently those who, by our own words and acts, ignore some of the basic principles of Americanism:

The right to criticize;

The right to hold unpopular beliefs;

The right to protest;

The right of independent thought.

The exercise of these rights should not cost one single American citizen his reputation or his right to a livelihood nor should he be in danger of losing his reputation or livelihood merely because he happens to know someone who holds unpopular beliefs. Who of us doesn't? Otherwise none of us could call our souls our own. Otherwise thought control would have set in.

The American people are sick and tired of being afraid to speak their minds lest they be politically smeared as "Communists" or "Fascists" by their opponents. Freedom of speech is not what it used to be in America. It has been so abused by some that it is not exercised by others.

The American people are sick and tired of seeing innocent people smeared and guilty people whitewashed. But there have been enough proved cases such as the Amerasia case, the Hiss case, the Coplon case, the Gold case, to cause nationwide distrust and suspicion that there may be something to the unproved, sensational accusations.

As a Republican, I say to my colleagues on this side of the aisle that the Republican Party faces a challenge today that is not unlike the challenge that it faced back in Lincoln's day. The Republican Party so successfully met that challenge that it emerged from the Civil War as the champion of a united nation—in addition to being a Party that unrelentingly fought loose spending and loose programs.

Today our country is being psychologically divided by the confusion and the suspicions that are bred in the United States Senate to spread like cancerous tentacles of "know nothing, suspect everything" attitudes. Today we have a Democratic Administration that has developed a mania for loose spending and loose programs. History is repeating itself—and the Republican Party again has the opportunity to emerge as the champion of unity and prudence.

The record of the present Democratic Administration has provided us with sufficient campaign issues without the necessity to resorting to political smears. America is rapidly losing its position as leader of the world simply because the Democratic Administration has pitifully failed to provide effective leadership.

The Democratic Administration has completely confused the American people by its daily contradictory grave warnings and optimistic assurances—that show the people that our Democratic Administration has no idea of where it is going.

The Democratic Administration has greatly lost the confidence of the American people by its complacency to the threat of communism here at home and the leak of vital secrets to Russia through key officials of the Democratic Administration. There are enough proved cases to make this point without diluting our criticism with unproved charges.

Surely these are sufficient reasons to make it clear to the American people that it is time for a change and that a Republican victory is necessary to the security of this country. Surely it is clear that this nation will continue to suffer as long as it is governed by the present ineffective Democratic Administration.

Yet to displace it with a Republican regime embracing a philosophy that lacks political integrity or intellectual honesty would prove equally disastrous to this nation. The nation sorely needs a Republican victory. But I don't want to see the Republican Party ride to political victory on the Four Horsemen of Calumny—Fear, Ignorance, Bigotry, and Smear.

I doubt if the Republican Party could—simply because I don't believe the American people will uphold any political party that puts political exploitation above national interest. Surely we Republicans aren't that desperate for victory.

I don't want to see the Republican Party win that way. While it might be a fleeting victory for the Republican Party, it would be a more lasting defeat for the American people. Surely it would ultimately be suicide for the Republican Party and the two-party system that has protected our American liberties from the dictatorship of a one-party system.

As members of the Minority Party, we do not have the primary authority to formulate the policy of our Government. But we do have the responsibility of rendering constructive criticism, of clarifying issues, of allaying fears by acting as responsible citizens.

As a woman, I wonder how the mothers, wives, sisters, and daughters feel about the way in which members of their families have been politically mangled in Senate debate—and I use the word "debate" advisedly.

As a United States Senator, I am not proud of the way in which the Senate has been made a publicity platform for irresponsible sensationalism. I am not proud of the reckless abandon in which unproved charges have been hurled from this side of the aisle. I am not proud of the obviously staged, undignified countercharges that have been attempted in retaliation from the other side of the aisle.

I don't like the way the Senate has been made a rendezvous for vilification, for selfish political gain at the sacrifice of individual reputations and national unity. I am not proud of the way we smear outsiders from the Floor of the Senate and hide behind the cloak of congressional immunity and still place ourselves beyond criticism on the Floor of the Senate.

As an American, I am shocked at the way Republicans and Democrats alike are playing directly into the Communist design of "confuse, divide, and conquer." As an American, I don't want a Democratic Administration "whitewash" or "coverup" any more than I want a Republican smear or witch hunt.

As an American, I condemn a Republican "Fascist" just as much as I condemn a Democrat "Communist." I condemn a Democrat "Fascist" just as much as I condemn a Republican "Communist." They are equally dangerous to you and me and to our country. As an

American, I want to see our nation recapture the strength and unity it once had when we fought the enemy instead of ourselves.

It is with these thoughts that I have drafted what I call a "Declaration of Conscience." I am gratified that Senator Tobey, Senator Aiken, Senator Morse, Senator Ives, Senator Thye, and Senator Hendrickson have concurred in that declaration and have authorized me to announce their concurrence.

ELEANOR ROOSEVELT
The United Nations as a Bridge
("There are things we can learn from other people")
United Nations Seminar
Brandeis University, Waltham, Massachusetts
December 17, 1954

Long a champion of civil rights and social activism, Eleanor Roosevelt (1884–1962) was America's beloved First Lady from 1933 to 1945. After the death of her husband, President Franklin D. Roosevelt, President Truman appointed her as United States representative to the United Nations General Assembly, where she served as the first chair of the organization's Human Rights Commission.

You hear people say, "Why hasn't the United Nations done this or that?" The United Nations functions just as well as the member nations make it function, and no better or worse. And so the first thing to look at is, I think, the kind of machinery that was set up, and what it was meant to do.

Now we have to go back in our minds to the time when the Charter was first planned. At that time the war was not over, and this was a dream, and everybody accepted it as a dream—an idea to set up an organization, the object of that organization being to keep peace.

Great areas of the world knew what it was like to have war on their doorsteps. We did not know what it was like, either to be occupied or to be bombed. That experience has made such a difference to many nations. I think we need to use our imaginations, because we really have to understand what the nations felt, what they feel today—where they actually were occupied or had great destruction within their own lands.

They had co-operated during the war; they believed that they were going to go on co-operating after the war. That was one of the great myths of the centuries.

They also believed that this organization they were setting up was to be an organization to maintain peace, not to make peace. Peace was going to be made, and then this organization would help to maintain it. What happened, of course, was that peace has never been found. And so this organization, which was not set up to meet certain questions, has had questions brought to it that were not in mind at the beginning.

But talk can have great value; you have to think of it as a bridge. You have to think of the General Assembly as a place where bridges are built between peoples.

We in the United States are an impatient people. We want to see results tomorrow. I am not sure sometimes that it isn't the people who can outwait the other people, who have the advantage. Frequently, moving too fast can set you back.

People are meeting in the United Nations that come from backgrounds where there have been certain customs and habits for generations. Some people grow impatient of these. We might think occasionally that other people find their way the best, and not our way. There are things we can learn from other people. You must have as a basis to all understanding, the willingness to learn and the willingness to listen.

Even though we have difficulties through having the Soviets as a part of the organization, just remember that it may be a very good thing. That is the bridge—if ever a time comes when there is a crack and we can perhaps meet people of another country, a Soviet or a satellite, it may be the one real way of increasing understanding. At the present time, they use the United Nations as a platform to boast about what they achieve. What they are told to say, they have to say, just exactly as they are told to say it. It must be hard to be that much of a slave. Their government wants to reach their own people; a speech made by a Soviet delegate is reported in full in the Soviet press. No answer is ever reported. These things are real difficulties.

When we look upon the failures in the United Nations, we should not be disheartened, because if we take the failure and learn, eventually we will use this machinery better and better. We will also learn one important thing, and that is, no machinery works unless people make it work.

And in a democracy like ours, it is the people who have to tell their representatives what they want them to do. And it is the acceptance of individual responsibility by each one of us that actually will make the United Nations machinery work. If we don't accept that, and if we don't do the job, we may well fail—but it lies in our hands. And I think that is the main thing for us to remember today.

We are the strongest nation in the world. We, whether we like it or not, are the leaders. And we lead not only in military and economic strength, but we lead in knowing what are our values, what are the things we believe in, and in being willing to live up to them, and being willing to accept the fact that living up to them here, we help ourselves, but we also help the world.

NIKITA SERGEYEVICH KHRUSHCHEV

The Personality Cult and Its Consequences

("The cult of the individual acquired such monstrous size
chiefly because Stalin himself . . . supported the
glorification of his own person")

Moscow, Union of Soviet Socialist Republics
February 24–25, 1956

The first public acknowledgement of the late Josef Stalin's criminal and tragic reign in the USSR came from a former member of Stalin's Politburo, the General Secretary Nikita Sergeyevich Khrushchev (1894–1971). In speaking at a "secret meeting" of the Communist Party's Twentieth Congress, Khrushchev tried to ensure that those fellow politicians attempting to use Stalin's posthumous political and social influence would be damaged. Khrushchev became premier in 1958. The following are excerpts from his two days of speeches.

Comrades! In the report of the Central Committee of the party at the twentieth congress, in a number of speeches by delegates to the Congress, as also formerly during the plenary CC/CPSU [Central Committee of the Community Party of the Soviet Union] sessions, quite a lot has been said about the cult of the individual and about its harmful consequences.

After Stalin's death the Central Committee of the party began to implement a policy of explaining concisely and consistently that it is impermissible and foreign to the spirit of Marxism-Leninism to elevate one person, to transform him into a superman possessing supernatural characteristics akin to those of a god. Such a man supposedly knows everything, sees everything, thinks for everyone, can do anything, is infallible in his behavior.

Such a belief about a man, and specifically about Stalin, was cultivated among us for many years.

At the present we are concerned with a question which has immense importance for the party now and for the future—[we are concerned] with how the cult of the person of Stalin has been gradually growing, the cult which became at a certain specific stage the source of a whole series of exceedingly serious and grave perversions of party principles, of party democracy, of revolutionary legality.

Because of the fact that not all as yet realize fully the practical consequences resulting from the cult of the individual, the great harm caused by the violation of the principle of collective direction of the party, and because of the accumulation of immense and limitless power in the hands of one person, the Central Committee of the party considers it absolutely necessary to make the material pertaining to this matter available to the twentieth congress of the Communist party of the Soviet Union.

In December, 1922, in a letter to the party congress Vladimir Ilyich [Lenin] wrote: "After taking over the position of Secretary General, Comrade Stalin accumulated in his hands immeasurable power and I am not certain whether he will be always able to use this power with the required care."

This letter, a political document of tremendous importance, known in the party history as Lenin's "testament," was distributed among the delegates to the twentieth party congress.

It was precisely during this period (1935–1937–1938) that the practice of mass repression through the Government apparatus was born, first against the enemies of Leninism—Trotskyites, Zinovievites, Bukharinites, long since politically defeated by the party, and subsequently also against many honest Communists, against those party cadres who had borne the heavy load of the Civil War, and the first and most difficult years of industrialization and collectivization, who actively fought against the Trotskyites and the rightists for the Leninist party line.

Stalin originated the concept "enemy of the people." This term automatically rendered it unnecessary that the ideological errors of a man or men engaged in a controversy be proven; this term made possible the use of the most cruel repression, violating all norms of revolutionary legality, against anyone who in any way disagreed with Stalin, against those who were only suspected of hostile intent, against those who had bad reputations in the main, and in actuality, the only proof of guilt used, against all norms of current legal science, was the "confession" of the accused himself; and, as subsequent probing proved, "confessions" were acquired through physical pressures against the accused.

It was determined that of the 139 members and candidates of the party's Central Committee who were elected at the seventeenth congress, ninety-eight persons, i.e., 70 per cent, were arrested and shot (mostly in 1937–38).

The same fate met not only the Central Committee members but also the majority of the delegates to the seventeenth party congress. Of 1,966 delegates with either voting or advisory rights, 1,108 persons were arrested on charges of antirevolutionary crimes, i.e., decidedly more than a majority. This very fact shows how absurd, wild and contrary to common sense were the charges of counter-revolutionary crimes made, as we now see, against a majority of participants at the seventeenth party congress.

After the criminal murder of Sergei M. Kirov, mass repressions and brutal acts of violation of Socialist legality began. On the evening of December 1, 1934, on Stalin's initiative (without the approval of the Political Bureau, which was passed two days later, casually) the secretary of the Presidium of the Central Executive Committee, Abel S. Yenukidze, signed the following directive:

1. Investigative agencies are directed to speed up the cases of those accused of the preparation or execution of acts of terror.
2. Judicial organs are directed not to hold up the execution of death sentences pertaining to crimes of this category in order to consider the possibility of pardon, because the Presidium of the Central Executive Committee of the U.S.S.R. does not consider as possible the receiving of petitions of this sort.
3. The organs of the Commissariat of Internal Affairs are directed to execute the death sentences against criminals of the above-mentioned category immediately after the passage of sentences.

This directive became the basis for mass acts of abuse against Socialist legality. During many of the fabricated court cases the accused were charged with "the preparation" of terroristic acts; this deprived them of any possibility that their cases might be re-examined, even when they stated before the court that their "confessions" were secured by force, and when, in a convincing manner, they disproved the accusations against them.

The majority of the Central Committee members and candidates elected at the seventeenth congress and arrested in 1937–1938 were expelled from the party illegally through the brutal abuse of the party statute, because the question of their expulsion was never studied at the Central Committee Plenum.

Now when the cases of some of these so-called "spies" and "saboteurs" were examined it was found that all their cases were fabricated. Confessions of guilt of many arrested and charged with enemy activity were gained with the help of cruel and inhuman tortures.

Comrade Eikhe was arrested April 29, 1938, on the basis of slanderous materials, without the sanction of the prosecutor of the U.S.S.R., which was finally received fifteen months after the arrest.

Eikhe was forced under torture to sign ahead of time a protocol of his confession prepared by the investigative judges in which he and several other eminent party workers were accused of anti-Soviet activity.

On October 1, 1939, Eikhe sent his declaration to Stalin in which he categorically denied his guilt and asked for an examination of his case. In the declaration he wrote:

> There is no more bitter misery than to sit in the jail of a government for which I have always fought.

On February 4 Eikhe was shot. It has been definitely established now that Eikhe's case was fabricated; he has been posthumously rehabilitated.

A large part of these cases are being reviewed now and a great part of them are being voided because they were baseless and falsified. Suffice it to say that from 1954 to the present time the Military Collegium of the Supreme Court has rehabilitated 7,679 persons, many of whom were rehabilitated posthumously.

The power accumulated in the hands of one person, Stalin, led to serious consequences during the great patriotic war.

A cable from our London Embassy dated June 18, 1941, stated:

> As of now Cripps is deeply convinced of the inevitability of armed conflict between Germany and the U.S.S.R. which will begin not later than the middle of June. According to Cripps, the Germans have presently concentrated 147 divisions (including air force and service units) along the Soviet borders.

Despite these particularly grave warnings, the necessary steps were not taken to prepare the country properly for defense and to prevent it from being caught unawares.

When the Fascist armies had actually invaded Soviet territory and military operations began, Moscow issued the order that Stalin, despite evident facts, thought that the war had not yet started, that this was only a provocative action on the part of several undisciplined sections of the German army, and that our reaction might serve as a reason for the Germans to begin the war.

Stalin was very much interested in the assessment of Comrade Zhukov as a military leader. He asked me often for my opinion of

Zhukov. I told him then, "I have known Zhukov for a long time; he is a good general and a good military leader."

After the war Stalin began to tell all kinds of nonsense about Zhukov, among others the following, "You praised Zhukov, but he does not deserve it. It is said that before each operation at the front Zhukov used to behave as follows: he used to take a handful of earth, smell it and say, 'We can begin the attack,' or the opposite, 'the planned operation cannot be carried out.'" I stated at that time, "Comrade Stalin, I do not know who invented this, but it is not true."

It is possible that Stalin himself invented these things for the purpose of minimizing the role and military talents of Marshal Zhukov.

All the more monstrous are the acts whose initiator was Stalin and which are rude violations of the basic Leninist principles of the nationality policy of the Soviet State. We refer to the mass deportations from their native places of whole nations, together with all Communists and Komsomols without any exception; this deportation action was not dictated by any military considerations.

The Ukrainians avoided meeting this fate only because there were too many of them and there was no place to which to deport them. Otherwise, he would have deported them also.

Let us also recall the "Affair of the Doctor Plotters." [Animation in the hall.] Actually there was no "affair" outside of the declaration of the woman doctor Timashuk, who was probably influenced or ordered by someone (after all, she was an unofficial collaborator of the organs of state security) to write Stalin a letter in which she declared that doctors were applying supposedly improper methods of medical treatment.

Such a letter was sufficient for Stalin to reach an immediate conclusion that there are doctor–plotters in the Soviet Union. He issued orders to arrest a group of eminent Soviet medical specialists. He personally issued advice on the conduct of the investigation and the method of interrogation of the arrested persons.

Stalin personally called the investigative judge, gave him instructions, advised him on which investigative methods should be used; these methods were simple—beat, beat and, once again, beat.

Comrades: The cult of the individual acquired such monstrous size chiefly because Stalin himself, using all conceivable methods, supported the glorification of his own person. This is supported by numerous facts. Once of the most characteristic examples of Stalin's self-glorification and of his lack of even elementary modesty is the edition of his "Short Biography," which was published in 1948.

"Stalin is the worthy continuer of Lenin's work, or, as it is said in our party, Stalin is the Lenin of today." You see how well it is said; not by the nation but by Stalin himself.

Comrades: We must abolish the cult of the individual decisively, once and for all; we must draw the proper conclusions concerning both ideological-theoretical and practical work.

It is necessary for this purpose:

First, in a Bolshevik manner to condemn and to eradicate the cult of the individual as alien to Marxism-Leninism and not consonant with the principles of party leadership and the norms of party life, and to fight inexorably all attempts at bringing back this practice in one form or another.

To return to and actually practice in all our ideological work the most important theses of Marxist-Leninist science about the people as the creator of history and as the creator of all material and spiritual good of humanity, about the decisive role of the Marxist party in the revolutionary fight for the transformation of society, about the victory of communism.

In this connection we will be forced to do much work to examine critically from the Marxist-Leninist viewpoint and to correct the widely spread erroneous views connected with the cult of the individual in the sphere of history, philosophy, economy and of the other sciences, as well as in the literature and the fine arts. It is especially necessary that in the immediate future we compile a serious textbook of the history of our party which will be edited in accordance with scientific Marxist objectivism, a textbook of the history of Soviet society, a book pertaining to the events of the civil war and the great patriotic war.

We are absolutely certain that our party, armed with the historical resolutions of the twentieth congress, will lead the Soviet people along the Leninist path to new successes, to new victories.

Long live the victorious banner of our party—Leninism!

DOUGLAS A. MACARTHUR

Sylvanus Thayer Award Acceptance Address
"Duty, Honor, Country"
("They teach you in this way to be an
officer and a gentleman")
West Point, New York
May 12, 1962

*During World War II, General MacArthur (1880–1964) was the Supreme
Commander of Allied Forces in the Southwest Pacific. In the Korean War, he
became the Commander of United Nations Forces, but soon lost that post for
criticizing government policy. MacArthur graduated from West Point in 1903
and in 1919 became its superintendent. "Since 1958," according to the award
web site, "the West Point Association of Graduates has presented the Sylvanus
Thayer Award to an outstanding citizen of the United States whose service and
accomplishments in the national interest exemplify personal devotion to the
ideals expressed in the West Point motto, 'Duty, Honor, Country.'"*

General Westmoreland, General Grove, distinguished guests, and
gentlemen of the Corps!

As I was leaving the hotel this morning, a doorman asked me,
"Where are you bound for, General?" And when I replied, "West
Point," he remarked, "Beautiful place. Have you ever been there
before?"

No human being could fail to be deeply moved by such a tribute
as this. Coming from a profession I have served so long, and a people
I have loved so well, it fills me with an emotion I cannot express. But
this award is not intended primarily to honor a personality, but to
symbolize a great moral code—the code of conduct and chivalry of
those who guard this beloved land of culture and ancient descent.
That is the animation of this medallion. For all eyes and for all time,
it is an expression of the ethics of the American soldier. That I should
be integrated in this way with so noble an ideal arouses a sense of
pride and yet of humility which will be with me always.

Duty, Honor, Country: Those three hallowed words reverently dictate what you ought to be, what you can be, what you will be. They are your rallying points: to build courage when courage seems to fail; to regain faith when there seems to be little cause for faith; to create hope when hope becomes forlorn.

Unhappily, I possess neither that eloquence of diction, that poetry of imagination, nor that brilliance of metaphor to tell you all that they mean.

The unbelievers will say they are but words, but a slogan, but a flamboyant phrase. Every pedant, every demagogue, every cynic, every hypocrite, every troublemaker, and I am sorry to say, some others of an entirely different character, will try to downgrade them even to the extent of mockery and ridicule.

But these are some of the things they do. They build your basic character. They mold you for your future roles as the custodians of the nation's defense. They make you strong enough to know when you are weak, and brave enough to face yourself when you are afraid. They teach you to be proud and unbending in honest failure, but humble and gentle in success; not to substitute words for actions, not to seek the path of comfort, but to face the stress and spur of difficulty and challenge; to learn to stand up in the storm but to have compassion on those who fall; to master yourself before you seek to master others; to have a heart that is clean, a goal that is high; to learn to laugh, yet never forget how to weep; to reach into the future yet never neglect the past; to be serious yet never to take yourself too seriously; to be modest so that you will remember the simplicity of true greatness, the open mind of true wisdom, the meekness of true strength. They give you a temper of the will, a quality of the imagination, a vigor of the emotions, a freshness of the deep springs of life, a temperamental predominance of courage over timidity, of an appetite for adventure over love of ease. They create in your heart the sense of wonder, the unfailing hope of what next, and the joy and inspiration of life. They teach you in this way to be an officer and a gentleman.

And what sort of soldiers are those you are to lead? Are they reliable? Are they brave? Are they capable of victory? Their story is known to all of you. It is the story of the American man-at-arms. My estimate of him was formed on the battlefield many, many years ago, and has never changed. I regarded him then as I regard him now—as one of the world's noblest figures, not only as one of the finest military characters, but also as one of the most stainless. His name and fame are the birthright of every American citizen. In his youth and strength, his love and loyalty, he gave all that mortality can give.

He needs no eulogy from me or from any other man. He has written his own history and written it in red on his enemy's breast. But when I think of his patience under adversity, of his courage under fire, and of his modesty in victory, I am filled with an emotion of admiration I cannot put into words. He belongs to history as furnishing one of the greatest examples of successful patriotism. He belongs to posterity as the instructor of future generations in the principles of liberty and freedom. He belongs to the present, to us, by his virtues and by his achievements. In twenty campaigns, on a hundred battlefields, around a thousand campfires, I have witnessed that enduring fortitude, that patriotic self-abnegation, and that invincible determination which have carved his statue in the hearts of his people. From one end of the world to the other he has drained deep the chalice of courage.

As I listened to those songs [of the glee club], in memory's eye I could see those staggering columns of the First World War, bending under soggy packs, on many a weary march from dripping dusk to drizzling dawn, slogging ankle-deep through the mire of shell-shocked roads, to form grimly for the attack, blue-lipped, covered with sludge and mud, chilled by the wind and rain, driving home to their objective, and for many, to the judgment seat of God.

I do not know the dignity of their birth, but I do know the glory of their death. They died unquestioning, uncomplaining, with faith in their hearts, and on their lips the hope that we would go on to victory. Always, for them: *Duty, Honor, Country;* always their blood and sweat and tears, as we sought the way and the light and the truth.

And twenty years after, on the other side of the globe, again the filth of murky foxholes, the stench of ghostly trenches, the slime of dripping dugouts; those boiling suns of relentless heat, those torrential rains of devastating storms; the loneliness and utter desolation of jungle trails; the bitterness of long separation from those they loved and cherished; the deadly pestilence of tropical disease; the horror of stricken areas of war; their resolute and determined defense, their swift and sure attack, their indomitable purpose, their complete and decisive victory—always victory. Always through the bloody haze of their last reverberating shot, the vision of gaunt, ghastly men reverently following your password of: *Duty, Honor, Country.*

The code which those words perpetuate embraces the highest moral laws and will stand the test of any ethics or philosophies ever promulgated for the uplift of mankind. Its requirements are for the things that are right, and its restraints are from the things that are wrong.

The soldier, above all other men, is required to practice the greatest act of religious training—sacrifice.

In battle and in the face of danger and death, he discloses those divine attributes which his Maker gave when he created man in his own image. No physical courage and no brute instinct can take the place of the Divine help which alone can sustain him.

However horrible the incidents of war may be, the soldier who is called upon to offer and to give his life for his country is the noblest development of mankind.

You now face a new world—a world of change. The thrust into outer space of the satellite, spheres, and missiles mark the beginning of another epoch in the long story of mankind. In the five or more billions of years the scientists tell us it has taken to form the earth, in the three or more billion years of development of the human race, there has never been a more abrupt or staggering evolution. We deal now not with things of this world alone, but with the illimitable distances and as yet unfathomed mysteries of the universe. We are reaching out for a new and boundless frontier.

We speak in strange terms: of harnessing the cosmic energy; of making winds and tides work for us; of creating unheard synthetic materials to supplement or even replace our old standard basics; to purify sea water for our drink; of mining ocean floors for new fields of wealth and food; of disease preventatives to expand life into the hundreds of years; of controlling the weather for a more equitable distribution of heat and cold, of rain and shine; of space ships to the moon; of the primary target in war, no longer limited to the armed forces of an enemy, but instead to include his civil populations; of ultimate conflict between a united human race and the sinister forces of some other planetary galaxy; of such dreams and fantasies as to make life the most exciting of all time.

And through all this welter of change and development, your mission remains fixed, determined, inviolable: it is to win our wars.

Everything else in your professional career is but corollary to this vital dedication. All other public purposes, all other public projects, all other public needs, great or small, will find others for their accomplishment. But you are the ones who are trained to fight. Yours is the profession of arms, the will to win, the sure knowledge that in war there is no substitute for victory; that if you lose, the nation will be destroyed; that the very obsession of your public service must be: *Duty, Honor, Country.*

Others will debate the controversial issues, national and international, which divide men's minds; but serene, calm, aloof, you stand as the Nation's war-guardian, as its lifeguard from the raging tides of international conflict, as its gladiator in the arena of battle. For a century and a half you have defended, guarded, and protected its hallowed traditions of liberty and freedom, of right and justice.

Let civilian voices argue the merits or demerits of our processes of government; whether our strength is being sapped by deficit financing, indulged in too long, by federal paternalism grown too mighty, by power groups grown too arrogant, by politics grown too corrupt, by crime grown too rampant, by morals grown too low, by taxes grown too high, by extremists grown too violent; whether our personal liberties are as thorough and complete as they should be. These great national problems are not for your professional participation or military solution. Your guidepost stands out like a ten-fold beacon in the night: *Duty, Honor, Country.*

You are the leaven which binds together the entire fabric of our national system of defense. From your ranks come the great captains who hold the nation's destiny in their hands the moment the war tocsin sounds. The Long Gray Line has never failed us. Were you to do so, a million ghosts in olive drab, in brown khaki, in blue and gray, would rise from their white crosses thundering those magic words: *Duty, Honor, Country.*

This does not mean that you are war-mongers.

On the contrary, the soldier, above all other people, prays for peace, for he must suffer and bear the deepest wounds and scars of war.

But always in our ears ring the ominous words of Plato, that wisest of all philosophers: "Only the dead have seen the end of war."

The shadows are lengthening for me. The twilight is here. My days of old have vanished, tone and tint. They have gone glimmering through the dreams of things that were. Their memory is one of wondrous beauty, watered by tears, and coaxed and caressed by the smiles of yesterday. I listen vainly, but with thirsty ears, for the witching melody of faint bugles blowing reveille, of far drums beating the long roll. In my dreams I hear again the crash of guns, the rattle of musketry, the strange, mournful mutter of the battlefield.

But in the evening of my memory, always I come back to West Point.

Always there echoes and re-echoes: *Duty, Honor, Country.*

Today marks my final roll call with you, but I want you to know that when I cross the river my last conscious thoughts will be of The Corps, and The Corps, and The Corps.

I bid you farewell.

JOHN F. KENNEDY
The Strategy for Peace
("I speak of peace . . . as the necessary
rational end of rational men")
American University, Washington, D.C.
June 10, 1963

*President Kennedy (1917–1963), aiming for "world peace" as he had in his
inaugural address in 1961, addresses American foreign policy during the cold
war and the possibility of negotiations with the Soviet Union regarding nuclear
weapons. The Nuclear Test Ban treaty was signed a month later. On November 22, 1963, he was assassinated in Dallas.*

It is with great pride that I participate in this ceremony of the Ameri-
can University sponsored by the Methodist Church, founded by
Bishop John Fletcher Hurst and first opened by President Woodrow
Wilson in 1914.

This is a young and growing university, but it has already fulfilled
Bishop Hurst's enlightened hope for the study of history and public
affairs in a city devoted to the making of history and to the conduct
of the public's business.

I have, therefore, chosen this time and place to discuss a topic on
which ignorance too often abounds and the truth is too rarely perceived—and that is the most important topic on earth: world peace.

What kind of peace do I mean and what kind of peace do we seek?
Not a Pax Americana enforced on the world by American weapons
of war. Not the peace of the grave or the security of the slave. I am
talking about genuine peace—the kind of peace that makes life on
earth worth living—and the kind that enables men and nations to
grow and to hope and build a better life for their children—not
merely peace for Americans but peace for all men and women—not
merely peace in our time but peace in all time.

I speak of peace because of the new face of war. Total war makes no
sense in an age where great powers can maintain large and relatively

invulnerable nuclear forces and refuse to surrender without resort to those forces. It makes no sense in an age when a single nuclear weapon contains almost ten times the explosive force delivered by all the Allied air forces in the second world war. It makes no sense in an age when the deadly poisons produced by a nuclear exchange would be carried by wind and water and soil and seed to the far corners of the globe and to generations yet unborn.

Today the expenditure of billions of dollars every year on weapons acquired for the purpose of making sure we never need them is essential to the keeping of peace. But surely the acquisition of such idle stockpiles—which can only destroy and can never create—is not the only, much less the most efficient, means of assuring peace.

I speak of peace, therefore, as the necessary rational end of rational men. I realize the pursuit of peace is not as dramatic as the pursuit of war—and frequently the words of the pursuer fall on deaf ears. But we have no more urgent task.

Some say that it is useless to speak of peace or world law or world disarmament—and that it will be useless until the leaders of the Soviet Union adopt a more enlightened attitude. I hope they do. I believe we can help them do it.

But I also believe that we must re-examine our own attitudes—as individuals and as a nation—for our attitude is as essential as theirs. And every graduate of this school, every thoughtful citizen who despairs of war and wishes to bring peace, should begin by looking inward—by examining his own attitude towards the course of the cold war and towards freedom and peace here at home.

First: Examine our attitude towards peace itself. Too many of us think it is impossible. Too many think it is unreal. But that is a dangerous, defeatist belief. It leads to the conclusion that war is inevitable—that mankind is doomed—that we are gripped by forces we cannot control.

We need not accept that view. Our problems are man-made. Therefore, they can be solved by man. And man can be as big as he wants. No problem of human destiny is beyond human beings. Man's reason and spirit have often solved the seemingly unsolvable—and we believe they can do it again.

I am not referring to the absolute, infinite concepts of universal peace and goodwill of which some fantasies and fanatics dream. I do not deny the value of hopes and dreams but we merely invite discouragement and incredulity by making that our only and immediate goal.

Let us focus instead on a more practical, more attainable peace—based not on a sudden revolution in human nature but on a gradual evolution in human institutions—on a series of concrete actions and effective agreements which are in the interests of all concerned.

There is no single, simple key to this peace—no grand or magic formula to be adopted by one or two powers. Genuine peace must be the product of many nations, the sum of many acts. It must be dynamic, not static, changing to meet the challenge of each new generation. For peace is a process—a way of solving problems.

With such a peace, there will still be quarrels and conflicting interests, as there are within families and nations. World peace, like community peace, does not require that each man love his neighbor—it requires only that they live together with mutual tolerance, submitting their disputes to a just and peaceful settlement. And history teaches us that enmities between nations, as between individuals, do not last forever. However fixed our likes and dislikes may seem, the tide of time and events will often bring surprising changes in the relations between nations and neighbors.

So let us persevere. Peace need not be impracticable—war need not be inevitable. By defining our goal more clearly—by making it seem more manageable and less remote—we can help all people to see it, to draw hope from it, and to move irresistibly towards it.

And second: let us re-examine our attitude towards the Soviet Union. It is discouraging to think that their leaders may actually believe what their propagandists write.

It is discouraging to read a recent authoritative Soviet text on military strategy and find, on page after page, wholly baseless and incredible claims—such as the allegation that "American imperialist circles are preparing to unleash different types of war . . . that there is a very real threat of a preventative war being unleashed by American imperialists against the Soviet Union . . . [and that] the political aims," and I quote, "of the American imperialists are to enslave economically and politically the European and other capitalist countries . . . [and] to achieve world domination . . . by means of aggressive wars."

Truly, as it was written long ago: "The wicked flee when no man pursueth." Yet it is sad to read these Soviet statements—to realize the extent of the gulf between us. But it is also a warning—a warning to the American people not to fall into the same trap as the Soviets, not to see only a distorted and desperate view of the other side, not to see conflict as inevitable, accommodation as impossible and communication as nothing more than an exchange of threats.

No government or social system is so evil that its people must be considered as lacking in virtue. As Americans, we find Communism profoundly repugnant as a negation of personal freedom and dignity. But we can still hail the Russian people for their many achievements—in science and space, in economic and industrial growth, in culture, in acts of courage.

Among the many traits the peoples of our two countries have in common, none is stronger than our mutual abhorrence of war. Almost unique among the major world powers, we have never been at war with each other. And no nation in the history of battle ever suffered more than the Soviet Union in the second world war. At least 20,000,000 lost their lives. Countless millions of homes and farms were burned or sacked. A third of the nation's territory, including two-thirds of its industrial base, was turned into a wasteland—a loss equivalent to the destruction of this country east of Chicago.

Today, should total war ever break out again—no matter how—our two countries will be the primary targets. It is an ironic but accurate fact that the two strongest powers are the two in the most danger of devastation. All we have built, all we have worked for, would be destroyed in the first 24 hours. And even in the cold war—which brings burdens and dangers to so many countries, including this nation's closest allies—our two countries bear the heaviest burdens. For we are both devoting massive sums of money to weapons that could be better devoted to contact ignorance, poverty and disease.

We are both caught up in a vicious and dangerous cycle with suspicion on one side breeding suspicion on the other, and new weapons begetting counter-weapons.

In short, both the United States and its allies, and the Soviet Union and its allies, have a mutually deep interest in a just and genuine peace and in halting the arms race. Agreements to this end are in the interests of the Soviet Union as well as ours—and even the most hostile nations can be relied upon to accept and keep those treaty obligations, and only those treaty obligations, which are in their own interest.

So, let us not be blind to our differences—but let us also direct attention to our common interests and the means by which those differences can be resolved. And if we cannot end now our differences, at least we can help make the world safe for diversity. For, in the final analysis, our most basic common link is that we all inhabit this small planet. We all breathe the same air. We all cherish our children's future. And we all are mortal.

Third: Let us re-examine our attitude towards the cold war, remembering we are not engaged in a debate, seeking to pile up debating points. We are not here distributing blame or pointing the finger of judgment. We must deal with the world as it is, and not as it might have been had the history of the last eighteen years been different.

We must, therefore, persevere in the search for peace in the hope that constructive changes within the Communist bloc might bring within reach solutions which now seem beyond us. We must conduct our affairs in such a way that it becomes in the Communists' interest to agree on a genuine peace. And above all, while defending our own vital interests, nuclear powers must avert those confrontations which bring an adversary to a choice of either a humiliating retreat or a nuclear war. To adopt that kind of course in the nuclear age would be evidence only of the bankruptcy of our policy—or of a collective death-wish for the world.

To secure these ends, America's weapons are non-provocative, carefully controlled, designed to deter and capable of selective use. Our military forces are committed to peace and disciplined in self-restraint. Our diplomats are instructed to avoid unnecessary irritants and purely rhetorical hostility.

For we can seek a relaxation of tensions without relaxing our guard. And, for our part, we do not need to use threats to prove that we are resolute. We do not need to jam foreign broadcasts out of fear our faith will be eroded. We are unwilling to impose our system on any unwilling people—but we are willing and able to engage in peaceful competition with any people on earth.

Meanwhile, we seek to strengthen the United Nations, to help solve its financial problems, to make it a more effective instrument for peace, to develop it into a genuine world security system—a system capable of resolving disputes on the basis of law, of insuring the security of the large and the small, and of creating conditions under which arms can finally be abolished.

At the same time we seek to keep peace inside the non-Communist world, where many nations, all of them our friends, are divided over issues which weaken Western unity, which invite Communist intervention or which threaten to erupt into war.

Our efforts in West New Guinea, in the Congo, in the Middle East and the Indian subcontinent have been persistent and patient despite criticism from both sides. We have also tried to set an example for others—by seeking to adjust small but significant differences with our closest neighbors in Mexico and Canada.

Speaking of other nations, I wish to make one point clear. We are bound to many nations by alliances. These alliances exist because our concern and theirs substantially overlap. Our commitment to defend Western Europe and West Berlin, for example, stands undiminished because of the identity of our vital interests. The United States will make no deal with the Soviet Union at the expense of other nations and other peoples, not merely because they are our partners, but also because their interests and ours converge.

Our interests converge, however, not only in defending the frontiers of freedom, but in pursuing the paths of peace.

It is our hope—and the purpose of allied policies—to convince the Soviet Union that she, too, should let each nation choose its own future, so long as that choice does not interfere with the choices of others. The Communist drive to impose their political and economic system on others is the primary cause of world tension today. For there can be no doubt that, if all nations could refrain from interfering in the self-determination of others, the peace would be much more assured.

This will require a new effort to achieve world law—a new context for world discussions. It will require increased understanding between the Soviets and ourselves. And increased understanding will require increased contact and communication.

One step in this direction is the proposed arrangement for a direct line between Moscow and Washington, to avoid on each side the dangerous delays, misunderstanding, and misreadings of the other's actions which might occur in a time of crisis.

We have also been talking to Geneva about other first-step measures of arms control, designed to limit the intensity of the arms race and reduce the risks of accidental war.

Our primary long-range interest in Geneva, however, is general and complete disarmament—designed to take place by stages, permitting parallel political developments to build the new institutions of peace which would take the place of arms. The pursuit of disarmament has been an effort of this Government since the 1920's. It has been urgently sought by the past three Administrations. And however dim the prospects are today, we intend to continue this effort—to continue it in order that all countries, including our own, can better grasp what the problems and the possibilities of disarmament are.

The only major area of these negotiations where the end is in sight—yet where a fresh start is badly needed—is in a treaty to outlaw nuclear tests. The conclusion of such a treaty—so near and yet so far—would check the spiraling arms race in one of its most dangerous areas. It would place the nuclear powers in a position to deal more effectively with one of the greatest hazards which man faces in 1963—the further spread of nuclear weapons. It would increase our security—it would decrease the prospects of war.

Surely this goal is sufficiently important to require our steady pursuit, yielding neither to the temptation to give up the whole effort nor the temptation to give up our insistence on vital and responsible safeguards.

I am taking this opportunity, therefore, to announce two important decisions in this regard:

First: Chairman Khrushchev, Prime Minister Macmillan and I have agreed that high-level discussions will shortly begin in Moscow towards early agreement on a comprehensive test ban treaty. Our hopes must be tempered with the caution of history—but with our hopes go the hopes of all mankind.

Second: To make clear our good faith and solemn convictions on the matter, I now declare that the United States does not propose to conduct nuclear tests in the atmosphere so long as other states do not do so. We will not be the first to resume. Such a declaration is no substitute for a formal, binding treaty—but I hope it will help us achieve one. Nor would such a treaty be a substitute for disarmament—but I hope it will help us achieve it.

Finally, my fellow Americans, let us examine our attitude towards peace and freedom here at home. The quality and spirit of our own society must justify and support our efforts abroad. We must show it in the dedication of our own lives—as many of you who are graduating today will have an opportunity to do, by serving without pay in the Peace Corps abroad or in the proposed National Service Corps here at home.

But wherever we are, we must all, in our daily lives, live up to the age-old faith that peace and freedom walk together. In too many of our cities today, the peace is not secure because freedom is incomplete.

It is the responsibility of the executive branch at all levels of government—local, state and national—to provide and protect that freedom for all of our citizens by all means within our authority. It is the responsibility of the legislative branch at all levels, wherever the authority is not now adequate, to make it adequate. And it is the responsibility of all citizens in all sections of this country to respect the rights of others and respect the law of the land.

All this is not unrelated to world peace. "When a man's ways please the Lord," the scriptures tell us, "he maketh even his enemies to be at peace with him." And is not peace, in the last analysis, basically a matter of human rights—the right to live out our lives without fear of devastation—the right to breathe air as nature provided it—the right of future generations to a healthy existence?

While we proceed to safeguard our national interests, let us also safeguard human interests. And the elimination of war and arms is clearly in the interest of both.

No treaty, however much it may be to the advantage of all, however tightly it may be worded, can provide absolute security against the risks of deception and evasion. But it can—if it is sufficiently effective in its enforcement and it is sufficiently in the interests of its signers—offer far more security and far fewer risks than an unabated, uncontrolled, unpredictable arms race.

The United States, as the world knows, will never start a war. We do not want a war. We do not now expect a war. This generation of Americans has already had enough—more than enough—of war and hate and oppression. We shall be prepared if others wish it. We shall be alert to try to stop it. But we shall also do our part to build a world of peace where the weak are safe and the strong are just.

We are not helpless before that task or hopeless of its success. Confident and unafraid, we labor on—not toward a strategy of annihilation but toward a strategy of peace. Thank you.

MARTIN LUTHER KING, JR.
I Have a Dream
("No, no, we are not satisfied, and we will not
be satisfied until justice rolls down like waters and
righteousness like a mighty stream")
Washington, D.C.
August 28, 1963

As president of the Southern Christian Leadership Conference, the Baptist pastor Dr. King (1929–1968) spoke at the Lincoln Memorial to the participants of the civil rights march on Washington, D.C. A native of Atlanta, King earned his undergraduate degree at Morehouse College and his Ph.D. at Boston University. He was an inspiring speaker as he advocated for racial justice and peace. In 1968, the Nobel Peace Prize winner was assassinated in Memphis.

I am happy to join with you today in what will go down in history as the greatest demonstration for freedom in the history of our nation.

Five score years ago, a great American, in whose symbolic shadow we stand, signed the Emancipation Proclamation. This momentous decree came as a great beacon light of hope to millions of Negro slaves who had been seared in the flames of withering injustice. It came as a joyous daybreak to end the long night of captivity.

But one hundred years later, we must face the tragic fact that the Negro is still not free. One hundred years later, the life of the Negro is still sadly crippled by the manacles of segregation and the chains of discrimination. One hundred years later, the Negro lives on a lonely island of poverty in the midst of a vast ocean of material prosperity. One hundred years later the Negro is still languishing in the corners of American society and finds himself an exile in his own land. So we have come here today to dramatize an appalling condition.

In a sense we have come to our nation's Capital to cash a check. When the architects of our republic wrote the magnificent words of the Constitution and the Declaration of Independence, they were signing a promissory note to which every American was to fall heir. This note was a promise that all men would be guaranteed the unalienable rights of life, liberty, and the pursuit of happiness.

It is obvious today that America has defaulted on this promissory note insofar as her citizens of color are concerned. Instead of honoring this sacred obligation, America has given the Negro people a bad check; a check which has come back marked "insufficient funds." But we refuse to believe that the bank of justice is bankrupt. We refuse to believe that there are insufficient funds in the great vaults of opportunity of this nation. So we have come to cash this check—a check that will give us upon demand the riches of freedom and the security of justice. We have also come to this hallowed spot to remind America of the fierce urgency of *now*. This is no time to engage in the luxury of cooling off or to take the tranquilizing drug of gradualism. *Now* is the time to make real the promise of Democracy. *Now* is the time to rise from the dark and desolate valley of segregation to the sunlit path of racial justice. *Now* is the time to open the doors of opportunity to all of God's children. *Now* is the time to lift our nation from the quicksands of racial injustice to the solid rock of brotherhood.

It would be fatal for the nation to overlook the urgency of the moment and to underestimate the determination of the Negro. This sweltering summer of the Negro's legitimate discontent will not pass until there is an invigorating autumn of freedom and equality. 1963 is not an end, but a beginning. Those who hope that the Negro needed to blow off steam and will now be content will have a rude awakening if the Nation returns to business as usual. There will be neither rest nor tranquility in America until the Negro is granted his citizenship rights. The whirlwinds of revolt will continue to shake the foundations of our Nation until the bright day of justice emerges.

But there is something that I must say to my people who stand on the warm threshold which leads into the palace of justice. In the process of gaining our rightful place we must not be guilty of wrongful deeds. Let us not seek to satisfy our thirst for freedom by drinking from the cup of bitterness and hatred. We must forever conduct our struggle on the high plane of dignity and discipline. We must not allow our creative protest to degenerate into physical violence. Again and again we must rise to the majestic heights of meeting physical force with soul force. The marvelous new militancy which has engulfed the Negro community must not lead us to a distrust of all white people, for many of our white brothers, as evidenced by their presence here today, have come to realize that their destiny is tied up

with our destiny and their freedom is inextricably bound to our freedom. We cannot walk alone.

And as we walk, we must make the pledge that we shall march
ahead. We cannot turn back. There are those who are asking the
devotees of civil rights, "When will you be satisfied?" We can never
be satisfied as long as the Negro is the victim of the unspeakable horrors of police brutality. We can never be satisfied as long as our bodies, heavy with the fatigue of travel, cannot gain lodging in the motels
of the highways and the hotels of the cities. We cannot be satisfied as
long as the Negro's basic mobility is from a smaller ghetto to a larger
one. We can never be satisfied as long as a Negro in Mississippi cannot vote and a Negro in New York believes he has nothing for
which to vote. No, no, we are not satisfied, and we will not be satisfied until justice rolls down like waters and righteousness like a
mighty stream.

I am not unmindful that some of you have come here out of great
trials and tribulations. Some of you have come fresh from narrow jail
cells. Some of you have come from areas where your quest for freedom left you battered by the storms of persecution and staggered by
the winds of police brutality. You have been the veterans of creative
suffering. Continue to work with the faith that unearned suffering is
redemptive.

Go back to Mississippi, go back to Alabama, go back to South
Carolina, go back to Georgia, go back to Louisiana, go back to the
slums and ghettos of our modern cities, knowing that somehow this
situation can and will be changed. Let us not wallow in the valley of
despair.

I say to you today, my friends, that in spite of the difficulties and
frustrations of the moment I still have a dream. It is a dream deeply
rooted in the American dream.

I have a dream that one day this nation will rise up and live out the
true meaning of its creed: "We hold these truths to be self-evident;
that all men are created equal."

I have a dream that one day on the red hills of Georgia the sons of
former slaves and the sons of former slaveowners will be able to sit
down together at the table of brotherhood.

I have a dream that one day even the state of Mississippi, a desert
state sweltering with the heat of injustice and oppression, will be
transformed into an oasis of freedom and justice.

I have a dream that my four little children will one day live in a
nation where they will not be judged by the color of their skin but
by the content of their character.

I have a dream today.

I have a dream that one day the state of Alabama, whose governor's lips are presently dripping with the words of interposition and nullification, will be transformed into a situation where little black boys and black girls will be able to join hand with little white boys and white girls and walk together as sisters and brothers.

I have a dream today.

I have a dream that one day every valley shall be exalted, every hill and mountain shall be made low, the rough places will be made plains, and the crooked places will be made straight, and the glory of the Lord shall be revealed, and all flesh shall see it together.

This is our hope. This is the faith with which I return to the South. With this faith we will be able to hew out of the mountain of despair a stone of hope. With this faith we will be able to transform the jangling discords of our nation into a beautiful symphony of brotherhood. With this faith we will be able to work together, to pray together, to struggle together, to go to jail together, to stand up for freedom together, knowing that we will be free one day.

This will be the day when all of God's children will be able to sing with new meaning "My country 'tis of thee, sweet land of liberty, of thee I sing. Land where my fathers died, land of the pilgrim's pride, from every mountainside, let freedom ring."

And if America is to be a great nation this must become true. So let freedom ring from the prodigious hilltops of New Hampshire. Let freedom ring from the mighty mountains of New York. Let freedom ring from the heightening Alleghenies of Pennsylvania!

Let freedom ring from the snowcapped Rockies of Colorado!

Let freedom ring from the curvaceous peaks of California!

But not only that; let freedom ring from Stone Mountain of Georgia!

Let freedom ring from Lookout Mountain of Tennessee!

Let freedom ring from every hill and mole hill of Mississippi. From every mountainside, let freedom ring.

When we let freedom ring, when we let it ring from every village and every hamlet, from every state and every city, we will be able to speed up that day when all of God's children, black men and white men, Jews and Gentiles, Protestants and Catholics, will be able to join hands and sing in the words of the old Negro spiritual, "Free at last! free at last! thank God almighty, we are free at last!"

CHE GUEVARA
Colonialism Is Doomed
(". . . the United States is not the champion of freedom,
but rather the perpetrator of exploitation and oppression
of the peoples of the world")
United Nations General Assembly
New York City
December 11, 1964

*The short, dramatic, and tragic life of Ernesto "Che" Guevara de la Serna
(1928–1967) has made him a folk hero. Born in Rosario, Argentina, he
became a doctor and through his medical work across South America he realized the extent of the continent's economic and political injustice. He became
a Cuban citizen after the Cuban Revolution of 1959 and was an important
spokesperson for the country. His speech that follows attacks American foreign
and internal policies.*

The Cuban delegation to this assembly has pleasure, first of all, in
fulfilling the pleasant duty of welcoming three new nations to the
large number of nations whose representatives are discussing the
problems of the world. We therefore greet through their Presidents
and Prime Ministers the people of Zambia, Malawi, and Malta, and
express the hope that from the outset these countries will be added to
the group of non-aligned countries which struggle against imperialism, colonialism, and neocolonialism.

We also wish to convey our congratulations to the President of this
assembly whose elevation to so high a post is of special significance
since it reflects this new historic stage or resounding triumphs for the
peoples of Africa, until recently subject to the colonial system of imperialism, and who, today, for the great part in the legitimate exercise
of self-determination, have become citizens of sovereign states. The
last hour of colonialism has struck, and millions of inhabitants of Africa, Asia, and Latin America rise to meet a new life, and assert their

unrestricted right to self-determination and to the independent development of their nations.

We wish you, Mr. President, the greatest success in the tasks entrusted to you by member states.

Cuba comes here to state its position on the most important controversial issues and will do so with the full sense of responsibility which the use of this rostrum implies, while at the same time responding to the unavoidable duty of speaking out, clearly and frankly.

We should like to see this assembly shake itself out of complacency and move forward. We should like to see the committees begin their work and not stop at the first confrontation. Imperialism wishes to convert this meeting into an aimless oratorical tournament, instead of using it to solve the grave problems of the world. We must prevent their doing so. This assembly should not be remembered in the future only by the number nineteen which identifies it. We feel that we have the right and the obligation to try to make this meeting effective because our country is a constant point of friction; one of the places where the principles supporting the rights of small nations to sovereignty are tested day by day, minute by minute; and at the same time our country is one of the barricades of freedom in the world, situated a few steps away from United States imperialism, to show with its actions, its daily example, that peoples can liberate themselves, can keep themselves free, in the existing conditions of the world.

Of course, there is now a socialist camp which becomes stronger day by day and has more powerful weapons of struggle. But additional conditions are required for survival: the maintenance of internal cohesion, faith in one's destiny, and the irreversible decision to fight to the death for the defense of one's country and revolution. These conditions exist in Cuba.

Of all the burning problems to be dealt with by this assembly, one which has special significance for us and whose solution we feel must be sought first, so as to leave no doubt in the minds of anyone, is that of peaceful coexistence among states with different economic and social systems. Much progress has been made in the world in this field. But imperialism, particularly United States imperialism, has tried to make the world believe that peaceful coexistence is the exclusive right of the great powers on earth. We repeat what our President said in Cairo, and which later took shape in the Declaration of the Second Conference of Heads of State or Government of Non-Aligned Countries; that there cannot be peaceful coexistence only among the powerful if we are to ensure world peace. Peaceful coexistence must be practiced by all states, independent of size, of the previous historic relations that linked them, and of the problems that may arise among some of them at a given moment."

At present the type of peaceful coexistence to which we aspire does not exist in many cases. The kingdom of Cambodia, merely because it maintained a neutral attitude and did not submit to the machinations of United States imperialism, has been subjected to all kinds of treacherous and brutal attacks from the Yankee bases in South Vietnam.

Laos, a divided country, has also been the object of imperialist aggression of every kind. The conventions concluded at Geneva have been violated, its peoples have been massacred from the air, and part of its territory is in constant danger from cowardly attacks by imperialist forces.

The Democratic Republic of Vietnam, which knows of the histories of aggressions as few people on earth, once again has seen its frontier violated, its installations attacked by enemy bomber and fighter planes, its naval posts attacked by the United States warships violating territorial waters.

At this moment, there hangs over the Democratic Republic of Vietnam the threat that the United States warmongers may openly extend to its territory the war that, for many years, they have been waging against the people of South Vietnam.

The Soviet Union and the People's Republic of China have given serious warning to the United States. Not only the peace of the world is in danger in this situation, but also the lives of millions of human beings in this part of Asia are being constantly threatened and subjected to the whim of the United States invader.

Peaceful coexistence has also been put to the test in a brutal manner in Cyprus, due to pressures from the Turkish Government and NATO, compelling the people and the government of Cyprus to make a firm and heroic stand in defense of their sovereignty.

In all these parts of the world imperialism attempts to impose its version of what coexistence should be. It is the oppressed peoples in alliance with the socialist camp which must show them the meaning of true coexistence, and it is the obligation of the United Nations to support them.

We must also say that it is not only in relations between sovereign states that the concept of peaceful coexistence must be clearly defined. As Marxists we have maintained that peaceful coexistence among nations does not encompass coexistence between the exploiters and the exploited, the oppressor and the oppressed.

Furthermore, a principle proclaimed by this Organization is that of the right to full independence of all forms of colonial oppression.

That is why we express our solidarity with the colonial peoples of so-called Portuguese Guinea, Angola, and Mozambique, who have been massacred for the crime of demanding their freedom, and we are prepared to help them to the extent of our ability in accordance with the Cairo Declaration.

We express our solidarity with the people of Puerto Rico and its great leader, Pedro Albizu Campos, who has been set free in another act of hypocrisy, at the age of seventy-two, after spending a lifetime in jail, now paralytic and almost without the ability to speak. Albizu Campos is a symbol of the still unredeemed but indomitable America. Years and years of prison, almost unbearable pressures in jail, mental torture, solitude, total isolation from his people and his family, the insolence of the conqueror and lackeys in the land of his birth—nothing at all broke his will. The delegation of Cuba, on behalf of its people, pays a tribute of admiration and gratitude to a patriot who bestows honor upon America.

The North Americans, for many years, have tried to convert Puerto Rico into a reflection of hybrid culture—the Spanish language with an English inflection, the Spanish language with hinges on its backbone, the better to bend before the United States soldier. Puerto Rican soldiers have been used as cannon-fodder in imperialist wars, as in Korea, and even been made to fire at their own brothers, as in the massacre perpetrated by the United States Army a few months ago against the helpless people of Panamane of the most recent diabolical acts carried out by Yankee imperialism. Yet despite that terrible attack against its will and its historic destiny, the people of Puerto Rico have preserved their culture, their Latin character, the national feelings, which in themselves give proof of the implacable will for independence that exists among the masses on the Latin American island.

We must also point out that the principle of peaceful coexistence does not imply a mockery of the will of the peoples, as is happening in the case of so-called British Guiana, where the government of Prime Minister Cheddi Jagan has been the victim of every kind of pressure and maneuver, while the achievement of independence has been delayed by the search for methods that would allow for the flouting of the will of the people while ensuring the docility of a Government different from the present one, put in by underhanded tactics, and then to grant an important "freedom" to this piece of American soil. Whatever roads Guiana may be compelled to follow to obtain independence, the moral and militant support of Cuba goes to its people.

Furthermore, we must point out that the islands of Guadaloupe and Martinique have been fighting for a long time for their autonomy without obtaining it. This state of affairs must not continue.

Once again we raise our voice to put the world on guard against what is happening in South Africa. The brutal policy of apartheid is being carried out before the eyes of the whole world. The peoples of Africa are being compelled to tolerate in that continent the concept, still official, of the superiority of one race over another and in the name of that racial superiority the murder of people with impunity. Can the United Nations do nothing to prevent this? I should like specifically to refer to the painful case of the Congo, unique in this history of the modern world, which shows how, with absolute impunity, with the most insolent cynicism, the rights of peoples can be flouted. The prodigious wealth of the Congo, which the imperialist nations wish to maintain under their control, is the direct reason for this. In his speech on his first visit to the United Nations, our comrade Fidel Castro said that the whole problem of coexistence among peoples was reduced to the undue appropriation of another's wealth. He said, "When this philosophy of despoilment disappears, the philosophy of war will have disappeared."

The philosophy of despoilment not only has not ceased, but rather it is stronger than ever, and that is why those who used the name of the United Nations to commit the murder of Lumumba, today, in the name of the defense of the white race, are assassinating thousands of Congolese. How can one forget how the hope that Patrice Lumumba placed in the United Nations was betrayed? How can one forget the machinations and maneuvers which followed in the wake of the occupation of that country by United Nations troops under whose auspices the assassins of this great African patriot acted with impunity? How can we forget that he who flouted the authority of the United Nations in the Congo, and not exactly for patriotic reasons, but rather by virtue of conflicts between imperialists, was Moise Tshombe, who initiated the secession in Katanga with Belgian support? And how can one justify, how can one explain, that at the end of all the United Nations activities there, Tshombe, dislodged from Katanga, returned as lord and master of the Congo? Who can deny the abject role that the imperialists compelled the United Nations to play?

To sum up, dramatic mobilizations were made to avoid the secession of Katanga, but today that same Katanga is in power! The wealth of the Congo is in imperialist hands and the expenses must be paid by honest nations. The merchants of war certainly do good business. That is why the government of Cuba supports the just attitude of the Soviet Union in refusing to pay the expenses of this crime.

And as if this were not enough, we now have flung in our faces recent events which have filled the world with horror and indignation. Who are the perpetrators? Belgian paratroopers transported by

United States plane, who took off from British bases. We remember as if it were yesterday that we saw a small country in Europe, a civilized and industrious country, the kingdom of Belgium, invaded by the hordes of Hitler. We learned with bitterness that these people were being massacred by the German imperialists, and our sympathy and affection went out to them. But the other side of the imperialist coin many did not then perceive. Perhaps the sons of Belgian patriots who died defending their country are now assassinating thousands of Congolese in the name of the white race, just as they suffered under the German heel because their blood was not purely Aryan. But the scales have fallen from our eyes and they now open upon new horizons, and we can see what yesterday, in our conditions of colonial servitude, we could not observe—that "Western civilization" disguises under its showy front a scene of hyenas and jackals. That is the only name that can be applied to those who have gone to fulfill "humanitarian" tasks in the Congo. Bloodthirsty butchers who feed on helpless people! That is what imperialism does to men; that is what marks the "white" imperialists.

The free men of the world must be prepared to avenge the crime committed in the Congo. It is possible that many of those soldiers who were converted into "supermen" by imperialist machinery, believe in good faith that they are defending the rights of a superior race, but in this assembly those peoples whose skins are darkened by a different sun, colored by different pigments, constitute the majority, and they fully and clearly understand that the difference between men does not lie in the color of their skins, but in the ownership of the means of production and in the relationship of production.

The Cuban delegation extends greetings to the peoples of Southern Rhodesia and Southwest Africa, oppressed by white colonialist minorities, to the peoples of Basutoland, Bechuanaland, Swaziland, French Somaliland, the Arabs of Palestine, Aden, and the Protectorates, Oman, and to all peoples in conflict with imperialism and colonialism; and we reaffirm our support.

I express also the hope that there will be a just solution to the conflict facing our sister republic of Indonesia in its relations with Malaysia.

One of the essential items before this conference is general and complete disarmament. We express our support of general and complete disarmament. Furthermore, we advocate the complete destruction of thermonuclear devices and the holding of a conference of all the nations of the world toward the fulfillment of this aspiration of all people. In his statement before this assembly, our Prime Minister said that arms races have always led to war. There are new atomic powers in the world, and the possibilities of a confrontation are grave.

We feel that a conference is necessary to obtain the total destruction of thermonuclear weapons and as a first step, the total prohibition of tests. At the same time there must be clearly established the obligation of all states to respect the present frontiers of other states and to refrain from indulging in any aggression even with conventional weapons.

In adding our voice to that of all peoples of the world who plead for general and complete disarmament, the destruction of all atomic arsenals, the complete cessation of thermonuclear devices and atomic tests of any kinds, we feel it necessary to stress, furthermore, that the territorial integrity of nations must be respected and the armed hand of imperialism, no less dangerous with conventional weapons, must be held back. Those who murdered thousands of defenseless citizens in the Congo did not use the atomic weapons. They used conventional weapons, and it was these conventional weapons, used by imperialists, which caused so many deaths.

Even if the measures advocated here were to become effective, thus making it unnecessary to say the following, we must still point out that we cannot adhere to any regional pact for denuclearization so long as the United States maintains aggressive bases on our territory, in Puerto Rico and in Panama, and in other American states where it feels it has the right to station them without any restrictions on conventional or nuclear weapons.

However, we feel we must be able to provide for our own defense in the light of the recent resolution of the Organization of American States against Cuba, which on the basis of the Treaty of Rio might permit aggression.

If such a conference to which we have just referred should achieve all these objectives—which unfortunately, would be rather difficult to do—it would be one of the most important developments in the history of mankind. To ensure this, the People's Republic of China must be represented, and that is why such a conference must be held. But it would be much simpler for the peoples of the world to recognize the undeniable truth that the People's Republic of China exists, that its rulers are the only representatives of the Chinese people, and to give it the place it deserves, which is, at present, usurped by a clique who control the province of Taiwan with United States aid.

The problem of the representation of China in the United Nations cannot, in any way, be considered as a case of a new admission to the organization, but rather as the restitution of their legitimate rights to the people of the People's Republic of China.

We repudiate strongly the concept of "two Chinas." The Chiang Kai-shek clique of Taiwan cannot remain in the United Nations. It must be expelled and the legitimate representative of the Chinese people put in.

We warn, also, against the insistence of the United States Government on presenting the problem of the legitimate representation of China in the United Nations as an "important question" so as to require a two-thirds majority of members present and voting.

The admission of the People's Republic of China to the United Nations is, in fact, an important question for the entire world, but not for the mechanics of the United Nations where it must constitute a mere question of procedure.

Thus will justice be done, but almost as important as attaining justice would be the fact that it would be demonstrated, once and for all, that this august Assembly uses its eyes to see with, its ears to hear with, and its tongue to speak with; and has definite standards in making its decisions.

The proliferation of atomic weapons among the member States of NATO, and especially the possession of these devices of mass destruction by the Federal Republic of Germany, would make the possibility of an agreement on disarmament even more remote, and linked to such an agreement is the problem of the peaceful reunification of Germany. So long as there is no clear understanding, the existence of two Germanies must be recognized: that of the Democratic Republic of Germany and the Federal Republic. The German problem can only be solved with the direct participation of the Democratic Republic of Germany with full rights in negotiations.

We shall touch lightly on the questions of economic development and international trade which take up a good part of the agenda. In this year, 1964, the Conference of Geneva was held, where a multitude of matters related to these aspects of international relations was dealt with. The warnings and forecasts of our delegation were clearly confirmed to the misfortune of the economically dependent countries.

We wish only to point out that insofar as Cuba is concerned, the United States of America has not implemented the explicit recommendations of that conference, and recently the United States Government also prohibited the sale of medicine to Cuba, thus divesting itself once and for all, of the mask of humanitarianism with which it attempted to disguise the aggressive nature of its blockade against the people of Cuba.

Furthermore, we once more state that these colonial machinations, which impede the development of the peoples, are not only expressed in political relations. The so-called deterioration of the terms of trade is nothing less than the result of the unequal exchange between countries producing raw materials and industrial countries which dominate markets and impose a false justice on an inequitable exchange of values.

So long as the economically dependent peoples do not free themselves from the capitalist markets, and as a bloc with the socialist countries, impose new terms of trade between the exploited and the exploiters, there will be no sound economic development, and in certain cases there will be retrogression, in which the weak countries will fall under the political domination of imperialists and colonialists.

Finally, it must be made clear that in the area of the Caribbean, maneuvers and preparations for aggression against Cuba are taking place; off the coast of Nicaragua above all, in Costa Rica, in the Panama Canal Zone, in the Vieques Islands of Puerto Rico, in Florida, and possibly in other parts of the territory of the United States, and also, perhaps, in Honduras, Cuban mercenaries are training, as well as mercenaries of other nationalities, with a purpose that cannot be peaceful.

After an open scandal, the government of Costa Rica, it is said, has ordered the elimination of all training fields for Cuban exiles in that country. No one knows whether this attitude is sincere, or whether it is simply a maneuver, because the mercenaries training there were about to commit some offense. We hope that full cognizance will be taken of the actual existence of those bases for aggression, which we denounced long ago, and that the world will think about the international responsibility of the government of a country which authorizes and facilitates the training of mercenaries to attack Cuba.

We must point out that news of the training of mercenaries at different places in the Caribbean and the participation of the United States Government in such acts is news that appears openly in United States newspapers. We know of no Latin American voice that has been lifted officially in protest against this. This shows the cynicism with which the United States moves its pawns.

The shrewd foreign ministers of the OAS has eyes to "see" Cuban emblems and find "irrefutable proof" in the Yankee weapons in Venezuela, but do not see the preparations for aggression in the United States, just as they did not hear the voice of President Kennedy, who explicitly declared himself to be the aggressor against Cuba at Playa Girón. In some cases it is a blindness provoked by the hatred of the ruling classes of the Latin American people against our revolution; in others, and these are even more deplorable, it is the result of the blinding light of Mammon.

As everyone knows, after the terrible upheaval called the "Caribbean crisis," the United States undertook certain given commitments with the Soviet Union which culminated in the withdrawal of certain types of weapons that the continued aggressions of that country—

such as the mercenary attack against Playa Girón and threats of invasion against our country—had compelled us to install in Cuba as a legitimate act of defense.

The Americans claimed, furthermore, that the United Nations should inspect our territory, which we refused and refuse emphatically since Cuba does not recognize the right of the United States, or of anyone else in the world, to determine what type of weapons Cuba may maintain within its borders.

In this connection, we would only abide by multilateral agreements, with equal obligations for all the parties concerned. Fidel Castro declared that "so long as the concept of sovereignty exists as the prerogative of nations and of independent peoples, and as a right of all peoples, we shall not accept the exclusion of our people from that right; so long as the world is governed by these principles, so long as the world is governed by those concepts which have universal validity because they are universally accepted by peoples, we shall not accept the attempt to deprive us of any of those rights and we shall renounce none of those rights."

The Secretary-General of the United Nations, U Thant, understood our reasons. Nevertheless, the United States presumed to establish a new prerogative, an arbitrary and illegal one; that of violating the air space of any small country. Thus, we see flying over our country U-2 aircraft and other types of espionage apparatus which fly over our airspace with impunity. We have issued all the necessary warnings for the cessation of the violation of our airspace as well as the provocations of the American navy against our sentry posts in the zone of Guantanamo, the "buzzing" by aircraft over our ships or ships of other nationalities in international waters, the piratical attacks against ships sailing under different flags, and the infiltration of spies, saboteurs and weapons in our island.

We want to build socialism; we have declared ourselves partisans of those who strive for peace; we have declared ourselves as falling within the group of non-aligned countries, although we are Marxist-Leninists, because the non-aligned countries, like ourselves, fight imperialism. We want peace; we want to build a better life for our people, and that is why we avoid answering, so far as possible, the planned provocations of the Yankee. But we know the mentality of United States rulers; they want to make us pay a very high price for that peace. We reply that price cannot go beyond the bounds of dignity.

And Cuba reaffirms once again the right to maintain on its territory the weapons it wishes and its refusal to recognize the right of any power on earth—no matter how powerful—to violate our soil, our territorial waters, or our airspace.

If, in any assembly, Cuba assumes obligations of a collective nature, it will fulfill them to the letter. So long as this does not happen, Cuba maintains all its rights, just as any other nation.

In the face of the demands of imperialism our Prime Minister posed the five necessary points for the existence of a sound peace in the Caribbean. They are as follows:

Cessation of the economic blockade and all economic and trade pressure by the United States in all parts of the world against our country.

Cessation of all subversive activities, launching and landing of weapons, and explosives by air and sea, organization of mercenary invasions, infiltration of spies and saboteurs, all of which acts are carried out from the territory of the United States and some accomplice countries.

Cessation of piratical attacks carried out from existing bases in the United States and Puerto Rico.

Cessation of all the violations of our airspace and our territorial waters by aircraft and warships of the United States.

Withdrawal from the Guantanamo naval base and restitution of the Cuban territory occupied by the United States.

None of these fundamental demands has been met, and our forces are still being provoked from the naval base at Guantanamo. That base has become a nest of thieves and the point from which they are introduced into our territory.

We would bore this assembly were we to give a detailed account of the large number of provocations of all kinds. Suffice it to say that including the first day of December, the number amounts to 1,323 in 1964 alone. The list covers minor provocations such as violation of the dividing line, launching of objects from the territory controlled by the North Americans, the commission of acts of sexual exhibitionism by North Americans of both sexes, verbal insults, others which are graver such as shooting off small-caliber weapons, the manipulation of weapons directed against our territory and offenses against our national emblem. The more serious provocations are those of crossing the dividing line and starting fires in installations on the Cuban side, seventy-eight rifle shots this year and the death of Ramon Lopez Pena, a soldier, from two shots fired from the United States post three and a half kilometers from the coast on the northern boundary.

This grave provocation took place at 19:07 hours on July 19, 1964, and our Prime Minister publicity stated on July 26 that if the event were to recur, he would give orders for our troops to repel the aggression. At the same time orders were given for the withdrawal of the advance line of Cuban forces to positions farther away from the dividing line and construction of the necessary housing.

One thousand three hundred and twenty-three provocations in 340 days amount to approximately four per day. Only a perfectly disciplined army with a morale such as ours could resist so many hostile acts without losing its self-control.

Forty-seven countries which met at the Second Conference of Heads of State or Government of the nonaligned countries at Cairo unanimously agreed that:

"Noting with concern that foreign military bases are, in practice, a means of bringing pressure on nations and retarding their emancipation and development, based on their own ideological, political, economic and cultural ideas . . . declares its full support to the countries which are seeking to secure the evacuation of foreign bases on their territory and calls upon all States maintaining troops and bases in other countries to remove them forthwith.

The Conference considers that the maintenance of Guantanamo (Cuba) of a military base of the United States of America, in defiance of the will of the Government and people of Cuba and in defiance of the provisions embodied in the Declaration of the Belgrade Conference, constitutes a violation of Cuba's sovereignty and territorial integrity.

Noting that the Cuban Government expresses its readiness to settle its dispute over the base at Guantanamo with the United States on an equal footing, the Conference urges the United States Government to negotiate the evacuation of their base with the Cuban Government."

The government of the United States has not responded to the above request of the Cairo Conference and presumes to maintain indefinitely its occupation by force of a piece of our territory from which it carries out acts of aggression such as those we mentioned earlier.

The Organization of American States—also called by some people the United States Ministry of Colonies—condemned us vigorously, although it had excluded us from its midst, and ordered its members to break off diplomatic and trade relations with Cuba. The OAS authorized aggression against our country at any time and under any pretext and violated the most fundamental international laws, completely disregarding the United Nations, Uruguay, Bolivia, Chile, and Mexico opposed that measure, and the government of the United States of Mexico refused to comply with the sanctions that had been approved. Since then we have no relations with any Latin American countries other than Mexico; thus the imperialists have carried out one of the stages preliminary to a plan of direct aggression.

We want to point out once again that our concern over Latin America is based on the ties that link us; the language we speak, our culture, and the common master we shared. But we have no other reason for desiring the liberation of Latin America from the colonial yoke of the United States. If any of the Latin American countries here decides to [resume relations it must be on the] basis of equality and not with the assumption that it is a gift to our government that we be recognized as a free country in the world, because we won the recognition of our freedom with our blood in the days of our struggles for liberation. We acquired it with our blood in the defense of our shores against Yankee invasion.

Although we reject any attempt to attribute to us interference in the internal affairs of other countries, we cannot deny that we sympathize with those people who strive for their freedom, and we must fulfill the obligation of our government and people to state clearly and categorically to the world that we morally support and feel as one with people everywhere who struggle to make a reality of the rights of full sovereignty proclaimed in the United Nations Charter.

It is the United States of America which intervenes. It has done so throughout the history of America. Since the end of the last century Cuba has known very well the truth of the matter; but it is known, too, by Venezuela, Nicaragua, Central America in general, Mexico, Haiti, and Santo Domingo. In recent years, besides our peoples, Panama has also known direct aggression, when the marines of the Canal opened fire against the defenseless people; Santo Domingo, whose coast was violated by the Yankee fleet to avoid an outbreak of the righteous fury of the people after the death of Trujillo; and Colombia, whose capital was taken by assault as a result of a rebellion provoked by the assassination nation of Gaitan.

There are masked interventions through military missions which participate in internal repression, organizing forces designed for that purpose in many countries, and also in coups d'etat which have been so frequently repeated on the American continent during the past few years. Specifically, United States forces took part in the repression of the peoples of Venezuela, Colombia, and Guatemala, who carry on an armed struggle for their freedom. In Venezuela not only do the Americans advise the army and the police, but they also direct acts of genocide from the air against the peasant population in vast rebel-held areas, and the United States companies established there exert pressures of every kind to increase direct interference.

The imperialists are preparing to repress the peoples of America and are setting up an "international" [network] of crime. The United States interfered in America while invoking the "defense of free institutions." The time will come when this assembly will acquire greater maturity and demand guarantees from the United States Government for the lives of the Negro and Latin American population who reside in that country, most of whom are native-born or naturalized United States citizens.

How can they presume to be the "guardians of liberty" when they kill their own children and discriminate daily against people because of the color of their skin; when they not only free the murderers of colored people, but even protect them, while punishing the colored population because they demand their legitimate rights as free men? We understand that today the assembly is not in a position to ask for explanations of these acts, but it must be clearly established that the government of the United States is not the champion of freedom, but rather the perpetrator of exploitation and oppression of the peoples of the world, and of a large part of its own population.

To the equivocating language with which some delegates have painted the case of Cuba and the Organization of American States, we reply with blunt words, that the governments pay for their treason.

Cuba, a free and sovereign state, with no chains binding it to anyone, with no foreign investments on its territory, with no proconsuls orienting its policy, can speak proudly in this assembly, proving the justice of the phrase by which we will always be known, "Free Territory of America."

Our example will bear fruit in our continent, as it is already doing to a certain extent already in Guatemala, Colombia, and Venezuela. The imperialists no longer have to deal with a small enemy, a contemptible force, since the people are no longer isolated.

As laid down in the Second Declaration of Havana:

"No people of Latin America is weak, because it is part of a family of 200 million brothers beset by the same miseries, who harbor the same feelings, have the same enemy, while they all dream of the same better destiny and have the support of all honest men and women in the world.

Future history will be written by the hungry masses of Indians, of landless peasants, of exploited workers; it will be written by the progressive masses, by the honest and brilliant intellectuals who abound in our unfortunate lands of Latin America, by the struggle of the masses and of ideas; an epic that will be carried forward by our peoples who have been ill-treated and despised by imperialism, our peoples who have until now gone unrecognized but who are awakening. We were considered an impotent and submissive flock; but now they are afraid of that flock, a gigantic flock of 200 million Latin Americans, which is sounding a warning note to the Yankee monopolist capitalists.

The hour of vindication, the hour it chose for itself, is now striking from one end to the other of the continent. That anonymous mass, that colored America, sombre, adamant, which sings throughout the continent the same sad, mournful song, now that mass is beginning definitely to enter into its own history, it is beginning to write it with its blood, to suffer and to die for it. Because now, in the fields, and in the mountains of America, in its plains and in its forests, in the solitude, and in the bustle of cities, on the shores of the great oceans and rivers, it is beginning to shape a world full of quickening hearts, who are ready to die for what is theirs, to conquer their rights which have been flouted for almost 500 years. History will have to tell the story of the poor of America, of the exploited of Latin America, who have decided to begin to write for themselves, forever, their own odyssey. We see them already walking along those roads, on foot, day after day, in long and endless marches, hundreds of kilometers, until they reach the ruling "Olympus" and wrest back their rights. We see them armed with stones, with sticks, with machetes, here, there, everywhere, daily occupying their lands, and taking root in the land that is theirs and defending it with their lives; we see them carrying banners, their banners running in the wind in the mountains and on the plains. And that wave of heightening fury, of just demands, of rights that have been flouted, is rising throughout Latin America, and no one can stem that tide; it will grow day by day because it is made up of the great multitude in every respect, those who with their work create the riches of the earth, and turn the wheel of history, those who are now awakening from their long, stupefying sleep.

For this great humanity has said "enough" and has started to move forward. And their march, the march of giants, cannot stop, will not stop until they have conquered their true independence, for which many have already died, and not uselessly. In any event, those who die will die like those in Cuba, at Playa Giron; they will die for their never-to-renounced, their only true independence."

This new will of a whole continent, America, shows itself in the cry proclaimed daily by our masses as the irrefutable expression of their decision to fight, to grasp and deter the armed hand of the invader. It is a cry that has the understanding and support of all the peoples of the world and especially of the socialist camp, headed by the Soviet Union.

That cry is: "Our country or death."

CÉSAR CHÁVEZ
The Mexican-American and the Church
("We ask the Church to sacrifice with the people for social
change, for justice, and for love of brother")
Delano, California
March 10, 1968

*When he ended his twenty-five day fast that brought attention to the mistreat-
ment of farm workers in central California, César Chávez (1927–1993), the
son of an Arizona grocer, the most famous and effective migrant farm-worker
labor leader of the century, a co-founder of the United Farm Workers, gave a
speech. In it, he discussed the lack of spiritual and economic support the
Catholic Church had given the farm workers, who were predominantly Catholic, during the strikes and protests.*

The place to begin is with our own experience with the Church in
the strike that has gone on for thirty-one months in Delano. For in
Delano the Church has been involved with the poor in a unique way
that should stand as a symbol to other communities. Of course, when
we refer to the Church we should define the word a little. We mean
the whole Church, the Church as an ecumenical body spread around
the world, and not just its particular form in a parish in a local
community.

The Church we are talking about is a tremendously powerful institution in our society, and in the world. That Church is one form
of the Presence of God on Earth, and so naturally it is powerful. It is
powerful by definition. It is a powerful moral and spiritual force
which cannot be ignored by any movement. Furthermore, it is an
organization with tremendous wealth. Since the Church is to be servant to the poor, it is our fault if that wealth is not channeled to help
the poor in our world. In a small way we have been able, in the
Delano strike, to work together with the Church in such a way as to
bring some of its moral and economic power to bear on those who

want to maintain the status quo, keeping farm workers in virtual en-slavement. In brief, here is what happened in Delano.

Some years ago, when some of us were working with the Community Service Organization, we began to realize the powerful effect which the Church can have on the conscience of the opposition. In scattered instances, in San Jose, Sacramento, Oakland, Los Angeles and other places, priests would speak out loudly and clearly against specific instances of oppression, and in some cases, stand with the people who were being hurt. Furthermore, a small group of priests, Frs. McDonald, McCollough, Duggan and others, began to pinpoint attention on the terrible situation of the farm workers in our state.

At about that same time, we began to run into the California Migrant Ministry in the camps and field. They were about the only ones there, and a lot of us were very suspicious, since we were Catholics and they were Protestants. However, they had developed a very clear conception of the Church. It was called to serve, to be at the mercy of the poor, and not to try to use them. After a while this made a lot of sense to us, and we began to find ourselves working side by side with them. In fact, it forced us to raise the question why our Church was not doing the same.

We would ask, why do the Protestants come out here and help the people, demand nothing, and give all their time to serving farm workers, while our own parish priests stay in their churches, where only a few people come, and usually feel uncomfortable? It was not until some of us moved to Delano and began working to build the National Farm Workers Association that we really saw how far removed from the people the parish Church was. In fact, we could not get any help at all from the priests of Delano. When the strike began, they told us we could not even use the Church's auditorium for the meetings. The farm workers' money helped build that auditorium! But the Protestants were there again, in the form of the California Migrant Ministry, and they began to help in little ways, here and there.

When the strike started in 1965, most of our friends forsook us for a while. They ran—or were just too busy to help. But the California Migrant Ministry held a meeting with its staff and decided that the strike was a matter of life or death for farm workers everywhere, and that even if it meant the end of the Migrant Ministry they would turn over their resources to the strikers. The political pressure on the Protestant Churches was tremendous and the Migrant Ministry lost a lot of money. But they stuck it out, and they began to point the way to the rest of the Church. In fact, when thirty of the strikers were arrested for shouting *"Huelga!,"* eleven ministers went to jail with them. They were in Delano that day at the request of Chris Hartmire, director of the California Migrant Ministry.

Then the workers began to raise the question: why ministers? Why not priests? What does the Bishop say? But the Bishop said nothing. But slowly the pressure of the people grew and grew, until finally we have in Delano a priest sent by the new Bishop, Timothy Manning, who is there to help minister to the needs of farm workers. His name is Father Mark Day and he is the Union's chaplain. Finally, our own Catholic Church has decided to recognize that we have our own peculiar needs, just as the growers have theirs. But outside of the local diocese, the pressure built up on growers to negotiate was tremendous. Though we were not allowed to have our own priest, the power of the ecumenical body of the Church was tremendous. The work of the Church, for example, in the Schenley, Di Giorgio, Perelly–Minetti strikes was fantastic. They applied pressure—and they mediated. When poor people get involved in a long conflict, such as a strike, or a civil rights drive, and the pressure increases each day, there is a deep need for spiritual advice. Without it we see families crumble, leadership weaken, and hard workers grow tired. And in such a situation the spiritual advice must be given by a friend, not by the opposition. What sense does it make to go to Mass on Sunday and reach out for spiritual help, and instead get sermons about the wickedness of your cause? That only drives one to question and to despair.

The growers in Delano have their spiritual problems . . . we do not deny that. They have every right to have priests and ministers who serve their needs. But we have different needs, and so we needed a friendly spiritual guide. And this is true in every community in this state where the poor face tremendous problems. But the opposition raises a tremendous howl about this. They don't want us to have our spiritual advisors, friendly to our needs. Why is this? Why indeed except that *there is tremendous spiritual and economic power in the church*. The rich know it, and for that reason they choose to keep it from the people.

The leadership of the Mexican-American Community must admit that we have fallen far short in our task of helping provide spiritual guidance for our people. We may say, I don't feel any such need. I can get along. But that is a poor excuse for not helping provide such help for others. For we can also say, I don't need any welfare help. I can take care of my own problems. But we are all willing to fight like hell for welfare aid for those who truly need it, who would starve without it. Likewise we may have gotten an education and not care about scholarship money for ourselves, or our children. But we would, we should, fight like hell to see to it that our state provides aid for any child needing it so that he can get the education he desires.

Likewise we can say we don't need the Church. That is our business. But there are hundreds of thousands of our people who desperately need some help from that powerful institution, the Church, and we are foolish not to help them get it. For example, the Catholic Charities agencies of the Catholic Church has millions of dollars earmarked for the poor. But often the money is spent for food baskets for the needy instead of for effective action to eradicate the causes of poverty. The men and women who administer this money sincerely want to help their brothers. It should be our duty to help direct the attention to the basic needs of the Mexican-Americans in our society . . . needs which cannot be satisfied with baskets of food, but rather with effective organizing at the grass roots level.

Therefore, I am calling for Mexican-American groups to stop ignoring this source of power. It is not just our right to appeal to the Church to use its power effectively for the poor, it is our duty to do so. It should be as natural as appealing to government . . . and we do that often enough.

Furthermore, we should be prepared to come to the defense of that priest, rabbi, minister, or layman of the Church, who out of commitment to truth and justice gets into a tight place with his pastor or bishop. It behooves us to stand with that man and help him see his trial through. It is our duty to see to it that his rights of conscience are respected and that no bishop, pastor or other higher body takes that God-given, human right away.

Finally, in a nutshell, what do we want the Church to do? We don't ask for more cathedrals. We don't ask for bigger churches or fine gifts. We ask for its presence with us, beside us, as Christ among us. We ask the Church to sacrifice with the people for social change, for justice, and for love of brother. We don't ask for words. We ask for deeds. We don't ask for paternalism. We ask for servanthood.

LYNDON BAINES JOHNSON
On Vietnam and on the Decision Not to Seek Reelection
("... I shall not seek, and I will not accept, the nomination
of my party for another term as your President")
National Broadcast
March 31, 1968

*Johnson (1908–1973) became the president of the United States after John
F. Kennedy's assassination. The Texas Democrat won the 1964 presidential
election against Barry Goldwater. In this dramatic televised speech, he surprised the nation with his announcement that he would not run again for
president. "Nineteen sixty-eight," he later wrote, "was one of the most ago-
nizing years any president ever spent in the White House. I sometimes felt
that I was living in a continuous nightmare."*

Good evening, my fellow Americans.

Tonight I want to speak to you of peace in Vietnam and Southeast
Asia.

No other question so preoccupies our people. No other dream so
absorbs the 250 million human beings who live in that part of the
world. No other goal motivates American policy in Southeast Asia.

For years, representatives of our Government and others have traveled the world seeking to find a basis for peace talks.

Since last September they have carried the offer that I made public
at San Antonio. And that offer was this:

That the United States would stop its bombardment of North
Vietnam when that would lead promptly to productive discussions—
and that we would assume that North Vietnam would not take military advantage of our restraint.

Hanoi denounced this offer, both privately and publicly. Even
while the search for peace was going on, North Vietnam rushed their
preparations for a savage assault on the people, the Government and
the allies of South Vietnam.

Their attack—during the Tet holidays—failed to achieve its principal objectives.

It did not collapse the elected Government of South Vietnam or shatter its army—as the Communists had hoped. It did not produce a "general uprising" among the people of the cities, as they had predicted.

The Communists were unable to maintain control of any of the more than 30 cities that they attacked, and they took very heavy casualties.

But they did compel the South Vietnamese and their allies to move certain forces from the countryside into the cities.

They caused widespread disruption and suffering. Their attacks, and the battles that followed, made refugees of half a million human beings.

The Communists may renew their attack any day. They are, it appears, trying to make 1968 the year of decision in South Vietnam—the year that brings, if not final victory or defeat, at least a turning point in the struggle.

This much is clear: If they do mount another round of heavy attacks, they will not succeed in destroying the fighting power of South Vietnam and its allies.

But tragically, this is also clear: Many men—on both sides of the struggle—will be lost. A nation that has already suffered 20 years of warfare will suffer once again. Armies on both sides will take new casualties. And the war will go on.

There is no need for this to be so. There is no need to delay the talks that could bring an end to this long and this bloody war.

Tonight, I renew the offer I made last August: to stop the bombardment of North Vietnam. We ask that talks begin promptly, that they be serious talks on the substance of peace. We assume that during those talks Hanoi will not take advantage of our restraint.

We are prepared to move immediately toward peace through negotiations. So tonight, in the hope that this action will lead to early talks, I am taking the first step to de-escalate the conflict. We are reducing—substantially reducing—the present level of hostilities, and we are doing so unilaterally and at once.

Tonight I have ordered our aircraft and our naval vessels to make no attacks on North Vietnam except in the area north of the demilitarized zone where the continuing enemy build-up directly threatens allied forward positions and where the movement of their troops and supplies are clearly related to that threat.

Even this very limited bombing of the North could come to an early end—if our restraint is matched by restraint in Hanoi. But I cannot in good conscience stop all bombing so long as to do so would immediately and directly endanger the lives of our men and our allies. Whether a complete bombing halt becomes possible in the future will be determined by events.

And tonight I call upon the United Kingdom and I call upon the Soviet Union—as co-chairman of the Geneva conferences and as permanent members of the United Nations Security Council— to do all they can to move from the unilateral act of de-escalation that I have just announced toward genuine peace in Southeast Asia.

The South Vietnamese know that further efforts are going to be required to expand their own armed forces; to move back into the countryside as quickly as possible; to increase their taxes; to select the very best men they have for civil and military responsibility; to achieve a new unity within their constitutional government, and to include in the national effort all those groups who wish to preserve South Vietnam's control over its own destiny.

President Thieu told his people last week, and I quote:

We must make greater efforts, we must accept more sacrifices, because as I have said many times, this is our country. The existence of our nation is at stake, and this is mainly a Vietnamese responsibility.

On many occasions I have told the American people that we would send to Vietnam those forces that are required to accomplish our mission there. So with that as our guide we have previously authorized a force level of approximately 525,000.

In order that these forces may reach maximum combat effectiveness, the Joint Chiefs of Staff have recommended to me that we should prepare to send during the next five months the support troops totaling approximately 13,500 men.

A portion of these men will be made available from our active forces. The balance will come from reserve component units, which will be called up for service.

Now let me give you my estimate of the chances for peace—the peace that will one day stop the bloodshed in South Vietnam. That will—all the Vietnamese people will be permitted to rebuild and develop their land. That will permit us to turn more fully to our own tasks here at home.

I cannot promise that the initiative that I have announced tonight will be completely successful in achieving peace any more than the 30 others that we have undertaken and agreed to in recent years.

One day, my fellow citizens, there will be peace in Southeast Asia. It will come because the people of Southeast Asia want it—those whose armies are at war tonight; those who, though threatened, have thus far been spared.

Peace will come because, Asians were willing to work for it and to sacrifice for it—and to die by the thousands for it.

But let it never be forgotten: peace will come also because America sent her sons to help secure it.

It has not been easy—far from it. During the past four and a half years, it has been my fate and my responsibility to be Commander in Chief. I have lived daily and nightly with the cost of this war. I know the pain that it has inflicted. I know perhaps better than anyone the misgivings it has aroused.

This I believe very deeply. Throughout my entire public career I have followed the personal philosophy that I am a free man, an American, a public servant and a member of my party—in that order—always and only.

For 37 years in the service of our nation, first as a Congressman, as a Senator and as Vice President, and now as your President, I have put the unity of the people first. I have put it ahead of any divisive partisanship. And in these times, as in times before, it is true that a house divided against itself by the spirit of faction, of party, of region, of religion, of race, is a house that cannot stand.

There is division in the American house now. There is divisiveness among us all tonight. And holding the trust that is mine, as President of all the people, I cannot disregard the peril of the progress of the American people and the hope and the prospect of peace for all peoples, so I would ask all Americans whatever their personal interest or concern to guard against divisiveness and all of its ugly consequences.

Fifty-two months and ten days ago, in a moment of tragedy and trauma, the duties of this office fell upon me.

I asked then for your help, and God's, that we might continue America on its course binding up our wounds, healing our history, moving forward in new unity, to clear the American agenda and to keep the American commitment for all of our people.

United we have kept that commitment. And united we have enlarged that commitment. And through all time to come I think America will be a stronger nation, a more just society, a land of greater opportunity and fulfillment because of what we have all done together in these years of unparalleled achievement.

Our reward will come in the life of freedom and peace and hope that our children will enjoy through ages ahead.

What we won when all of our people united just must not now be lost in suspicion and distrust and selfishness and politics among any of our people. And believing this as I do I have concluded that I should not permit the Presidency to become involved in the partisan divisions that are developing in this political war.

With American sons in the fields far away, with America's future under challenge right here at home, with our hopes and the world's hopes for peace in the balance every day, I do not believe that I should devote an hour or a day of my time to any personal partisan causes or to any duties other than the awesome duties of this office—the Presidency of your country.

Accordingly, I shall not seek, and I will not accept, the nomination of my party for another term as your President. But let men everywhere know, however, that a strong and a confident and a vigilant America stands ready tonight to seek an honorable peace; and stands ready tonight to defend an honored cause, whatever the price, whatever the burden, whatever the sacrifice that duty may require.

Thank you for listening. Good night and God bless all of you.

SHIRLEY CHISHOLM
Equal Rights for Women
(". . . in the political world I have been far oftener
discriminated against because I am a woman than
because I am black")
United States House of Representatives
Washington, D.C.
May 21, 1969

*The Brooklyn native Shirley Chisholm (1924–2005) served in the House of
Representatives from 1969 to 1983, the first African-American woman to be
elected to Congress. She entered the primaries for the Democratic nomination
for the presidency in 1972.*

Mr. Speaker, when a young woman graduates from college and starts
looking for a job, she is likely to have a frustrating and even demean-
ing experience ahead of her. If she walks into an office for an interview, the first question she will be asked is, "Do you type?"

There is a calculated system of prejudice that lies unspoken behind
that question. Why is it acceptable for women to be secretaries, li-
brarians, and teachers, but totally unacceptable for them to be managers, administrators, doctors, lawyers, and Members of Congress?

The unspoken assumption is that women are different. They do
not have executive ability, orderly minds, stability, leadership skills,
and they are too emotional.

It has been observed before, that society, for a long time, discriminated
against another minority, the blacks, on the same basis—that they were
different and inferior. The happy little homemaker and the contented
"old darkey" on the plantation were both produced by prejudice.

As a black person, I am no stranger to race prejudice. But the truth
is that in the political world I have been far oftener discriminated
against because I am a woman than because I am black.

Prejudice against blacks is becoming unacceptable although it will
take years to eliminate it. But it is doomed because, slowly, white

America is beginning to admit that it exists. Prejudice against women is still acceptable. There is very little understanding yet of the immorality involved in double pay scales and the classification of most of the better jobs as "for men only."

More than half of the population of the United States is female. But women occupy only two percent of the managerial positions. They have not even reached the level of tokenism yet. No women sit on the AFL-CIO council or Supreme Court. There have been only two women who have held Cabinet rank, and at present there are none. Only two women now hold ambassadorial rank in the diplomatic corps. In Congress, we are down to one Senator and ten Representatives.

Considering that there are about three and a half million more women in the United States than men, this situation is outrageous.

It is true that part of the problem has been that women have not been aggressive in demanding their rights. This was also true of the black population for many years. They submitted to oppression and even cooperated with it. Women have done the same thing. But now there is an awareness of this situation particularly among the younger segment of the population.

As in the field of equal rights for blacks, Spanish-Americans, the Indians, and other groups, laws will not change such deep-seated problems overnight, but they can be used to provide protection for those who are most abused, and to begin the process of evolutionary change by compelling the insensitive majority to reexamine its unconscious attitudes.

It is for this reason that I wish to introduce today a proposal that has been before every Congress for the last forty years and that sooner or later must become part of the basic law of the land—the equal rights amendment.

Let me note and try to refute two of the commonest arguments that are offered against this amendment. One is that women are already protected under the law and do not need legislation. Existing laws are not adequate to secure equal rights for women. Sufficient proof of this is the concentration of women in lower paying, menial, unrewarding jobs and their incredible scarcity in the upper level jobs. If women are already equal, why is it such an event whenever one happens to be elected to Congress?

It is obvious that discrimination exists. Women do not have the opportunities that men do. And women that do not conform to the system, who try to break with the accepted patterns, are stigmatized as "odd" and "unfeminine." The fact is that a woman who aspires to be chairman of the board, or a Member of the House, does so for exactly the same reasons as any man. Basically, these are that she thinks she can do the job and she wants to try.

A second argument often heard against the equal rights amendment is that it would eliminate legislation that many States and the Federal Government have enacted giving special protection to women and that it would throw the marriage and divorce laws into chaos.

As for the marriage laws, they are due for a sweeping reform, and an excellent beginning would be to wipe the existing ones off the books. Regarding special protection for working women, I cannot understand why it should be needed. Women need no protection that men do not need. What we need are laws to protect working people, to guarantee them fair pay, safe working conditions, protection against sickness and layoffs, and provision for dignified, comfortable retirement. Men and women need these things equally. That one sex needs protection more than the other is a male supremacist myth as ridiculous and unworthy of respect as the white supremacist myths that society is trying to cure itself of at this time.

PIERRE TRUDEAU
Notes for a National Broadcast
(". . . within Canada there is ample room for opposition
and dissent, but none for intimidation and terror")
October 16, 1970

*As prime minister of Canada, Trudeau (1919–2000) addressed his nation
on "The October Crisis," a political kidnapping in the province of Quebec.
It happened that one of the two men who were kidnapped was murdered; the
kidnappers, members of the Front de Liberation du Quebec, were later
arrested.*

I am speaking to you at a moment of grave crisis, when violent and
fanatical men are attempting to destroy the unity and the freedom of
Canada. One aspect of that crisis is the threat which has been made
on the lives of two innocent men. These are matters of the utmost
gravity and I want to tell you what the government is doing to deal
with them.

What has taken place in Montreal in the past two weeks is not
unprecedented. It has happened elsewhere in the world on several
recent occasions; it could happen elsewhere within Canada. But Canadians have always assumed that it could not happen here and as a
result we are doubly shocked that it has.

Our assumption may have been naive, but it was understandable;
understandable because democracy flourishes in Canada; understandable because individual liberty is cherished in Canada.

Notwithstanding these conditions—partly because of them—it has
now been demonstrated to us by a few misguided persons just how
fragile a democratic society can be, if democracy is not prepared to
defend itself, and just how vulnerable to blackmail are tolerant, compassionate people.

Because the kidnappings and the blackmail are most familiar to
you, I shall deal with them first.

The governments of Canada and Quebec have been told by groups of self-styled revolutionaries that they intend to murder in cold blood two innocent men unless their demands are met. The kidnappers claim they act as they do in order to draw attention to instances of social injustice. But I ask them whose attention are they seeking to attract. The Government of Canada? The Government of Quebec? Every government in this country is well aware of the existence of deep and important social problems. And every government to the limit of its resources and ability is deeply committed to their solution. But not by kidnappings and bombings. By hard work. And if any doubt exists about the good faith or the ability of any government, there are opposition parties ready and willing to be given an opportunity to govern. In short, there is available everywhere in Canada an effective mechanism to change governments by peaceful means. It has been employed by disenchanted voters again and again.

Who are the kidnap victims? To the victims' families they are husbands and fathers. To the kidnappers their identity is immaterial. The kidnappers' purposes would be served equally well by having in their grip you or me, or perhaps some child. Their purpose is to exploit the normal, human feelings of Canadians and to bend those feelings of sympathy into instruments for their own violent and revolutionary ends.

What are the kidnappers demanding in return for the lives of these men? Several things. For one, they want their grievances aired by force in public on the assumption, no doubt, that all right-thinking persons would be persuaded that the problems of the world can be solved by shouting slogans and insults.

They want more, they want the police to offer up as a sacrificial lamb a person whom they assume assisted in the lawful arrest and proper conviction of certain of their criminal friends.

They also want money. Ransom money.

They want still more. They demand the release from prison of seventeen criminals, and the dropping of charges against six other men, all of whom they refer to as "political prisoners." Who are these men who are held out as latter-day patriots and martyrs? Let me describe them to you.

Three are convicted murderers; five others were jailed for manslaughter; one is serving a life imprisonment after having pleaded guilty to numerous charges related to bombings; another has been convicted of seventeen armed robberies; two were once paroled but are now back in jail awaiting trial on charges of robberies.

Yet we are being asked to believe that these persons have been unjustly dealt with, that they have been imprisoned as a result of their political opinions, and that they deserve to be freed immediately, without recourse to due process of law.

The responsibility of deciding whether to release one or other of these criminals is that of the Federal Government. It is a responsibility that the government will discharge according to law. To bow to the pressures of these kidnappers who demand that the prisoners be released would be not only an abdication of responsibility, it would lead to an increase in terrorist activities in Quebec. It would be as well an invitation to terrorism and kidnapping across the country. We might well find ourselves facing an endless series of demands for the release of criminals from jails, from coast to coast, and we would find that the hostages could be innocent members of your family or mine.

At the moment the FLQ is holding hostage two men in the Montreal area, one a British diplomat, the other a Quebec cabinet minister. They are threatened with murder. Should governments give in to this crude blackmail we would be facing the breakdown of the legal system, and its replacement by the law of the jungle. The government's decision to prevent this from happening is not taken just to defend an important principle, it is taken to protect the lives of Canadians from dangers of the sort I have mentioned. Freedom and personal security are safeguarded by laws; those laws must be respected in order to be effective.

If it is the responsibility of government to deny the demands of the kidnappers, the safety of the hostages is without question the responsibility of the kidnappers. Only the most twisted form of logic could conclude otherwise. Nothing that either the Government of Canada or the Government of Quebec has done or failed to do, now or in the future, could possibly excuse any injury to either of these two innocent men. The guns pointed at their heads have FLQ fingers on the triggers. Should any injury result, there is no explanation that could condone the acts. Should there be harm done to these men, the government promises unceasing pursuit of those responsible.

During the past twelve days, the governments of Canada and Quebec have been engaged in constant consultations. The course followed in this matter had the full support of both governments, and of the Montreal municipal authorities. In order to save the lives of Mr. Cross and Mr. Laporte, we have engaged in communications with the kidnappers.

The offer of the federal government to the kidnappers of safe conduct out of Canada to a country of their choice, in return for the delivery of the hostages has not yet been taken up, neither has the offer of the Government of Quebec to recommend parole for the five prisoners eligible for parole.

This offer of safe conduct was made only because Mr. Cross and Mr. Laporte might be able to identify their kidnappers and to assist in their prosecution. By offering the kidnappers safe exit from Canada we removed from them any possible motivation for murdering their hostages.

Let me turn now to the broader implications of the threat represented by the FLQ and similar organizations.

If a democratic society is to continue to exist, it must be able to root out the cancer of an armed, revolutionary movement that is bent on destroying the very basis of our freedom. For that reason the government, following an analysis of the facts, including requests of the Government of Quebec and the City of Montreal for urgent action, decided to proclaim the War Measures Act. It did so at 4:00 a.m. this morning, in order to permit the full weight of government to be brought quickly to bear on all those persons advocating or practicing violence as a means of achieving political ends.

The War Measures Act gives sweeping powers to the government. It also suspends the operation of the Canadian Bill of Rights. I can assure you that the government is most reluctant to seek such powers, and did so only when it became crystal clear that the situation could not be controlled unless some extraordinary assistance was made available on an urgent basis.

The authority contained in the act will permit governments to deal effectively with the nebulous yet dangerous challenge to society represented by the terrorist organizations. The criminal law as it stands is simply not adequate to deal with systematic terrorism.

The police have therefore been given certain extraordinary powers necessary for the effective detection and elimination of conspiratorial organizations which advocate the use of violence. These organizations, and membership in them, have been declared illegal. The powers include the right to search and arrest without warrant, to detain suspected persons without the necessity of laying specific charges immediately, and to detain persons without bail.

These are strong powers and I find them as distasteful as I am sure do you. They are necessary, however, to permit the police to deal with persons who advocate or promote the violent overthrow of our democratic system. In short, I assure you that the government recognizes its grave responsibilities in interfering in certain cases with civil liberties, and that it remains answerable to the people of Canada for its actions. The government will revoke this proclamation as soon as possible.

As I said in the House of Commons this morning, the government will allow sufficient time to pass to give it the necessary experience to assess the type of statute which may be required in the present circumstances.

It is my firm intention to discuss then with the leaders of the opposition parties the desirability of introducing legislation of a less comprehensive nature. In this respect I earnestly solicit from the leaders and from all honorable members constructive suggestions for the amendment of the regulations. Such suggestions will be given careful consideration for possible inclusion in any new statute.

I recognize, as I hope do others, that this extreme position into which governments have been forced is in some respects a trap. It is a well-known technique of revolutionary groups who attempt to destroy society by unjustified violence to goad the authorities into inflexible attitudes. The revolutionaries then employ this evidence of alleged authoritarianism as justification for the need to use violence in their renewed attacks on the social structure. I appeal to all Canadians not to become so obsessed by what the government has done today in response to terrorism that they forget the opening play in this vicious game. That play was taken by the revolutionaries; they chose to use bombing, murder and kidnapping.

The threat posed by the FLQ terrorists and their supporters is out of all proportion to their numbers. This follows from the fact that they act stealthily and because they are known to have in their possession a considerable amount of dynamite. To guard against the very real possibility of bombings directed at public buildings or utilities in the immediate future, the Government of Quebec has requested the assistance of the Canadian Armed Forces to support the police in several places in the Province of Quebec. These forces took up their positions yesterday.

Violence, unhappily, is no stranger to this decade. The speech from the Throne opening the current session of Parliament a few days ago said that "we live in a period of tenseness and unease." We must not overlook the fact, moreover, that violence is often a symptom of deep social unrest. This government has pledged that it will introduce legislation which deals not just with symptoms but with the social causes which often underlie or serve as an excuse for crime and disorder.

It was in that context that I stated in the House of Commons a year ago that there was no need anywhere in Canada for misguided or misinformed zealots to resort to acts of violence in the belief that only in this fashion could they accomplish change. There may be some places in the world where the law is so inflexible and so insensitive as to prompt such beliefs. But Canada is not such a place. I said then, and I repeat now, that those who would defy the law and ignore the opportunities available to them to right their wrongs and satisfy their claims will receive no hearing from this government.

We shall ensure that the laws passed by Parliament are worthy of respect. We shall also ensure that those laws are respected.

We have seen in many parts of Canada all too much evidence of violence in the name of revolution in the past twelve months. We are now able to see some of the consequences of violence. Persons who invoke violence are raising deliberately the level of hate in Canada. They do so at a time when the country must eliminate hate, and must exhibit tolerance and compassion in order to create the kind of society which we all desire. Yet those who disrespect legal processes create a danger that law-abiding elements of the community, out of anger and out of fear, will harden their attitudes and refuse to accommodate any change or remedy any shortcomings. They refuse because fear deprives persons of their normal sense of compassion and their normal sense of justice.

This government is not acting out of fear. It is acting to prevent fear from spreading. It is acting to maintain the rule of law without which freedom is impossible. It is acting to make clear to kidnappers and revolutionaries and assassins that in this country laws are made and changed by the elected representatives of all Canadians—not by a handful of self-selected dictators—those who gain power through terror, rule through terror. The government is acting, therefore, to protect your life and your liberty.

The government is acting as well to ensure the safe return of Mr. James Cross and Mr. Pierre Laporte. I speak for millions of Canadians when I say to their courageous wives and families how much we sympathize with them for the nightmare to which they have been subjected, and how much we all hope and pray that it will soon conclude.

Canada remains one of the most wholesome and humane lands on this earth. If we stand firm, this current situation will soon pass. We will be able to say proudly, as we have for decades, that within Canada there is ample room for opposition and dissent, but none for intimidation and terror.

There are very few times in the history of any country when all persons must take a stand on critical issues. This is one of those times; this is one of those issues. I am confident that those persons who unleashed this tragic sequence of events with the aim of destroying our society and dividing our country will find that the opposite will occur. The result of their acts will be a stronger society in a unified country. Those who would have divided us will have united us.

I sense the unease which grips many Canadians today. Some of you are upset, and this is understandable. I want to reassure you that the authorities have the situation well in hand. Everything that needs to be done is being done; every level of government in this country is well prepared to act in your interests.

CHAIM HERZOG
Response to "Zionism Is Racism"
("I come here to denounce the two great evils which
menace society in general and a society of nations in
particular . . . hatred and ignorance")
United Nations, New York City
November 10, 1975

*Herzog (1918–1997) was born and raised in Ireland, the son of the chief
rabbi there. He moved to Palestine in 1935, and after the Six-Day War in
1967 served as a military governor of the West Bank. In the speech that follows, as Israel's Ambassador to the United Nations, he protested a U.N.
resolution that condemned Israel's history and equated Zionism with racism.
He became the sixth president of Israel in 1983.*

Mr. President,

It is symbolic that this debate, which may well prove to be a turning point in the fortunes of the United Nations and a decisive factor
in the possible continued existence of this organization, should take
place on November 10.

Tonight, thirty-seven years ago, has gone down in history as
Kristallnacht, the Night of the Crystals. This was the night in 1938
when Hitler's Nazi storm-troopers launched a coordinated attack on
the Jewish community in Germany, burned the synagogues in all its
cities and made bonfires in the streets of the Holy Books and the
Scrolls of the Holy Law and Bible.

It was the night when Jewish homes were attacked and heads of
families taken away, many of them never to return. It was the night
when the windows of all Jewish businesses and stores were smashed,
covering the streets in the cities of Germany with a film of broken
glass which dissolved into the millions of crystals which gave that
night its name. It was the night which led eventually to the cremato-
ria and the gas chambers, Auschwitz, Birkenau, Dachau, Buchenwald, Theresienstadt and others. It was the night which led to the
most terrifying holocaust in the history of man.

It is indeed befitting Mr. President, that this debate, conceived in the desire to deflect the Middle East from its moves towards peace and born of a deep pervading feeling of anti-Semitism, should take place on the anniversary of this day. It is indeed befitting, Mr. President, that the United Nations, which began its life as an anti-Nazi alliance, should thirty years later find itself on its way to becoming the world center of anti-Semitism. Hitler would have felt at home on a number of occasions during the past year, listening to the proceedings in this forum, and above all to the proceedings during the debate on Zionism.

It is sobering to consider to what level this body has been dragged down if we are obliged today to contemplate an attack on Zionism. For this attack constitutes not only an anti-Israeli attack of the foulest type, but also an assault in the United Nations on Judaism—one of the oldest established religions in the world, a religion which has given the world the human values of the Bible, and from which two other great religions, Christianity and Islam, sprang.

Is it not tragic to consider that we here at this meeting in the year 1975 are contemplating what is a scurrilous attack on a great and established religion which has given to the world the Bible with its Ten Commandments the great prophets of old, Moses, Isaiah, Amos; the great thinkers of history, Maimonides, Spinoza, Marx, Einstein; many of the masters of the arts and as high a percentage of the Nobel Prize-winners in the world, in the sciences, in the arts and in the humanities as has been achieved by any people on earth? . . .

The resolution against Zionism was originally one condemning racism and colonialism, a subject on which we could have achieved consensus, a consensus which is of great importance to all of us and to our African colleagues in particular. However, instead of permitting this to happen, a group of countries, drunk with the feeling of power inherent in the automatic majority and without regard to the importance of achieving a consensus on this issue, railroaded the UN in a contemptuous maneuver by the use of the automatic majority into bracketing Zionism with the subject under discussion.

I do not come to this rostrum to defend the moral and historical values of the Jewish people. They do not need to be defended. They speak for themselves. They have given to mankind much of what is great and eternal. They have done for the spirit of man more than can readily be appreciated by a forum such as this one.

I come here to denounce the two great evils which menace society in general and a society of nations in particular. These two evils are hatred and ignorance. These two evils are the motivating force behind the proponents of this resolution and their supporters. These two evils characterize those who would drag this world organization, the ideals of which were first conceived by the prophets of Israel, to the depths to which it has been dragged today.

The key to understanding Zionism is in its name. The easternmost of the two hills of ancient Jerusalem during the tenth century B.C.E. was called Zion. In fact, the name Zion, referring to Jerusalem, appears 152 times in the Old Testament. The name is overwhelmingly a poetic and prophetic designation. The religious and emotional qualities of the name arise from the importance of Jerusalem as the Royal City and the City of the Temple. "Mount Zion" is the place where God dwells. Jerusalem, or Zion, is a place where the Lord is King, and where He has installed His king, David.

King David made Jerusalem the capital of Israel almost three thousand years ago, and Jerusalem has remained the capital ever since. During the centuries the term "Zion" grew and expanded to mean the whole of Israel. The Israelites in exile could not forget Zion. The Hebrew Psalmist sat by the waters of Babylon and swore: "If I forget thee, O Jerusalem, let my right hand forget her cunning." This oath has been repeated for thousands of years by Jews throughout the world. It is an oath which was made over seven hundred years before the advent of Christianity and over twelve hundred years before the advent of Islam, and Zion came to mean the Jewish homeland, symbolic of Judaism, of Jewish national aspirations.

While praying to his God every Jew, wherever he is in the world, faces towards Jerusalem. For over two thousand years of exile these prayers have expressed the yearning of the Jewish people to return to their ancient homeland, Israel. In fact, a continuous Jewish presence, in larger or smaller numbers, has been maintained in the country over the centuries.

Zionism is the name of the national movement of the Jewish people and is the modern expression of the ancient Jewish heritage. The Zionist ideal, as set out in the Bible, has been, and is, an integral part of the Jewish religion.

Zionism is to the Jewish people what the liberation movements of Africa and Asia have been to their own people.

Zionism is one of the most dynamic and vibrant national movements in human history. Historically it is based on a unique and unbroken connection, extending some four thousand years, between the People of the Book and the Land of the Bible.

In modern times, in the late nineteenth century, spurred by the twin forces of anti-Semitic persecution and of nationalism, the Jewish people organized the Zionist movement in order to transform their dream into reality. Zionism as a political movement was the revolt of an oppressed nation against the depredation and wicked discrimination and oppression of the countries in which anti-Semitism flourished. It is no coincidence that the co-sponsors and supporters of this resolution include countries who are guilty of the horrible crimes of anti-Semitism and discrimination to this very day.

Support for the aim of Zionism was written into the League of Nations Mandate for Palestine and was again endorsed by the United Nations in 1947, when the General Assembly voted by overwhelming majority for the restoration of Jewish independence in our ancient land.

The re-establishment of Jewish independence in Israel, after centuries of struggle to overcome foreign conquest and exile, is a vindication of the fundamental concepts of the equality of nations and of self-determination. To question the Jewish people's right to national existence and freedom is not only to deny to the Jewish people the right accorded to every other people on this globe, but it is also to deny the central precepts of the United Nations.

As a former Foreign Minister of Israel, Abba Eban, has written:

"Zionism is nothing more—but also nothing less—than the Jewish people's sense of origin and destination in the land linked eternally with its name. It is also the instrument whereby the Jewish nation seeks an authentic fulfillment of itself. And the drama is enacted in twenty states comprising a hundred million people in four and a half million square miles, with vast resources. The issue therefore is not whether the world will come to terms with Arab nationalism. The question is at what point Arab nationalism, with its prodigious glut of advantage, wealth and opportunity, will come to terms with the modest but equal rights of another Middle Eastern nation to pursue its life in security and peace."

The vicious diatribes on Zionism voiced here by Arab delegates may give this Assembly the wrong impression that while the rest of the world supported the Jewish national liberation movement the Arab world was always hostile to Zionism. This is not the case. Arab leaders, cognizant of the rights of the Jewish people, fully endorsed the virtues of Zionism. Sherif Hussein, the leader of the Arab world during World War I, welcomed the return of the Jews to Palestine. His son, Emir Feisal, who represented the Arab world in the Paris Peace Conference, had this to say about Zionism:

"We Arabs, especially the educated among us, look with deepest sympathy on the Zionist movement. . . . We will wish the Jews a hearty welcome home. . . . We are working together for a reformed and revised Near East, and our two movements complement one another. The movement is national and not imperialistic. There is room in Syria for us both. Indeed, I think that neither can be a success without the other."

It is perhaps pertinent at this point to recall that when the question of Palestine was being debated in the United Nations in 1947, the Soviet Union strongly supported the Jewish independence struggle. It is particularly relevant to recall some of Andrei Gromyko's remarks:

"As we know, the aspirations of a considerable part of the Jewish people are linked with the problem of Palestine and of its future administration. This fact scarcely requires proof. . . . During the last war, the Jewish people underwent exceptional sorrow and suffering. Without any exaggeration, this sorrow and suffering are indescribable. It is difficult to express them in dry statistics on the Jewish victims of the fascist aggressors. The Jews in the territories where the Hitlerites held sway were subjected to almost complete physical annihilation. The total number of Jews who perished at the hands of the Nazi executioners is estimated at approximately six million. . . .

"The United Nations cannot and must not regard this situation with indifference, since this would be incompatible with the high principles proclaimed in its Charter, which provides for the defense of human rights, irrespective of race, religion or sex. . . .

"The fact that no Western European State has been able to ensure the defense of the elementary rights of the Jewish people and to safeguard it against the violence of the fascist executioners explains the aspirations of the Jews to establish their own State. It would be unjust not to take this into consideration and to deny the right of the Jewish people to realize this aspiration."

How sad it is to see here a group of nations, many of whom have but recently freed themselves of colonial rule, deriding one of the most noble liberation movements of this century, a movement which not only gave an example of encouragement and determination to the peoples struggling for independence but also actively aided many of them either during the period of preparation for their independence or immediately thereafter.

Here you have a movement which is the embodiment of a unique pioneering spirit, of the dignity of labor, and of enduring human values, a movement which has presented to the world an example of social equality and open democracy being associated in this resolution with abhorrent political concepts.

We in Israel have endeavored to create a society which strives to implement the highest ideals of society—political, social and cultural—for all the inhabitants of Israel, irrespective of religious belief, race or sex.

Show me another pluralistic society in this world in which despite all the difficult problems, Jew and Arab live together with such a degree of harmony, in which the dignity and rights of man are observed before the law, in which no death sentence is applied, in which freedom of speech, of movement, of thought, of expression are guaranteed, in which even movements which are opposed to our national aims are represented in our Parliament.

The Arab delegates talk of racism. What has happened to the 800,000 Jews who lived for over two thousand years in the Arab lands, who formed some of the most ancient communities long before the advent of Islam? Where are they now?

The Jews were once one of the important communities in the countries of the Middle East, the leaders of thought, of commerce, of medical science. Where are they in Arab society today? You dare talk of racism when I can point with pride to the Arab ministers who have served in my government; to the Arab deputy speaker of my Parliament; to Arab officers and men serving of their own volition in our border and police defense forces, frequently commanding Jewish troops; to the hundreds of thousands of Arabs from all over the Middle East crowding the cities of Israel every year; to the thousands of Arabs from all over the Middle East coming for medical treatment to Israel; to the peaceful coexistence which has developed; to the fact that Arabic is an official language in Israel on a par with Hebrew; to the fact that it is as natural for an Arab to serve in public office in Israel as it is incongruous to think of a Jew serving in any public office in an Arab country, indeed being admitted to many of them. Is that racism? It is not! That, Mr. President, is Zionism.

Zionism is our attempt to build a society, imperfect though it may be, in which the visions of the prophets of Israel will be realized. I know that we have problems. I know that many disagree with our government's policies. Many in Israel too disagree from time to time with the government's policies . . . and are free to do so because Zionism has created the first and only real democratic state in a part of the world that never really knew democracy and freedom of speech.

This malicious resolution, designed to divert us from its true purpose, is part of a dangerous anti-Semitic idiom which is being insinuated into every public debate by those who have sworn to block the current move towards accommodation and ultimately towards peace in the Middle East. This, together with similar moves, is designed to sabotage the efforts of the Geneva Conference for peace in the Middle East and to deflect those who are moving along the road towards peace from their purpose. But they will not succeed, for I can but reiterate my government's policy to make every move in the direction towards peace, based on compromise.

We are seeing here today but another manifestation of the bitter anti-Semitic, anti-Jewish hatred which animates Arab society. Who would have believed that in this year, 1975, the malicious falsehoods of the "elders of Zion" would be distributed officially by Arab governments? Who would have believed that we would today contemplate an Arab society which teaches the vilest anti-Jewish hate in the kindergartens? . . . We are being attacked by a society which is motivated by the most extreme form of racism known in the world today. This is the racism which was expressed so succinctly in the words of the leader of the PLO, Yassir Arafat, in his opening address at a symposium in Tripoli, Libya: "There will be no presence in the region other than the Arab presence." In other words, in the Middle East from the Atlantic Ocean to the Persian Gulf only one presence is allowed, and that is Arab presence. No other people, regardless of how deep are its roots in the region, is to be permitted to enjoy its right to self-determination.

Look at the tragic fate of the Kurds of Iraq. Look what happened to the black population in southern Sudan. Look at the dire peril in which an entire community of Christians finds itself in Lebanon. Look at the avowed policy of the PLO, which calls in its Palestine Covenant of 1964 for the destruction of the State of Israel, which denies any form of compromise on the Palestine issue and which, in the words of its representative only the other day in this building, considers Tel Aviv to be occupied territory. Look at all this, and you see before you the root cause of the twin evils of this world at work, the blind hatred of the Arab proponents of this resolution, and the abysmal ignorance and wickedness of those who support them.

The issue before this Assembly is neither Israel nor Zionism. The issue is the fate of this organization. Conceived in the spirit of the prophets of Israel, born out of an anti-Nazi alliance after the tragedy of World War II, it has degenerated into a forum which was this last week described by [Paul Johnson] one of the leading writers in a foremost organ of social and liberal thought in the West as "rapidly becoming one of the most corrupt and corrupting creations in the whole history of human institutions . . . almost without exception those in the majority came from states notable for racist oppression of every conceivable hue." He goes on to explain the phenomenon of this debate:

"Israel is a social democracy, the nearest approach to a free socialist state in the world; its people and government have a profound respect for human life, so passionate indeed that, despite every conceivable provocation, they have refused for a quarter of a century to execute a single captured terrorist. They also have an ancient but vigorous culture, and a flourishing technology. The combination of national qualities they have assembled in their brief existence as a state is a perpetual and embittering reproach to most of the new countries whose representatives swagger about the UN building. So Israel is envied and hated; and efforts are made to destroy her. The extermination of the Israelis has long been the prime objective of the Terrorist International; they calculate that if they can break Israel, then all the rest of civilization is vulnerable to their assaults. . . .

"The melancholy truth, I fear, is that the candles of civilization are burning low. The world is increasingly governed not so much by capitalism, or communism, or social democracy, or even tribal barbarism, as by a false lexicon of political clichés, accumulated over half a century and now assuming a kind of degenerate sacerdotal authority. . . .We all know what they are. . . ."

Over the centuries it has fallen to the lot of my people to be the testing agent of human decency, the touchstone of civilization, the crucible in which enduring human values are to be tested. A nation's level of humanity could invariably be judged by its behavior towards its Jewish population. Persecution and oppression have often enough begun with the Jews, but it has never ended with them. The anti-Jewish pogroms in Czarist Russia were but the tip of the iceberg which revealed the inherent rottenness of a regime that was soon to disappear in the storm of revolution. The anti-Semitic excesses of the Nazis merely foreshadowed the catastrophe which was to befall mankind in Europe. . . .

On the issue before us, the world has divided itself into good and bad, decent and evil, human and debased. We, the Jewish people, will recall in history our gratitude to those nations who stood up and were counted and who refused to support this wicked proposition. I know that this episode will have strengthened the forces of freedom and decency in this world and will have fortified the free world in their resolve to strengthen the ideals they so cherish. I know that this episode will have strengthened Zionism as it has weakened the United Nations.

As I stand on this rostrum, the long and proud history of my people unravels itself before my inward eye. I see the oppressors of our people over the ages as they pass one another in evil procession into oblivion. I stand here before you as the representative of a strong and flourishing people which has survived them all and which will survive this shameful exhibition and the proponents of this resolution.

The great moments of Jewish history come to mind as I face you, once again outnumbered and the would-be victim of hate, ignorance and evil. I look back on those great moments. I recall the greatness of a nation which I have the honor to represent in this forum. I am mindful at this moment of the Jewish people throughout the world wherever they may be, be it in freedom or in slavery, whose prayers and thoughts are with me at this moment.

I stand here not as a supplicant. Vote as your moral conscience dictates to you. For the issue is neither Israel nor Zionism. The issue is the continued existence of this organization, which has been dragged to its lowest point of discredit by a coalition of despots and racists.

The vote of each delegation will record in history its country's stand on anti-Semitic racism and anti-Judaism. You yourselves bear the responsibility for your stand before history, for as such will you be viewed in history. We, the Jewish people, will not forget.

For us, the Jewish people, this is but a passing episode in a rich and event-filled history. We put our trust in our Providence, in our faith and beliefs, in our time-hallowed tradition, in our striving for social advance and human values, and in our people wherever they may be. For us, the Jewish people, this resolution based on hatred, falsehood and arrogance, is devoid of any moral or legal value.

HARVEY MILK
The Hope Speech
("Without hope, not only gays, but the blacks, the seniors,
the handicapped, the us'es, the us'es will give up")
San Diego, California
March 10, 1978

*Harvey Milk (1930–1978), a Korean War veteran born on Long Island,
New York, moved in the early 1970s to San Francisco, where he owned a
small business. He began taking an interest in politics, and in 1977 became
the first openly gay person in the United States to be elected to civil office, as
city and county supervisor in San Francisco. He and the mayor of San Francisco, George Moscone, were assassinated in 1978.*

My name is Harvey Milk and I'm here to recruit you.

I've been saving this one for years. It's a political joke. I can't help
it—I've got to tell it. I've never been able to talk to this many political
people before, so if I tell you nothing else you may be able to go
home laughing a bit.

This ocean liner was going across the ocean and it sank. And there was
one little piece of wood floating and three people swam to it and they
realized only one person could hold on to it. So they had a little debate
about which was the person. It so happened the three people were the
Pope, the President, and Mayor Daley. The Pope said he was titular head
of one of the great religions of the world and he was spiritual adviser to
many, many millions and he went on and pontificated and they thought
it was a good argument. Then the President said he was leader of the
largest and most powerful nation of the world. What takes place in this
country affects the whole world and they thought that was a good argument. And Mayor Daley said he was mayor of the backbone of the
United States and what took place in Chicago affected the world, and
what took place in the archdiocese of Chicago affected Catholicism.
And they thought that was a good argument. So they did it the democratic way and voted. And Daley won, seven to two.

About six months ago, Anita Bryant in her speaking to God said that the drought in California was because of the gay people. On November 9, the day after I got elected, it started to rain. On the day I got sworn in, we walked to City Hall and it was kinda nice, and as soon as I said the word "I do," it started to rain again. It's been raining since then and the people of San Francisco figure the only way to stop it is to do a recall petition. That's a local joke.

So much for that. Why are we here? Why are gay people here? And what's happening? What's happening to me is the antithesis of what you read about in the papers and what you hear about on the radio. You hear about and read about this movement to the right. That we must band together and fight back this movement to the right. And I'm here to go ahead and say that what you hear and read is what they want you to think because it's not happening. The major media in this country has talked about the movement to the right so much that they've got even us thinking that way. Because they want the legislators to think that there is indeed a movement to the right and that the Congress and the legislators and the city councils will start to move to the right the way the major media want them. So they keep on talking about this move to the right.

So let's look at 1977 and see if there was indeed a move to the right. In 1977, gay people had their rights taken away from them in Miami. But you must remember that in the week before Miami and the week after that, the word homosexual or gay appeared in every single newspaper in this nation in articles both pro and con. In every radio station, in every TV station and every household. For the first time in the history of the world, everybody was talking about it, good or bad. Unless you have dialogue, unless you open the walls of dialogue, you can never reach to change people's opinion. In those two weeks, more good and bad, but *more* about the word homosexual and gay was written than probably in the history of mankind. Once you have dialogue starting, you know you can break down the prejudice. In 1977 we saw a dialogue start. In 1977, we saw a gay person elected in San Francisco. In 1977 we saw the state of Mississippi decriminalize marijuana. In 1977, we saw the convention of conventions in Houston. And I want to know where the movement to the right is happening.

What that is is a record of what happened last year. What we must do is make sure that 1978 continues the movement that is really happening that the media don't want you to know about, that is the movement to the left. It's up to CDC to put the pressures on Sacramento—not to just bring flowers to Sacramento—but to break down the walls and the barriers so the movement to the left continues and progress continues in the nation. We have before us coming up several issues we must speak out on. Probably the most important issue outside the Briggs—which we will come to—but we do know what will take place this June. We know there's an issue on the ballot called Jarvis-Gann. We hear the taxpayers talk about it on both sides. But what you don't hear is that it's probably the most racist issue on the ballot in a long time. In the city and county of San Francisco, if it passes and we indeed have to lay off people, who will they be? The last in, not the first in, and who are the last in but the minorities? Jarvis-Gann is a racist issue. We must address that issue. We must not talk away from it. We must not allow them to talk about the money it's going to save, because look at who's going to save the money and who's going to get hurt.

We also have another issue that we've started in some of the north counties and I hope in some of the south counties it continues. In San Francisco elections we're asking—at least we hope to ask—that the U.S. government put pressure on the closing of the South African consulate. That must happen. There is a major difference between an embassy in Washington which is a diplomatic bureau, and a consulate in major cities. A consulate is there for one reason only—to promote business, economic gains, tourism, investment. And every time you have business going to South Africa, you're promoting a regime that's offensive.

In the city of San Francisco, if everyone of 51 percent of that city were to go to South Africa, they would be treated as second-class citizens. That is an offense to the people of San Francisco and I hope all my colleagues up there will take every step we can to close down that consulate and hope that people in other parts of the state follow us in that lead. The battles must be started some place and CDC is the greatest place to start the battles.

I know we are pressed for time so I'm going to cover just one more little point. That is to understand why it is important that gay people run for office and that gay people get elected. I know there are many people in this room who are running for central committee who are gay. I encourage you. There's a major reason why. If my non-gay friends and supporters in this room understand it, they'll probably understand why I've run so often before I finally made it. Y'see right now, there's a controversy going on in this convention about the governor. Is he speaking out enough? Is he strong enough for gay rights? And there is a controversy and for us to say it is not would be foolish. Some people are satisfied and some people are not.

You see there is a major difference—and it remains a vital difference—between a friend and a gay person, a friend in office and a gay person in office. Gay people have been slandered nationwide. We've been tarred and we've been brushed with the picture of pornography. In Dade County, we were accused of child molestation. It's not enough anymore just to have friends represent us. No matter how good that friend may be.

The black community made up its mind to that a long time ago. That the myths against blacks can only be dispelled by electing black leaders, so the black community could be judged by the leaders and not by the myths or black criminals. The Spanish community must not be judged by Latin criminals or myths. The Asian community must not be judged by Asian criminals or myths. The Italian community should not be judged by the mafia, myths. And the time has come when the gay community must not be judged by our criminals and myths.

Like every other group, we must be judged by our leaders and by those who are themselves gay, those who are visible. For invisible, we remain in limbo—a myth, a person with no parents, no brothers, no sisters, no friends who are straight, no important positions in employment. A tenth of a nation supposedly composed of stereotypes and would-be seducers of children—and no offense meant to the stereotypes. But today, the black community is not judged by its friends, but by its black legislators and leaders. And we must give people the chance to judge us by our leaders and legislators. A gay person in office can set a tone, can command respect not only from the larger community, but from the young people in our own community who need both examples and hope.

The first gay people we elect must be strong. They must not be content to sit in the back of the bus. They must not be content to accept pablum. They must be above wheeling and dealing. They must be—for the good of all of us—independent, unbought. The anger and the frustrations that some of us feel is because we are misunderstood, and friends can't feel that anger and frustration. They can sense it in us, but they can't feel it. Because a friend has never gone through what is known as coming out. I will never forget what it was like coming out and having nobody to look up toward. I remember the lack of hope—and our friends can't fulfill that.

I can't forget the looks on faces of people who've lost hope. Be they gay, be they seniors, be they blacks looking for an almost-impossible job, be they Latins trying to explain their problems and aspirations in a tongue that's foreign to them. I personally will never forget that people are more important than buildings. I use the word "I" because I'm proud. I stand here tonight in front of my gay sisters, brothers and friends because I'm proud of you. I think it's time that we have many legislators who are gay and proud of that fact and do not have to remain in the closest. I think that a gay person, up-front, will not walk away from a responsibility and be afraid of being tossed out of office. After Dade County, I walked among the angry and the frustrated night after night and I looked at their faces. And in San Francisco, three days before Gay Pride Day, a person was killed just because he was gay. And that night, I walked among the sad and the frustrated at City Hall in San Francisco and later that night as they lit candles on Castro Street and stood in silence, reaching out for some symbolic thing that would give them hope. These were strong people, people whose faces I knew from the shop, the streets, meetings and people who I never saw before but I knew. They were strong, but even they needed hope.

And the young gay people in the Altoona, Pennsylvanias and the Richmond, Minnesotas who are coming out and hear Anita Bryant on television and her story. The only thing they have to look forward to is hope. And you have to give them hope. Hope for a better world, hope for a better tomorrow, hope for a better place to come to if the pressures at home are too great. Hope that all will be all right. Without hope, not only gays, but the blacks, the seniors, the handicapped, the us'es, the us'es will give up. And if you help elect to the central committee and other offices, more gay people, that gives a green light to all who feel disenfranchised, a green light to move forward. It means hope to a nation that has given up, because if a gay person makes it, the doors are open to everyone.

So if there is a message I have to give, it is that if I've found one overriding thing abut my personal election, it's the fact that if a gay person can be elected, it's a green light. And you and you and you, you have to give people hope. Thank you very much.

URSULA K. LE GUIN
A Left-Handed Commencement Address
("Why should a free woman with a college education
either fight Machoman or serve him?")
Mills College
Oakland, California
May 19, 1983

*Ursula K. Le Guin is a prolific author of science fiction and fantasy novels
and a poet. She was born in Berkeley, California, in 1929, the daughter of
the anthropologist Alfred Kroeber.*

I want to thank the Mills College Class of '83 for offering me a rare
chance: to speak aloud in public in the language of women.

I know there are men graduating, and I don't mean to exclude
them, far from it. There is a Greek tragedy where the Greek says to
the foreigner, "If you don't understand Greek, please signify by
nodding." Anyhow, commencements are usually operated under
the unspoken agreement that everybody graduating is either male or
ought to be. That's why we are all wearing these twelfth-century
dresses that look so great on men and make women look either like
a mushroom or a pregnant stork. Intellectual tradition is male. Public speaking is done in the public tongue, the national or tribal
language; and the language of our tribe is the men's language. Of
course women learn it. We're not dumb. If you can tell Margaret
Thatcher from Ronald Reagan, or Indira Gandhi from General
Somoza, by anything they say, tell me how. This is a man's world,
so it talks a man's language. The words are all words of power.
You've come a long way, baby, but no way is long enough. You
can't even get there by selling yourself out: because there is theirs,
not yours.

Maybe we've had enough words of power and talk about the battle
of life. Maybe we need some words of weakness. Instead of saying
now that I hope you will all go forth from this ivory tower of college

172

into the Real World and forge a triumphant career or at least help your husband to and keep our country strong and be a success in everything—instead of talking about power, what if I talked like a woman right here in public? It won't sound right. It's going to sound terrible. What if I said what I hope for you is first, if—only if—you want kids, I hope you have them. Not hordes of them. A couple, enough. I hope they're beautiful. I hope you and they have enough to eat, and a place to be warm and clean in, and friends, and work you like doing. Well, is that what you went to college for? Is that all? What about success?

Success is somebody else's failure. Success is the American Dream we can keep dreaming because most people in most places, including thirty million of ourselves, live wide awake in the terrible reality of poverty. No, I do not wish you success. I don't even want to talk about it. I want to talk about failure.

Because you are human beings you are going to meet failure. You are going to meet disappointment, injustice, betrayal, and irreparable loss. You will find you're weak where you thought yourself strong. You'll work for possessions and then find they possess you. You will find yourself—as I know you already have—in dark places, alone, and afraid.

What I hope for you, for all my sisters and daughters, brothers and sons, is that you will be able to live there, in the dark place. To live in the place that our rationalizing culture of success denies, calling it a place of exile, uninhabitable, foreign.

Well, we're already foreigners. Women as women are largely excluded from, alien to, the self-declared male norms of this society, where human beings are called Man, the only respectable god is male, the only direction is up. So that's their country; let's explore our own. I'm not talking about sex; that's a whole other universe, where every man and woman is on their own. I'm talking about society, the so-called man's world of institutionalized competition, aggression, violence, authority, and power. If we want to live as women, some separatism is forced upon us: Mills College is a wise embodiment of that separatism. The war-games world wasn't made by us or for us; we can't even breathe the air there without masks. And if you put the mask on you'll have a hard time getting it off. So how about going on doing things our own way, as to some extent you did here at Mills? Not *for* men and the male power hierarchy—that's their game. Not *against* men, either—that's still playing by their rules. But *with* any men who are with us: that's our game. Why should a free woman with a college education either fight Machoman or serve him? Why should she live her life on his terms?

Machoman is afraid of our terms, which are not all rational, positive, competitive, etc. And so he has taught us to despise and deny them. In our society, women have lived, and have been despised for living, the whole side of life that includes and takes responsibility for helplessness, weakness, and illness, for the irrational and the irreparable, for all that is obscure, passive, uncontrolled, animal, unclean—the valley of the shadow, the deep, the depths of life. All that the Warrior denies and refuses is left to us and the men who share it with us and therefore, like us, can't play doctor, only nurse, can't be warriors, only civilians, can't be chiefs, only Indians. Well so that is our country. The night side of our country. If there is a day side to it, high sierras, prairies of bright grass, we only know pioneers' tales about it, we haven't got there yet. We're never going to get there by imitating Machoman. We are only going to get there by going our own way, by living there, by living through the night in our own country.

So what I hope for you is that you live there not as prisoners, ashamed of being women, consenting captives of a psychopathic social system, but as natives. That you will be at home there, keep house there, be your own mistress, with a room of your own. That you will do your work there, whatever you're good at, art or science or tech or running a company or sweeping under the beds, and when they tell you that it's second-class work because a woman is doing it, I hope you tell them to go to hell and while they're going to give you equal pay for equal time. I hope you live without the need to dominate, and without the need to be dominated. I hope you are never victims, but I hope you have no power over other people. And when you fail, and are defeated, and in pain, and in the dark, then I hope you will remember that darkness is your country, where you live, where no wars are fought and no wars are won, but where the future is. Our roots are in the dark; the earth is our country. Why did we look up for blessing—instead of around, and down? What hope we have lies there. Not in the sky full of orbiting spy-eyes and weaponry, but in the earth we have looked down upon. Not from above, but from below. Not in the light that blinds, but in the dark that nourished, where human beings grow human souls.

RALPH NADER
The Megacorporate World of Ronald Reagan
(". . . the Reagan government is the consummate promoter
of the rich and powerful when the latter are arrayed against
the interests of the rest of America")
The National Press Club
Washington, D.C.
June 6, 1984

*Though Nader (b. 1934) later gained notoriety for his participation in the
2000 U.S. presidential election, his first and great claim to fame was as a
consumer advocate. For decades the Harvard-educated lawyer continually
brought to light corporate wrongdoing and helped make American homes and
roads safer.*

Many years ago, when some of our nation's political leaders were
wise, Thomas Jefferson said that the purpose of representative government was to curb "the excesses of the monied interests." Many
decades later, in 1936, Franklin D. Roosevelt, one of the last presidents to hold corporations accountable for the state of the economy,
promised that while "the malefactors of great wealth" had met their
match in the previous four years, they would meet their master in the
following four years.

Ronald Reagan has the opposite plan in mind. During Mr. Reagan's first term, "the malefactors of great wealth," now described as
big business or multinational corporations, have regularly met their
obedient servant in the white house. The power of "the monied interests" has become ever more focused on turning representative
government into a versatile accounts receivable for too many mis-
managed, speculating, negligent, avaricious, unsafe or downright
criminal companies. This Reagan-corporatist revolution, whereby
business regulates government in pursuit of private profit at the expense of the legitimate interests of Americans as taxpayers, consumers
and citizens, has little to do with being conservative. It has everything

175

to do with building a government of the Exxons, by the General Motors, and for the DuPonts.

So systematic, recurrent and widespread are these retrograde policies against basic, historic American values, as shall be noted shortly, that political commentators have wondered aloud how Mr. Reagan can still be so much in the running for re-election. The implication in their observations is proper: Presidents should be judged for what they do, not for what they say, or what they say they do. These commentators still expect a framework of accountability around the White House that includes the departments and agencies of the Executive Branch directed largely by presidential appointees or Schedule C personnel.

"The Teflon President"—one of those very apt descriptions by Democrats that ironically serve to encourage their discouragement about November—has a strategy for irresponsible power that invites closer scrutiny.

Rule One is never get openly involved in the details. He who rises by details falls by details could be his motto. Stay abstract, using heroic phrases of reassurance and national pride.

Rule Two is amiability—especially in "Aw shucks" demeanor with lots of even-toned voice, pendant smiles and head shrugs. Remember Reagan in China. When asked by American reporters what he thought of Peking censoring his remarks on Chinese television, he replied with a slight smile: "You fellows do it all the time." Imagine how Nixon would have been treated had he tried that one.

Rule Three is insulate the President from impromptu media exposure. His aides even joke about it, as Lyn Nofziger did on the campaign trail in 1980 when he told reporters, "I've got Ronnie under house arrest from you guys."

Rule Four is induced condescension. If people think they are so much smarter than you, they don't expect much and they forgive more.

Rule Five is create a banality of wrongdoing, of cruelty, of hypocrisy, of selling the country short. Banality avoids the constant search for novelty by the media and helps opposing politicians throw up their hands in despair. Any President whose administration can incite the response of the jaded—"So what else is new"—is already almost out of the woods. Banality is nourished by a numbing frequency of abuses whose very quantity depreciate their provocative impact.

Rule Six is seize the semantics and wrap the national symbols around one's own political ideology.

Rule Seven is be blessed by an opposition party that has largely surrendered the basic contention of its politics—namely that of challenging the mal-distribution of power between the haves and have nots. The formula which used to win again and again for the Democrats— that they were the party of the people and the Republicans were the party of the rich—is no longer used. It fails because these are times of massive campaign finance beggary and a giant corporate lock on an economy increasingly within corporate prerogative to transfer operations overseas or close down plant by plant. People see this overlap by the two parties in currying the favor of business interests. Deprived of distinct political choice, citizens begin to doubt the credibility of the party out of office when it claims it will be different. The candidates who can convince us that there will be a difference on concrete policy after concrete policy will move people's minds.

The radical regime of Ronald Reagan does provide a background against which there indeed can be significant choices affecting the perceived needs and rights of citizens. Here are some of the directions pursued by the Reagan-Big Business axis:

The concentration of power within government and business has increased in both political and economic manifestations. The corporate merger movement, given the green light by Reagan, is moving from rabid to frenzied. Nine of the ten largest mergers in U.S. history have occurred under the permissive reign of Reagan. It is difficult to know what limits Reagan would put on mergers, most of which promise no greater efficiencies, no economies of scale, no market discipline of bad management (without golden parachutes) and no new jobs. His former Justice Department antitrust chief, William Baxter, said: "There is nothing written in the sky that says the world would not be a perfectly satisfactory place if there were only one hundred companies, provided each had one percent of every product and service market." Nothing written in the sky, but there is much written in the anti-monopoly laws, their legislative history and judicial decisions that would give pause to such a concentrated political economy. Corporate bigness makes its demands on small business and the consumer in prices, in political manipulation, and in being too big to fail without a bailout. The loss of the family farm in the tens of thousands each year to agribusiness and banks receives no attention from this former rural Illinois native who extolls this way of life when he wants votes and forgets it after the election.

Over at the Federal Communications Commission, with Mr. Reagan's full support, his appointees, led by Chairman Mark Fowler, want to eliminate the few viewer's rights under the Fairness and Equal Time Doctrines. They want to repeal 7–7–7 limitation (7 am, 7 fm and 7 tv) stations which can be under a single owner and allow a vastly greater concentration of electronic media ownership.

Within the Federal Government there is greater concentration of power from many agencies to one—the White House Office of Management and Budget. The OMB makes political judgments, invites back door "ex parte" meetings with business lobbyists, excludes the public from its right to know and respond under the Administrative Procedures Act, and generally translates unilateral white house dictates. OMB does this in violation of fair play, and by some expert opinion, in violation of administrative laws as well. The Reagan Government also shuts Americans out of its decision-making processes by ending legal aid for poorer petitioners before regulatory agencies such as the Federal Trade Commission. They do so by using every technical objection to deny citizens legal standing to challenge their government, and by giving early preferential notice of proposals to their industrial and commercial friends. If there is any company on the Fortune 100 list that objects to these anti-democratic powerplays, it has kept a very low visibility.

There is a wholesale repudiation of the historic role of the American Government's duty to protect or expand the public's health and safety. Health and safety laws go unenforced or underenforced below even laggard levels of the past. The Food and Drug Administration's enforcement level is down about 50 percent, as are the enforcement actions against dirty meat and poultry plants and violators of motor vehicle regulations. The enforcement record of OSHA—the job safety agency—is a disgrace made worse by Reaganite reductions in serious inspections and redrawing what constitutes sanctionable violations. Since taking office, Reagan has not issued a single new worker health standard to limit any chemical or gas, though dozens in January 1981 were nearly ready to be issued to reduce cancer, emphysema, and other diseases and injuries in the workplace. These diseases claim about 100,000 American lives a year. Only one motor vehicle standard has emerged—that dealing with rear mounted lights on automobiles, while several critical lifesavers were revoked or shunted aside. The list can go on and on to demonstrate that Mr. Reagan has little interest in saving American lives when it inconveniences his corporate masters.

With the stroke of Transportation Secretary Drew Lewis' pen, a lifesaving, crash protection standard was illegally repealed (according to a 9–0 decision by the U.S. Supreme Court). Thousands of Americans are now dying or being seriously injured every year in frontal collisions by their non-crashworthy cars. Mr. Reagan campaigned against this humane and economical engineering system right along with General Motors which pressed upon him this macabre position. The pattern recurs in one industry after another. What do the pesticide companies want? Just follow the Reagan trail of waivers and exceptions for dangerous pesticides, the absence of regulatory action against suspected farm chemicals, the virtual cessation of testing foods for pesticide residues and the reduction of research for non-toxic ways of controlling pests.

The sordid behavior of Reagan's Environmental Protection Agency in bowing to corporate polluters on demand has been reported many times. But Mr. Reagan's responsibility needs to be made clearer. EPA Chief Ann Gorsuch did the president's bidding. It was the Reagan White House that stopped the new EPA Chief William Ruckelshaus from doing anything to reduce the sources of acid rain. It is Mr. Reagan and the corporate polluters who oppose overdue implementation of stricter safety standards for America's drinking water—now contaminated with heavy metals and cancer-causing chemicals. The corporate polluters want the air and water pollution laws severely weakened. Many polls conclude that the overwhelming majority of people want them strengthened. Ronald Reagan joins with his corporate patrons on these issue as well. Even in the field of toxic waste dumps, scarring and poisoning the America that he professes to revere, Mr. Reagan exerts no leadership. For the Great Communicator, there is no time for compassionate recognition of victims of corporate abuses, corporate cancer and other forms of industrial violence. It is as if there needed to be proof that the contamination of America's air and water were the products of an International Communist Conspiracy before Mr. Reagan would leap into action. Alas, for those sick or dying under Reagan—"The Real King of The Special Interests," as a *Washington Post* headline put it—there is no such relief ahead.

Mr. Reagan's insensitivity seems at times to go beyond taking orders from business. It reaches to uncharted realms of indifference and irresponsibility that congeal to form a type of intellectual incontinence. Some view his hard line determination against law and order for corporations and his softness on corporate crime as the result of an ideologically indentured mind. It is perfectly attuned to his political creators—the multimillionaires of the Southern California kitchen cabinet who, like they'd acquired a sure winner horse, selected, groomed, trained and financed him for Sacramento, and finally for Washington. It is all that but more.

How else can anyone explain why Mr. Reagan would so mistreat the most vulnerable in our society when he could so easily defend their right to live in health, safety, and dignity? Infants and children surely cannot be expected "to vote with their feet," Mr. Reagan. Yet, in 1981, he pushed to drop requirements that gasoline refiners reduce the amount of lead in gasoline. Too many little children in this country already have the devastating symptoms of lead poisoning; more lead violence cannot be allowed in their bodies. What of asbestos in thousands of school buildings? Despite visible protests from concerned parents, Mr. Reagan and Mr. Stockman refused to ask Congress to appropriate any money to help seal or remove exposed asbestos surfaces spinning off deadly microscopic particles into those young lungs. This Commander-in-Chief, who has never met a weapons system he didn't like, wanted to abolish the Consumer Product Safety Commission—a tiny agency with a major mission of protecting children from household and other product hazards. With an annual budget worth less than two hours of Pentagon expenditures, the CPSC did not fit within Mr. Reagan's definition of defense in depth. Fortunately, Congress disagreed, so just the budget was cut. There is more. After mothers of brain-damaged infants lobbied through Congress a bill to have the Food and Drug Administration establish quality control standards for commercial infant formula, Mr. Reagan's White House delayed the issuance of these regulations for eighteen months. Without press exposure, the delay may have been longer. Because of the lack of care and compassion so characteristic of this Administration, three million additional cans of deficient formula were sold to unsuspecting parents.

Two years ago, health officials at the Food and Drug Administration wanted to require aspirin makers to place a label on their product warning about Reye's Syndrome, a disease causing convulsions and sometimes death in some children who take aspirin when they have chicken pox or the flu. The White House OMB intervened on behalf of aspirin manufacturers and blocked both the move and distribution through supermarkets of a half million copies of pamphlets cautioning parents. Again there was wide publicity of this intragovernment struggle but Mr. Reagan let the aspirin industry prevail.

It was said about Woodrow Wilson that he disliked individuals but loved humanity. The reverse seems to apply to Mr. Reagan, with the qualification that the individuals are those friends who share his dogmas or who are politically useful symbols during photo opportunities. He brought back, with calculated media exposure, two Korean children who needed medical operations. Would that he wield his great powers as President on behalf of America's infants and children instead of reducing special nutrition programs for impoverished pregnant women, mothers and their newly born.

He must know by now that polls consistently are showing sizeable majorities of people dislike his policies though they think he is a nice fellow. As long as that anomaly continues, he has little incentive to sensitize himself by meeting with active-victim groups such as the disabled. He has little incentive to ask his speech writers for genuine declarations of his compassionate recognition of their plight and determination to alleviate pain and prevent further trauma and disease.

Recently a young pediatrician took a long unpaid leave of absence from his California practice to crusade for reinstatement of the Crash Protection Standard (commonly called the Airbag Rule). He has received some mass media coverage of his efforts. He held a well-prepared vigil of physicians at Lafayette Park one Saturday afternoon and delivered a "visual letter" on video tape to the President. The White House, I subsequently learned, did not even bother to do the routine thing and forward it to the Secretary of Transportation. The doctor wondered why he and his fellow physicians could not see the President on a matter that public health specialists have called "the single most effective domestic life saving decision that the administration is in a position to make this year and perhaps for many years." I could have told the physician, recalling the list of past visitors to the President, that he did not quality for a meeting since he had not won a boxing championship, performed a decisive slamdunk or won an Emmy.

Mr. Reagan is consistent with his pitiless deregulatory generalities. Had Congress not stopped him, he would have abolished crucial health and safety requirements imposed on the heavily tax-supported nursing home industry. Instead of firmer enforcement efforts and more adequate standards, he was content to leave defenseless the more than one million elderly in nursing homes.

So extreme is the President's corporatism that he is finding more genuine conservative groups taking sharp issue with his policies. In a little reported evolution that may change the future complexion of American politics, organizations who call themselves conservative populists are teaming up with their progressive counterparts to oppose corporate bailouts. Last year this coalition defeated the breeder reactor boondoggle—a high Reagan priority. In 1981, it nearly defeated the legislation regarding the Alaska gas pipeline that would coerce consumers into paying for the pipeline even if the project isn't completed and consumers did not receive any natural gas. The synfuel industry's welfare project is under similar pressure, though its predicted mismanagement and awful economics appear to be self-dismantling. This new coalition put up a strong fight against the Reaganite bailout of the big U.S. banks that made such imprudent loans at sky-high interest rates to foreign countries. Reagan, who spent years lecturing around the country for General Electric on the virtues of sink or swim free enterprise, has become the most prominent advocate of big business bailouts in American history.

If this all goes against his philosophic grain, it demonstrates the contrary power of giant business over his government. His formerly strong belief in states' rights is surrendered when companies want his backing for a weaker federal law replacing the adaptable common law in the fifty states that gives people injured by dangerous products rights to sue and recover compensation from manufacturers. It is surrendered when the banks demand that his agencies preempt stronger state regulations designed to protect depositors and borrowers. It is surrendered again when the nuclear industry wants him to strip state and local governments of their police power over the transportation of radioactive materials through their communities. Corporatizing the ex-conservative Ronald Reagan is a routine matter these days, even when Wall Street's economic and tax policy demands result in placing Main Street, with its small businesses, at a comparative disadvantage.

The simplest of international decencies are rejected by the Reagan administration in obeisance to the multinationals. Mr. Carter's executive order requiring notification to foreign governments was revoked early in this republican administration. The order had been intended to restrain the export from this country of hazardous products illegal for domestic sale but not for export (e.g., certain drugs, pesticides) or to stop outright illegal exports. Now, with Mr. Reagan's knowledge and support, a clutch of global corporations, State and Commerce Department officials, and this government's United Nations' mission is working to stop the United Nations' draft guidelines on consumer protection. These principles of consumer safety and economic rights (the freedom to form consumer associations and the like) are drawn heavily from U.S. law and practice. They are just principles, having no force of authority but meant to have a moral impact on many countries and companies. Apparently, however, suggesting that the world has something to learn from U.S. consumer protection achievements over the past century is too provocative for the corporate statists in the Reagan camp. They seem unmindful of the disasters that have occurred in Third World countries, not a few generated by Western corporations taking advantage of the absence of indigenous consumer safeguards.

Such unmindfulness has become a habit. The Reagan government is the only member of the United Nations to vote against a U.N. resolution seeking to deter the kind of dumping of hazardous materials as occurred with the export of tris-treated (a carcinogen) children's pajamas from the U.S. All our allies voted the other way. The World Health Organization, with just one dissent, that of Ronald Reagan, approved a code for better marketing practices for infant formula promotion. This code was stimulated by the death of millions of Third World babies during the seventies linked to over-promotion of infant formulas through scare techniques and other deceptions in conjunction with unsanitary village water sources. This tragedy has been reported in the context of the Nestlé boycott that was recently settled with international children's defense groups after Nestlé agreed to modify its actions.

Every president has a unique mission of trust imposed upon him by certain conservation laws, some of them enacted by Republican-dominated congresses and presidents early in this century. I refer to the federal lands onshore and offshore with those glorious wildernesses and natural resources for present and future generations of Americans to enjoy and preserve. These lands comprise one-third of our nation from the pristine wilds of Alaska to the barren deserts of Arizona (a prime solar energy region someday). Does Mr. Reagan use his communications skills to graphically etch in the minds of more Americans the grandeur and permanence of his public trust? No, although he no longer talks about his support of the Sagebrushers who want the states to have these lands on their way to private ownership and exploitation.

Instead, he launched, through his agent James Watt, the biggest natural resource giveaway program to corporations in modern American History. The Reagan-Watt team wanted to lease billions of acres of offshore lands so fast that the oil company beneficiaries-to-be had to say, "Whoa, we can't absorb that rapid a transfer." So they settled for merely massive leaseholds on public lands whose oil and gas potential the government could not independently verify. In a glutted market of declining prices, Reagan-Watt proposed to lease as much coal in fifteen months as eleven administrations have done in the sixty-three years since the government began to lease its coal-bearing lands. These men knew that the coal and oil companies already were sitting on existing federal coal leases without producing any coal. What these companies want is not to produce but to control huge reserves of the people's resources at giveaway prices obtained in a depressed market. Reagan was all too eager to deliver, until organized civic opposition retired Watt and cooled off an election-sensitive President.

One would at the very least expect Mr. Reagan to want to give taxpayers (that majority of the taxpayers who will pay more in total taxes in 1984 than in 1980) value for what they paid government contractors to develop. Not at all. By presidential directive, agencies are urged to turn over to companies exclusive patent rights to government-financed discoveries to the fullest extent permissible. This is one of many areas of corporate privilege to which the Reaganites neglect to apply their cost-benefit formula. But the formula is so often rigged to cater to corporations, one shouldn't be surprised when it is not applied at all.

The curtain around Reagan's corporate state is one of intense secrecy whose function of excluding the public's participation and monitoring is nourished by a rising base of zero data. This administration does not want to know what corporations do; it has stopped collecting much data about the large oil companies. It has stopped collecting data about line of business reporting by conglomerates. Referring to across-the-board cuts in federal statistical gathering services, University of Chicago Dean William Kruskal wrote: "When a vessel is in stormy seas, it is foolhardy to cut corners on radar, navigational equipment, good maps, and ample, well-trained crews." Coupled with not wanting to know, the government has defined as trade secrets whatever information companies want withheld from the public, even though it is supplied to the government for particular proceedings affecting the public.

The price of government reports and pamphlets has skyrocketed to levels reachable only by the affluent or desperate. Look at the government printing office's price list and you will see pamphlets of only a few pages selling for over two dollars each. Price hikes have driven the number of publications requested from the government's consumer information center in fiscal year 1984 to half of what they were in fiscal 1982. Many publications, such as the popular *Car Book,* have been discontinued. Citizens wanting to be placed on mailing lists of the FCC or the ICC for agency press releases are referred to private contractors who will sell you this service. The principle of the broadest possible distribution of information about what the government is doing and deciding has been destroyed. The pretext is that the user should pay and as printing volume declines the prices go up in a vicious circle of exclusion. The government pays almost $100 million a year for marching bands. (That's twice as much as the cost of administering the Freedom of Information Act and there are no viewer fees charged there.)

To top off Reagan's Darkness at Noon, the basic research and development which elevates awareness of hazards to be averted and opportunities to be developed have been severely weakened due to industry demands. Thus, the experimental Safety Vehicle Program and the Fuel Economy Research Program have been closed. Sharply reduced are research undertakings in energy conservation, cancer prevention, drug safety, toxic chemicals and consumer product safety. Such inquiries could lead to stronger future safety standards—a prospect companies usually like to cut off at the pass. What is so deplorable about Mr. Reagan is that his supine relations with business brings out the worst in corporate behavior. Executives see that they do not have to do safety research or be concerned about compliance with laws that are about to be enforced. General Motors' Chairman, Roger Smith, disbanded the company's crack air-bag technology development section unit in April 1981, after learning that Transportation Secretary Drew Lewis was going to scrap the Automatic Crash Protection Regulation. Companies that stretch to advance the cause of safety, as have State Farm and Allstate, receive no plaudits, no medals, no encouragement from the man in the White House. If anything, these firms think they may be inviting resentment for their efforts.

All in all, the Reagan government is the consummate promoter of the rich and powerful when the latter are arrayed against the interests of the rest of America. We must not forget that it is not just Reagan who occupies that eminent political office. It is the network of collegial business interests who have learned so well that the essence of privilege in America's marketplace today requires control over the government's powers and its public wealth. Subsidies, monopolistic licenses, protectionism, selective enforcement, lucrative contracts, loan guarantees, bailouts, and the free results of expensive research and development are among the dispensations of modern Uncle Sugar in Washington, D.C. Together these goodies make a bustling bazaar of corporate welfare and largess that requires nurturing and enlargement. Toward this objective it helps to have your own business agent in the White House. It helps to have someone who does not raise American's expectation levels.

Americans have every right to some solutions to their everyday afflictions, some value for their everyday tax dollars and some voice for their everyday concerns, some remedies for their everyday injustices, and some civic mechanisms for building their futures.

The empowerment and widespread exercise of citizenship is a prerequisite for a sound, democratic society. Leadership that empowers more people, that reduces the severe concentration of power and information, and that lifts a nation into missions of accomplishment which will increase justice, happiness and opportunity—that is the leadership citizens must demand by involving themselves in a national political campaign. So too, the media should rise to their higher responsibility to report the White House and not just mimeograph its rhetoric.

Our history has demonstrated that the well-being of society springs from the growth of daily, active citizenship that provides an enabling environment for good leaders to come forth. Every significant social movement in this century has sprung from active citizens fighting for their cause—women's suffrage, workers' rights, civil rights, environmental and consumer protection, peace. Put in today's terms, citizens in our country need to spend more time being citizens. That is the real bottom line.

RONALD REAGAN
The Berlin Wall
("Mr. Gorbachev, tear down this wall")
Berlin, West Germany
June 12, 1987

Ronald Reagan (1911–2004) was born in Illinois and became a Hollywood movie star in the late 1930s. In 1966 he was elected governor of California, and in 1980 the fortieth president of the United States. He was a master speaker, and at the Brandenburg Gate of the Berlin Wall, a symbol of Soviet repression, he upstaged the general secretary of the USSR, Mikhail Gorbachev. The Wall came down on November 9, 1989.

Chancellor Kohl, Governing Mayor Diepgen, ladies and gentlemen:

Twenty-four years ago, President John F. Kennedy visited Berlin, speaking to the people of this city and the world at the City Hall. Well, since then two other presidents have come, each in his turn, to Berlin. And today I, myself, make my second visit to your city.

We come to Berlin, we American presidents, because it's our duty to speak, in this place, of freedom. But I must confess, we're drawn here by other things as well: by the feeling of history in this city, more than 500 years older than our own nation; by the beauty of the Grunewald and the Tiergarten; most of all, by your courage and determination. Perhaps the composer Paul Lincke understood something about American presidents. You see, like so many presidents before me, I come here today because wherever I go, whatever I do: *Ich hab noch einen Koffer in Berlin.* [I still have a suitcase in Berlin.]

Our gathering today is being broadcast throughout Western Europe and North America. I understand that it is being seen and heard as well in the East. To those listening throughout Eastern Europe, a special word: Although I cannot be with you, I address my remarks to you just as surely as to those standing here before me. For I join you, as I join your fellow countrymen in the West, in this firm, this unalterable belief: *Es gibt nur ein Berlin.* [There is only one Berlin.]

Behind me stands a wall that encircles the free sectors of this city, part of a vast system of barriers that divides the entire continent of Europe. From the Baltic, south, those barriers cut across Germany in a gash of barbed wire, concrete, dog runs, and guard towers. Farther south, there may be no visible, no obvious wall. But there remain armed guards and checkpoints all the same—still a restriction on the right to travel, still an instrument to impose upon ordinary men and women the will of a totalitarian state. Yet it is here in Berlin where the wall emerges most clearly; here, cutting across your city, where the news photo and the television screen have imprinted this brutal division of a continent upon the mind of the world. Standing before the Brandenburg Gate, every man is a German, separated from his fellow men. Every man is a Berliner, forced to look upon a scar.

President von Weizsacker has said, "The German question is open as long as the Brandenburg Gate is closed." Today I say: As long as the gate is closed, as long as this scar of a wall is permitted to stand, it is not the German question alone that remains open, but the question of freedom for all mankind. Yet I do not come here to lament. For I find in Berlin a message of hope, even in the shadow of this wall, a message of triumph.

In this season of spring in 1945, the people of Berlin emerged from their air-raid shelters to find devastation. Thousands of miles away, the people of the United States reached out to help. And in 1947 Secretary of State—as you've been told—George Marshall announced the creation of what would become known as the Marshall Plan. Speaking precisely 40 years ago this month, he said: "Our policy is directed not against any country or doctrine, but against hunger, poverty, desperation, and chaos."

In the Reichstag a few moments ago, I saw a display commemorating this 40th anniversary of the Marshall Plan. I was struck by the sign on a burnt-out, gutted structure that was being rebuilt. I understand that Berliners of my own generation can remember seeing signs like it dotted throughout the western sectors of the city. The sign read simply: "The Marshall Plan is helping here to strengthen the free world." A strong, free world in the West, that dream became real. Japan rose from ruin to become an economic giant. Italy, France, Belgium—virtually every nation in Western Europe saw political and economic rebirth; the European Community was founded.

In West Germany and here in Berlin, there took place an economic miracle, the Wirtschaftswunder. Adenauer, Erhard, Reuter, and other leaders understood the practical importance of liberty—that just as truth can flourish only when the journalist is given freedom of speech, so prosperity can come about only when the farmer and businessman enjoy economic freedom. The German leaders reduced tariffs, expanded free trade, lowered taxes. From 1950 to 1960 alone, the standard of living in West Germany and Berlin doubled.

Where four decades ago there was rubble, today in West Berlin there is the greatest industrial output of any city in Germany—busy office blocks, fine homes and apartments, proud avenues, and the spreading lawns of parkland. Where a city's culture seemed to have been destroyed, today there are two great universities, orchestras and an opera, countless theaters, and museums. Where there was want, today there's abundance—food, clothing, automobiles—the wonderful goods of the Ku'damm. From devastation, from utter ruin, you Berliners have, in freedom, rebuilt a city that once again ranks as one of the greatest on earth. The Soviets may have had other plans. But my friends, there were a few things the Soviets didn't count on—*Berliner Herz, Berliner Humor, ja, und Berliner Schnauze.* [Berliner heart, Berliner humor, yes, and a Berliner Schnauze.]

In the 1950s, Khrushchev predicted: "We will bury you." But in the West today, we see a free world that has achieved a level of prosperity and well-being unprecedented in all human history. In the Communist world, we see failure, technological backwardness, declining standards of health, even want of the most basic kind—too little food. Even today, the Soviet Union still cannot feed itself. After these four decades, then, there stands before the entire world one great and inescapable conclusion: Freedom leads to prosperity. Freedom replaces the ancient hatreds among the nations with comity and peace. Freedom is the victor.

And now the Soviets themselves may, in a limited way, be coming to understand the importance of freedom. We hear much from Moscow about a new policy of reform and openness. Some political prisoners have been released. Certain foreign news broadcasts are no longer being jammed. Some economic enterprises have been permitted to operate with greater freedom from state control.

Are these the beginnings of profound changes in the Soviet state? Or are they token gestures, intended to raise false hopes in the West, or to strengthen the Soviet system without changing it? We welcome change and openness; for we believe that freedom and security go together, that the advance of human liberty can only strengthen the cause of world peace. There is one sign the Soviets can make that would be unmistakable, that would advance dramatically the cause of freedom and peace.

General Secretary Gorbachev, if you seek peace, if you seek prosperity for the Soviet Union and Eastern Europe, if you seek liberalization:

Come here to this gate! Mr. Gorbachev, open this gate! Mr. Gorbachev, tear down this wall!

I understand the fear of war and the pain of division that afflict this continent—and I pledge to you my country's efforts to help overcome these burdens. To be sure, we in the West must resist Soviet expansion. So we must maintain defenses of unassailable strength. Yet we seek peace; so we must strive to reduce arms on both sides.

Beginning ten years ago, the Soviets challenged the Western alliance with a grave new threat, hundreds of new and more deadly SS-20 nuclear missiles, capable of striking every capital in Europe. The Western alliance responded by committing itself to a counter-deployment unless the Soviets agreed to negotiate a better solution; namely, the elimination of such weapons on both sides. For many months, the Soviets refused to bargain in earnestness. As the alliance, in turn, prepared to go forward with its counter-deployment, there were difficult days—days of protests like those during my 1982 visit to this city—and the Soviets later walked away from the table.

But through it all, the alliance held firm. And I invite those who protested then—I invite those who protest today—to mark this fact: Because we remained strong, the Soviets came back to the table. And because we remained strong, today we have within reach the possibility, not merely of limiting the growth of arms, but of eliminating, for the first time, an entire class of nuclear weapons from the face of the earth.

As I speak, NATO ministers are meeting in Iceland to review the progress of our proposals for eliminating these weapons. At the talks in Geneva, we have also proposed deep cuts in strategic offensive weapons. And the Western allies have likewise made far-reaching proposals to reduce the danger of conventional war and to place a total ban on chemical weapons.

While we pursue these arms reductions, I pledge to you that we will maintain the capacity to deter Soviet aggression at any level at which it might occur. And in cooperation with many of our allies, the United States is pursuing the Strategic Defense Initiative—research to base deterrence not on the threat of offensive retaliation, but on defenses that truly defend; on systems, in short, that will not target populations, but shield them. By these means we seek to increase the safety of Europe and all the world. But we must remember a crucial fact: East and West do not mistrust each other because we are armed; we are armed because we mistrust each other. And our differences are not about weapons but about liberty. When President Kennedy spoke at the City Hall those 24 years ago, freedom was encircled, Berlin was under siege. And today, despite all the pressures upon this city, Berlin stands secure in its liberty. And freedom itself is transforming the globe.

In the Philippines, in South and Central America, democracy has been given a rebirth. Throughout the Pacific, free markets are working miracle after miracle of economic growth. In the industrialized nations, a technological revolution is taking place—a revolution marked by rapid, dramatic advances in computers and telecommunications.

In Europe, only one nation and those it controls refuse to join the community of freedom. Yet in this age of redoubled economic growth, of information and innovation, the Soviet Union faces a choice: It must make fundamental changes, or it will become obsolete.

Today thus represents a moment of hope. We in the West stand ready to cooperate with the East to promote true openness, to break down barriers that separate people, to create a safe, freer world. And surely there is no better place than Berlin, the meeting place of East and West, to make a start. Free people of Berlin: Today, as in the past, the United States stands for the strict observance and full implementation of all parts of the Four Power Agreement of 1971. Let us use this occasion, the 750th anniversary of this city, to usher in a new era, to seek a still fuller, richer life for the Berlin of the future. Together, let us maintain and develop the ties between the Federal Republic and the Western sectors of Berlin, which is permitted by the 1971 agreement.

And I invite Mr. Gorbachev: Let us work to bring the Eastern and Western parts of the city closer together, so that all the inhabitants of all Berlin can enjoy the benefits that come with life in one of the great cities of the world.

To open Berlin still further to all Europe, East and West, let us expand the vital air access to this city, finding ways of making commercial air service to Berlin more convenient, more comfortable, and more economical. We look to the day when West Berlin can become one of the chief aviation hubs in all central Europe.

With our French and British partners, the United States is prepared to help bring international meetings to Berlin. It would be only fitting for Berlin to serve as the site of United Nations meetings, or world conferences on human rights and arms control or other issues that call for international cooperation.

There is no better way to establish hope for the future than to enlighten young minds, and we would be honored to sponsor summer youth exchanges, cultural events, and other programs for young Berliners from the East. Our French and British friends, I'm certain, will do the same. And it's my hope that an authority can be found in East Berlin to sponsor visits from young people of the Western sectors.

One final proposal, one close to my heart: Sport represents a source of enjoyment and ennoblement, and you may have noted that the Republic of Korea—South Korea—has offered to permit certain events of the 1988 Olympics to take place in the North. International sports competitions of all kinds could take place in both parts of this city. And what better way to demonstrate to the world the openness of this city than to offer in some future year to hold the Olympic games here in Berlin, East and West? In these four decades, as I have said, you Berliners have built a great city. You've done so in spite of threats—the Soviet attempts to impose the East-mark, the blockade. Today the city thrives in spite of the challenges implicit in the very presence of this wall. What keeps you here? Certainly there's a great deal to be said for your fortitude, for your defiant courage. But I believe there's something deeper, something that involves Berlin's whole look and feel and way of life—not mere sentiment. No one could live long in Berlin without being completely disabused of illusions. Something instead, that has seen the difficulties of life in Berlin but chose to accept them, that continues to build this good and proud city in contrast to a surrounding totalitarian presence that refuses to release human energies or aspirations. Something that speaks with a powerful voice of affirmation, that says yes to this city, yes to the future, yes to freedom. In a word, I would submit that what keeps you in Berlin is love—love both profound and abiding.

Perhaps this gets to the root of the matter, to the most fundamental distinction of all between East and West. The totalitarian world produces backwardness because it does such violence to the spirit, thwarting the human impulse to create, to enjoy, to worship. The totalitarian world finds even symbols of love and of worship an affront. Years ago, before the East Germans began rebuilding their churches, they erected a secular structure: the television tower at Alexander Platz. Virtually ever since, the authorities have been working to correct what they view as the tower's one major flaw, treating the glass sphere at the top with paints and chemicals of every kind. Yet even today when the sun strikes that sphere—that sphere that towers over all Berlin—the light makes the sign of the cross. There in Berlin, like the city itself, symbols of love, symbols of worship, cannot be suppressed.

As I looked out a moment ago from the Reichstag, that embodiment of German unity, I noticed words crudely spray-painted upon the wall, perhaps by a young Berliner: "This wall will fall. Beliefs become reality." Yes, across Europe, this wall will fall. For it cannot withstand faith; it cannot withstand truth. The wall cannot withstand freedom.

And I would like, before I close, to say one word. I have read, and I have been questioned since I've been here about certain demonstrations against my coming. And I would like to say just one thing, and to those who demonstrate so. I wonder if they have ever asked themselves that if they should have the kind of government they apparently seek, no one would ever be able to do what they're doing again.

Thank you and God bless you all.

NELSON MANDELA

Address to a Rally in Cape Town on His Release from Prison
(". . . the future of our country can only be
determined by a body which is democratically
elected on a non-racial basis")
Cape Town, South Africa
February 11, 1990

Nelson Rolihlahla Mandela (born 1918), the lifelong anti-apartheid activist, spent twenty-seven years in prison for his opposition to the white minority government of South Africa and its policies of racial discrimination. In 1990, President F. W. de Klerk, under domestic and international pressure, ordered Mandela's release and lifted the ban on his political organization, the African National Congress. After resuming leadership of the ANC, negotiations between Mandela and de Klerk led to the dismantling of apartheid and paved the way for major political reform. In 1993, Mandela and de Klerk were jointly awarded the Nobel Peace Prize; in 1996, Mandela was chosen president in South Africa's first open democratic elections. ⋆

Friends, comrades and fellow South Africans.

I greet you all in the name of peace, democracy and freedom for all.

I stand here before you not as a prophet but as a humble servant of you, the people. Your tireless and heroic sacrifices have made it possible for me to be here today. I therefore place the remaining years of my life in your hands.

On this day of my release, I extend my sincere and warmest gratitude to the millions of my compatriots and those in every corner of the globe who have campaigned tirelessly for my release.

I send special greetings to the people of Cape Town, this city which has been my home for three decades. Your mass marches and

---

⋆Note by Stephen J. McKenna, *The World's Great Speeches* (1999).

other forms of struggle have served as a constant source of strength to all political prisoners.

I salute the African National Congress. It has fulfilled our every expectation in its role as leader of the great march to freedom.

I salute our President, Comrade Oliver Tambo, for leading the ANC even under the most difficult circumstances.

I salute the rank and file members of the ANC. You have sacrificed life and limb in the pursuit of the noble cause of our struggle.

I salute combatants of Umkhonto we Sizwe, like Solomon Mahlangu and Ashley Kriel, who have paid the ultimate price for the freedom of all South Africans.

I salute the South African Communist Party for its sterling contribution to the struggle for democracy. You have survived forty years of unrelenting persecution. The memory of great communists like Moses Kotane, Yusuf Dadoo, Bram Fischer and Moses Mabhida will be cherished for generations to come.

I salute General Secretary Joe Slovo, one of our finest patriots. We are heartened by the fact that the alliance between ourselves and the Party remains as strong as it always was.

I salute the United Democratic Front, the National Education Crisis Committee, the South African Youth Congress, the Transvaal and Natal Indian Congresses and COSATU and the many other formations of the Mass Democratic Movement.

I also salute the Black Sash and the National Union of South African Students. We note with pride that you have acted as the conscience of white South Africa. Even during the darkest days in the history of our struggle you held the flag of liberty high. The large-scale mass mobilization of the past few years is one of the key factors which led to the opening of the final chapter of our struggle.

I extend my greetings to the working class of our country. Your organized strength is the pride of our movement. You remain the most dependable force in the struggle to end exploitation and oppression.

I pay tribute to the many religious communities who carried the campaign for justice forward when the organizations for our people were silenced.

I greet the traditional leaders of our country—many of you continue to walk in the footsteps of great heroes like Hintsa and Sekhukune.

I pay tribute to the endless heroism of youth, you, the young lions. You, the young lions, have energized our entire struggle.

I pay tribute to the mothers and wives and sisters of our nation. You are the rock-hard foundation of our struggle. Apartheid has inflicted more pain on you than on anyone else.

On this occasion, we thank the world community for their great contribution to the anti-apartheid struggle. Without your support our struggle would not have reached this advanced stage. The sacrifice of the frontline states will be remembered by South Africans forever.

My salutations would be incomplete without expressing my deep appreciation for the strength given to me during my long and lonely years in prison by my beloved wife and family. I am convinced that your pain and suffering was far greater than my own.

Before I go any further I wish to make the point that I intend making only a few preliminary comments at this stage. I will make a more complete statement only after I have had the opportunity to consult with my comrades.

Today the majority of South Africans, black and white, recognize that apartheid has no future. It has to be ended by our own decisive mass action in order to build peace and security. The mass campaign of defiance and other actions of our organization and people can only culminate in the establishment of democracy. The destruction caused by apartheid on our sub-continent is incalculable. The fabric of family life of millions of my people has been shattered. Millions are homeless and unemployed. Our economy lies in ruins and our people are embroiled in political strife. Our resort to the armed struggle in 1960 with the formation of the military wing of the ANC, Umkhonto we Sizwe, was a purely defensive action against the violence of apartheid. The factors which necessitated the armed struggle still exist today. We have no option but to continue. We express the hope that a climate conducive to a negotiated settlement will be created soon so that there may no longer be the need for the armed struggle.

I am a loyal and disciplined member of the African National Congress. I am therefore in full agreement with all of its objectives, strategies and tactics.

The need to unite the people of our country is as important a task now as it always has been. No individual leader is able to take on this enormous task on his own. It is our task as leaders to place our views before our organization and to allow the democratic structures to decide. On the question of democratic practice, I feel duty bound to make the point that a leader of the movement is a person who has been democratically elected at a national conference. This is a principle which must be upheld without any exceptions.

Today, I wish to report to you that my talks with the government have been aimed at normalizing the political situation in the country. We have not as yet begun discussing the basic demands of the struggle. I wish to stress that I myself have at no time entered into negotiations about the future of our country except to insist on a meeting between the ANC and the government.

Mr. de Klerk has gone further than any other Nationalist president in taking real steps to normalize the situation. However, there are further steps as outlined in the Harare Declaration that have to be met before negotiations on the basic demands of our people can begin. I reiterate our call for, inter alia, the immediate ending of the State of Emergency and the freeing of all, and not only some, political prisoners. Only such a normalized situation, which allows for free political activity, can allow us to consult our people in order to obtain a mandate.

The people need to be consulted on who will negotiate and on the content of such negotiations. Negotiations cannot take place above the heads or behind the backs of our people. It is our belief that the future of our country can only be determined by a body which is democratically elected on a non-racial basis. Negotiations on the dismantling of apartheid will have to address the overwhelming demand of our people for a democratic, non-racial and unitary South Africa. There must be an end to white monopoly on political power and a fundamental restructuring of our political and economic systems to ensure that the inequalities of apartheid are addressed and our society thoroughly democratized.

It must be added that Mr. de Klerk himself is a man of integrity who is acutely aware of the dangers of a public figure not honoring his undertakings. But as an organization we base our policy and strategy on the harsh reality we are faced with. And this reality is that we are still suffering under the policy of the Nationalist government.

Our struggle has reached a decisive moment. We call on our people to seize this moment so that the process towards democracy is rapid and uninterrupted. We have waited too long for our freedom. We can no longer wait. Now is the time to intensify the struggle on all fronts. To relax our efforts now would be a mistake which generations to come will not be able to forgive. The sight of freedom looming on the horizon should encourage us to redouble our efforts.

It is only through disciplined mass action that our victory can be assured. We call on our white compatriots to join us in the shaping of a new South Africa. The freedom movement is a political home for you too. We call on the international community to continue the campaign to isolate the apartheid regime. To lift sanctions now would be to run the risk of aborting the process towards the complete eradication of apartheid.

Our march to freedom is irreversible. We must not allow fear to stand in our way. Universal suffrage on a common voters' roll in a united democratic and non-racial South Africa is the only way to peace and racial harmony.

In conclusion I wish to quote my own words during my trial in 1964. They are as true today as they were then:

I have fought against white domination and I have fought against black domination. I have cherished the ideal of a democratic and free society in which all persons live together in harmony and with equal opportunities. It is an ideal which I hope to live for and to achieve. But if needs be, it is an ideal for which I am prepared to die.

VÁCLAV HAVEL
Address to a Joint Session of Congress
("We still don't know how to put morality ahead of
politics, science and economics")
Washington, D.C.
February 21, 1990

The Czech playwright, born in Prague in 1936, spent almost five years in prison for protesting injustice and participating in the human rights group Charter 77. In this speech in Washington, he describes his surprise and sense of responsibility upon becoming the president of free Czechoslovakia after the country's Velvet Revolution. (The country divided into the Czech Republic and Slovakia in 1993.)

My advisors have advised me, on this important occasion, to speak in Czech. I don't know why. Perhaps they wanted you to enjoy the sweet sounds of my mother tongue.

The last time they arrested me, on October 27 of last year, I didn't know whether it was for two days or two years.

Exactly one month later, when the rock musician Michael Kocab told me that I would probably be proposed as a presidential candidate, I thought it was one of his usual jokes.

On the 10th of December 1989, when my actor friend Jiri Bartoska, in the name of the Civic Forum, nominated me as a candidate for the office of President of the Republic, I thought it was out of the question that the parliament we had inherited from the previous regime would elect me.

Twelve days later, when I was unanimously elected President of my country, I had no idea that in two months I would be speaking in front of this famous and powerful assembly, and that what I say would be heard by millions of people who have never heard of me and that hundreds of politicians and political scientists would study every word I say.

When they arrested me on October 27, I was living in a country ruled by the most conservative Communist government in Europe, and our society slumbered beneath the pall of a totalitarian system. Today, less than four months later, I am speaking to you as the representative of a country that has set out on the road to democracy, a country where there is complete freedom of speech, which is getting ready for free elections, and which wants to create a prosperous market economy and its own foreign policy.

It is all very strange indeed.

But I have not come here to speak of myself or my feelings, or merely to talk about my own country. I have used this small example of something I know well, to illustrate something general and important.

We are living in very odd times. The human face of the world is changing so rapidly that none of the familiar political speedometers are adequate.

We playwrights, who have to cram a whole human life or an entire historical era into a two-hour play, can scarcely understand this rapidity ourselves. And if it gives us trouble, think of the trouble it must give to political scientists, who spend their whole lives studying the realm of the probable.

Let me try to explain why I think the velocity of the changes in my country, in Central and Eastern Europe, and of course in the Soviet Union itself, has made such a significant impression on the face of the world today, and why it concerns the fate of us all, including you Americans. I would like to look at this, first from the political point of view, and then from a point of view that we might call philosophical.

Twice in this century, the world has been threatened by a catastrophe; twice this catastrophe was born in Europe, and twice you Americans, along with others, were called upon to save Europe, the whole world and yourselves. The first rescue mission—among other things—provided significant help to us Czechs and Slovaks.

Thanks to the great support of your President Wilson, our first president, Tomás Garrigue Masaryk, could found our modern independent state. He founded it, as you know, on the same principles on which the United States of America had been founded, as Masaryk's manuscripts held by the Library of Congress testify.

At the same time, the United States was making enormous strides. It became the most powerful nation on earth, and it understood the responsibility that flowed from this. Proof of this are the hundreds of thousands of your young citizens who gave their lives for the liberation of Europe, and the graves of American airmen and soldiers on Czechoslovak soil.

But something else was happening as well: the Soviet Union appeared, grew, and transformed the enormous sacrifices of its people suffering under totalitarian rule into a strength that, after World War Two, made it the second most powerful nation in the world. It was a country that nightly gave people nightmares, because no one knew what would occur to its rulers next and what country they would decide to conquer and drag into their sphere of influence, as it is called in political language.

All of this taught us to see the world in bipolar terms, as two enormous forces, one a defender of freedom, the other a source of nightmares. Europe became the point of friction between these two powers and thus it turned into a single enormous arsenal divided into two parts. In this process, one half of the arsenal became part of that nightmarish power, while the other—the free part—bordering on the ocean and having no wish to be driven into it, was compelled, together with you, to build a complicated security system, to which we probably owe the fact that we still exist.

So you may have contributed to the salvation of us Europeans, of the world and thus of yourselves for a third time: you have helped us to survive until today—without a hot war this time—but merely a cold one.

And now what is happening is happening: the totalitarian system in the Soviet Union and in most of its satellites is breaking down and our nations are looking for a way to democracy and independence. The first act in this remarkable drama began when Mr. Gorbachev and those around him, faced with the sad reality of their country, initiated their policy of *perestroika*. Obviously they had no idea either what they were setting in motion or how rapidly events would unfold. We knew a lot about the enormous number of growing problems that slumbered beneath the honeyed, unchanging mask of socialism. But I don't think any of us knew how little it would take for these problems to manifest themselves in all their enormity, and for the longings of these nations to emerge in all their strength. The mask fell away so rapidly that, in the flood of work, we have literally no time even to be astonished.

What does all this mean for the world in the long run? Obviously a number of things. This is, I am firmly convinced, an historically irreversible process, and as a result Europe will begin again to seek its own identity without being compelled to be a divided armory any longer. Perhaps this will create the hope that sooner or later your boys will no longer have to stand on guard for freedom in Europe, or come to our rescue, because Europe will at last be able to stand guard over itself. But that is still not the most important thing: the main thing is, it seems to me, that these revolutionary changes will enable us to escape from the rather antiquated straitjacket of this bipolar view of the world, and to enter at last into an era of multipolarity. That is, into an era in which all of us—large and small, former slaves and former masters—will be able to create what your great President Lincoln called "the family of man." Can you imagine what a relief this would be to that part of the world which for some reason is called the Third World, even though it is the largest?

I don't think it's appropriate simply to generalize, so let me be specific:

1) As you certainly know, most of the big wars and other conflagrations over the centuries have traditionally begun and ended on the territory of modern Czechoslovakia, or else they are somehow related to that area. Let the Second World War stand as the most recent example. This is understandable: whether we like it or not, we are located in the very heart of Europe, and thanks to this, we have no view of the sea, and no real navy. I mention this because political stability in our country has traditionally been important for the whole of Europe. This is still true today. Our government of national understanding, our present Federal Assembly, the other bodies of the state and I myself will personally guarantee this stability until we hold free elections, planned for June. We understand the terribly complex reasons, domestic political reasons above all, why the Soviet Union cannot withdraw its troops from our territory as quickly as they arrived in 1968. We understand that the arsenals built there over the past twenty years cannot be dismantled and removed overnight. Nevertheless, in our bilateral negotiations with the Soviet Union, we would like to have as many Soviet units as possible moved out of our country before the elections, in the interests of political stability. The more successful our negotiations, the more those who are elected in our places will be able to guarantee political stability in our country even after the elections.

2) I often hear the question: how can the United States of America help us today? My reply is as paradoxical as the whole of my life has been: you can help us most of all if you help the Soviet Union on its irreversible, but immensely complicated road to democracy. It is far more complicated than the road possible to its former European satellites. You yourselves know best how to support, as rapidly as possible, the non-violent evolution of this enormous, multi-national body politic towards democracy and autonomy for all of its peoples. Therefore, it is not fitting for me to offer you any advice. I can only say that the sooner, the more quickly, and the more peacefully the Soviet Union begins to move along the road towards genuine political pluralism,

respect for the rights of nations to their own integrity and to a work-ing—that is a market—economy, the better it will be, not just for Czechs and Slovaks, but for the whole world. And the sooner you yourselves will be able to reduce the burden of the military budget borne by the American people. To put it metaphorically: the millions you give to the East today will soon return to you in the form of billions in savings.

3) It is not true that the Czech writer Václav Havel wishes to dissolve the Warsaw Pact tomorrow and the NATO [North Atlantic Treaty Organization] the day after that, as some eager nationalists have written. Václav Havel merely thinks what he has already said here, that for another hundred years, American soldiers shouldn't have to be separated from their mothers just because Europe is incapable of being a guarantee of world peace, which it ought to be, in order to make some amends, at least, for having given the world two world wars. Sooner or later Europe must recover and come into its own, and decide for itself how many of whose soldiers it needs so that its own security, and all the wider implications of that security, may radiate peace into the whole world. Václav Havel cannot make decisions about things it is not proper for him to decide. He is merely putting in a good word for genuine peace, and for achieving it quickly.

4) Czechoslovakia thinks that the planned summit conference of countries participating in the Helsinki process should take place soon, and that in addition to what it wants to accomplish, it should aim to hold the so-called Helsinki Two conference earlier than 1992, as originally planned. Above all, we feel it could be something far more significant than has so far seemed possible. We think that Helsinki Two should become something equivalent to the European peace conference, which has not yet been held; one that would finally put a formal end to the Second World War and all its unhappy consequences. Such a conference would officially bring a future democratic Germany, in the process of unifying itself, into a new pan-European structure which could decide about its own security system. This system would naturally require some connection with that part of the glove we might label the "Helsinki" part, stretching westward from Vladivostock all the way to Alaska. The borders of the European states, which by the way should become gradually less important, should finally be legally guaranteed by a common, regular treaty. It should be more than obvious that the basis for such a treaty would have to be general respect for human rights, genuine political pluralism and genuinely free elections.

5) Naturally we welcome the initiative of President Bush, which was essentially accepted by Mr. Gorbachev as well, according to

which the number of American and Soviet troops in Europe should be radically reduced. It is a magnificent shot in the arm for the Vienna disarmament talks and creates favorable conditions not only for our own efforts to achieve the quickest possible departure of Soviet troops from Czechoslovakia, but indirectly as well for our own intention to make considerable cuts in the Czechoslovak army, which is disproportionately large in relation to our population. If Czechoslovakia were forced to defend itself against anyone, which we hope will not happen, then it will be capable of doing so with a considerably smaller army, because this time its defense would be—not only after decades but even centuries—supported by the common and indivisible will of both its nations and its leadership. Our freedom, independence and our new-born democracy have been purchased at great cost, and we will not surrender them. For the sake of order, I should add that whatever steps we take are not intended to complicate the Vienna disarmament talks, but on the contrary to facilitate them.

6) Czechoslovakia is returning to Europe. In the general interest and in its own interest as well, it wants to coordinate this return—both politically and economically—with the other returnees, which means, above all, with its neighbors the Poles and the Hungarians. We are doing what we can to coordinate these returns. And at the same time, we are doing what we can so that Europe will be capable of really accepting us, its wayward children. Which means that it may open itself to us, and may begin to transform its structures—which are formally European but de facto Western European—in that direction, but in such a way that it will not be to its detriment, but rather to its advantage.

7) I have already said this in our parliament, and I would like to repeat it here, in this Congress, which is architecturally far more attractive: for many years, Czechoslovakia—as someone's meaningless satellite—has refused to face up honestly to its co-responsibility for the world. It has a lot to make up for. If I dwell on this and so many important things here, it is only because I feel—along with my fellow citizens—a sense of culpability for our former responsible passivity, and a rather ordinary sense of indebtedness.

8) Last but not least, we are of course delighted that your country is so readily lending its support to our fresh efforts to renew democracy. Both our peoples were deeply moved by the generous offers made a few days ago in Prague at the Charles University, one of the oldest in Europe, by your Secretary of State, Mr. James Baker. We are ready to sit down and talk about them.

Ladies and gentlemen, I've only been president for two months and I haven't attended any schools for presidents. My only school was life itself. Therefore I don't want to burden you any longer with my political thoughts, but instead I will move on to an area that is more familiar to me, to what I would call the philosophical aspect of those changes that still concern everyone, although they are taking place in our corner of the world.

As long as people are people, democracy in the full sense of the word will always be no more than an ideal; one may approach it as one would a horizon, in ways that may be better or worse, but it can never be fully attained. In this sense you too are merely approaching democracy. You have thousands of problems of all kinds, as other countries do. But you have one great advantage: you have been approaching democracy uninterruptedly for more than two hundred years, and your journey towards that horizon has never been disrupted by a totalitarian system. Czechs and Slovaks, despite their humanistic traditions that go back to the first millenium, have approached democracy for a mere twenty years, between the two world wars, and now for the three and a half months since the seventeenth of November of last year.

The advantage that you have over us is obvious at once.

The communist type of totalitarian system has left both our nations, Czechs and Slovaks—as it has all the nations of the Soviet Union and the other countries the Soviet Union subjugated in its time—a legacy of countless dead, an infinite spectrum of human suffering, profound economic decline, and above all enormous human humiliation. It has brought us horrors that fortunately you have not known.

At the same time, however—unintentionally, of course—it has given us something positive: a special capacity to look, from time to time, somewhat further than someone who has not undergone this bitter experience. A person who cannot move and live a somewhat normal life because he is pinned under a boulder has more time to think about his hopes than someone who is not trapped in this way.

What I am trying to say is this: we must all learn many things from you, from how to educate our offspring, how to elect our representatives, all the way to how to organize our economic life so that it will lead to prosperity and not to poverty. But it doesn't have to be merely assistance from the well-educated, the powerful and the wealthy to someone who has nothing and therefore has nothing to offer in return.

We too can offer something to you: our experience and the knowledge that has come from it.

This is a subject for books, many of which have already been written and many of which have yet to be written. I shall therefore limit myself to a single idea.

The specific experience I'm talking about has given me one great certainty: consciousness precedes Being, and not the other way around, as the Marxists claim.

For this reason, the salvation of this human world lies nowhere else than in the human heart, in the human power to reflect, in human meekness and in human responsibility.

Without a global revolution in the sphere of human consciousness, nothing will change for the better in the sphere of our Being as humans, and the catastrophe towards which this world is headed, whether it be ecological, social, demographic or a general breakdown of civilization, will be unavoidable. If we are no longer threatened by world war, or by the danger that the absurd mountains of accumulated nuclear weapons might blow up the world, this does not mean that we have definitively won. We are in fact far from definitive victory.

We are still a long way from that "family of man"; in fact, we seem to be receding from the ideal rather than drawing closer to it. Interests of all kinds: personal, selfish, state, national, group and, if you like, company interests still considerably outweigh genuinely common and global interests. We are still under the sway of the destructive and vain belief that man is the pinnacle of creation, and not just a part of it, and that therefore everything is permitted. There are still many who say they are concerned not for themselves, but for the cause, while they are demonstrably out for themselves and not for the cause at all. We are still destroying the planet that was entrusted to us, and its environment. We still close our eyes to the growing social, ethnic and cultural conflicts in the world. From time to time we say that the anonymous megamachinery we have created for ourselves no longer serves us, but rather has enslaved us, yet we still fail to do anything about it.

In other words, we still don't know how to put morality ahead of politics, science and economics. We are still incapable of understanding that the only genuine backbone of all our actions—if they are to be moral—is responsibility. Responsibility to something higher than my family, my country, my firm, my success. Responsibility to the order of Being, where all our authority is indelibly recorded and where, and only where, they will be properly judged.

The interpreter or mediator between us and this higher authority is what is traditionally referred to as human conscience.

If I subordinate my political behavior to this imperative mediated to me by my conscience, I can't go far wrong. If on the contrary I were not guided by this voice, not even ten presidential schools with two thousand of the best political scientists in the world could help me.

This is why I ultimately decided—after resisting for a long time—to accept the burden of political responsibility.

I'm not the first, nor will I be the last, intellectual to do this. On the contrary, my feeling is that there will be more and more of them all the time. If the hope of the world lies in human consciousness, then it is obvious that intellectuals cannot go on forever avoiding their share of responsibility for the world and hiding their distaste for politics under an alleged need to be independent.

It is easy to have independence in your program and then leave others to carry that program out. If everyone thought that way pretty soon no one would be independent.

I think that you Americans should understand this way of thinking. Wasn't it the best minds of your country, people you could call intellectuals, who wrote your famous Declaration of Independence, your Bill of Human Rights and your Constitution and who—above all—took upon themselves the practical responsibility for putting them into practice? The worker from Branik in Prague that your President referred to in his State of the Union message this year is far from being the only person in Czechoslovakia, let alone in the world, to be inspired by those great documents. They inspire us all. They inspire us despite the fact that they are over two hundred years old. They inspire us to be citizens.

[*Speaking English*] When Thomas Jefferson wrote that "Governments are instituted among Men, deriving their just Powers from the Consent of the Governed," it was a simple and important act of the human spirit. What gave meaning to the act, however, was the fact that the author backed it up with his life. It was not just his words, it was his deeds as well.

I will end where I began: history has accelerated. I believe that once again, it will be the human mind that will notice this acceleration, give it a name, and transform those words into deeds.

Thank you.

MOTHER TERESA

National Prayer Breakfast Speech
(". . . the greatest destroyer of love and peace is abortion")
Washington, D.C.
February 3, 1994

Mother Teresa of Calcutta (1910–1997), born Agnesë Gonxhe Bojaxhiu in what was then Albania, took her vows as a nun when she was twenty. She won the 1971 Nobel Peace Prize for her decades of work with the poor in Calcutta and as creator of the order the Missionaries of Charity. In 1994, at the annual National Prayer Breakfast in Washington, with President Bill Clinton and other prominent politicians and religious leaders in attendance, Mother Teresa spoke out against abortion.

On the last day, Jesus will say to those at his right hand, "Come, enter the Kingdom. For I was hungry and you gave me food, I was thirsty and you gave me drink, I was sick and you visited me."

Then Jesus will turn to those on his left hand and say, "Depart from me because I was hungry and you did not feed me, I was thirsty and you did not give me drink, I was sick and you did not visit me."

These will ask him "When did we see you hungry, or thirsty, or sick, and did not come to your help?"

And Jesus will answer them, "Whatever you neglected to do unto the least of these you neglected to do unto me!"

Let us thank God for the opportunity He has given us today to have come here to pray together. We have come here especially to pray for peace, joy and love. We are reminded that Jesus came to bring the good news to the poor. He had told us what that good news was when he said, "My peace I leave with you, My peace I give unto you." He came not to give the peace of the world, which is only that we don't bother each other. He came to give peace of the heart which comes from loving, from doing good to others.

And God loved the world so much that he gave His Son. God gave His Son to the Virgin Mary, and what did she do with Him? As soon as Jesus came into Mary's life, immediately she went in haste to give that good news. And as she came into the house of her cousin, Elizabeth, Scripture tells us that the unborn child—the child in the womb of Elizabeth—leapt with joy.

While still in the womb of Mary, Jesus brought peace to John the Baptist, who leapt for joy in the womb of Elizabeth. And as if that were not enough—as if it were not enough that God the Son should become one of us and bring peace and joy while still in the womb—Jesus also died on the Cross to show that greater love.

He died for you and for me, and for that leper and for that man dying of hunger and that naked person lying in the street—not only of Calcutta, but of Africa, of everywhere. Our Sisters serve these people in 105 countries throughout the world. Jesus insisted that we love one another as He loves each one of us. Jesus gave His life to love us, and He tells us very clearly, "Love as I have loved you."

Jesus died on the Cross because that is what it took for Him to do good for us—to save us from our selfishness and sin. He gave up everything to do the Father's will, to show us that we, too, must be willing to give everything to do God's will, to love one another as He loves each of us.

St. John says you are a liar if you love God and you don't love your neighbor. How can you love God whom you do not see, if you do not love your neighbor whom you see, whom you touch, with whom you live?

Jesus makes Himself the hungry one, the naked one, the homeless one, the unwanted one, and He says, "You did it to me."

I can never forget the experience I had in visiting a home where they kept all these old parents of sons and daughters who had just put them into an institution and, maybe, forgotten them. I saw that in the home these old people had everything: good food, comfortable place, television—everything. But everyone was looking toward the door. And I did not see a single one with a smile on his face.

I turned to Sister and I asked, "Why do these people, who have every comfort here—why are they all looking toward the door? Why are they not smiling?" (I am so used to seeing the smiles on our people. Even the dying ones smile.) And Sister said, "This is the way it is, nearly every day. They are expecting that a son or daughter will come visit them."

See, this neglect to love brings spiritual poverty. Maybe in our family we have someone who is feeling lonely, who is feeling sick, who is feeling worried. Are we willing to give until it hurts, in order to be with our families? Or do we put our own interests first?

I was surprised in the West to see so many boys and girls given to drugs. And I tried to find out why. Why is it like that when those in the West have so many more things than those in the East? And the answer was: "Because there was no one in the family to receive them."

Our children depend on us for everything: their health, their nutrition, their security, their coming to know and love God. For all of this, they look to us with trust, hope and expectation. But often father and mother are so busy that they have no time for their children, or perhaps they are not even married, or have given up on their marriage. So the children go to the streets, and get involved in drugs, or other things.

We are talking of love of the child, which is where love and peace must begin.

But I feel that the greatest destroyer of peace today is abortion, because it is a war against the child—a direct killing of the innocent child—murder by the mother herself. And if we accept that a mother can kill her own child, how can we tell other people not to kill one another?

How do we persuade a woman not to have an abortion? As always, we must persuade her with love. The father of that child, whoever he is, must also give until it hurts. By abortion, the mother does not learn to love, but kills even her own child to solve her problems. And by abortion, the father is told that he does not have to take any responsibility at all for the child he has brought into the world.

Any country that accepts abortion is not teaching the people to love, but to use any violence to get what they want. That is why the greatest destroyer of love and peace is abortion.

And for this I appeal in India and I appeal everywhere: "Let us bring the child back." The child is God's gift to the family. Each child is created in the special image and likeness of God for greater things—to love and to be loved. This is the only way that our children are the only hope for the future. As other people are called to God, only their children can take their places.

But what does God say to us? He says, "Even if a mother could forget her child, I will not forget you. I have carved you in the palm of My hand." We are carved in the palm of His hand—that unborn child has been carved in the hand of God from conception, and is called by God to love and to be loved, not only now in this life, but forever. God can never forget us.

From our children's home in Calcutta alone, we have saved over three thousand children from abortion. These children have brought such love and joy to their adopting parents and have grown up so full of love and joy.

I know that couples have to plan their family and for that there is natural family planning. The way to plan the family is natural family planning, not contraception. In destroying the power of giving life, of loving; through contraception, a husband or wife is doing something to self. This turns the attention to self and so it destroys the gift of love in him or her. In loving, the husband and wife must turn the attention to each other as happens in natural family planning, and not to self, as happens in contraception. Once that living love is destroyed by contraception, abortion follows very easily.

That is why I never give a child to a family that has used contraception, because if the mother has destroyed the power of loving, how will she love my child? I also know there are great problems in the world, that many spouses do not love each other enough to practice natural family planning. We cannot solve the problems in the world, but let us never bring in the worst problem of all, to destroy love, to destroy life.

The poor are very great people. They can teach us so many beautiful things. Once one of them came to thank us for teaching her natural family planning and said: "You people who have practiced chastity, you are the best people to teach us natural family planning because it is nothing more than self-control out of love for each other." And what this poor person said is very true. These poor people maybe have nothing to eat, maybe they have not a home to live in, but they can still be great people when they are spiritually rich.

One evening, we went out and we picked up four people from the street. And one of them was in the most terrible condition. I told the Sisters: "You take care of the other three. I will take care of the one who looks worse." So I did for her all that my love can do. I put her in bed, and there was a beautiful smile on her face. She took hold of my hand, and she said one thing only: "Thank you." Then she died.

I could not help but examine my conscience before her. I asked, "What would I say if I were in her place?" And my answer was very simple. I would have tried to draw a little attention to myself. I would have said, "I am hungry, I am dying, I am cold, I am in pain," or something like that. But she gave me much more—she gave me her grateful love. And she died with a smile on her face.

Then there was a man we picked up from a drain, half eaten by worms. And after we had brought him to the home, he only said, "I have lived like an animal in the street, but I am going to die as an angel, loved and cared for." Then after we had removed all the worms from this body, all he said—with a big smile—was: "Sister, I am going home to God." And he died.

It was so wonderful to see the greatness of that man, who could speak like that without blaming anybody, without comparing anything. Like an angel—this is the greatness of people who are spiritually rich, even when they are materially poor.

And so here I am talking with you. I want you to find the poor here, right in your own home first. And begin love there. Bear the good news to your own people first. And find out about your next-door neighbors. Do you know who they are?

I had the most extraordinary experience of love of a neighbor from a Hindu family. A gentlemen came to our house and said, "Mother Teresa, there is a family who have not eaten for so long. Do something." So I took some rice and went there immediately. And I saw the children, their eyes shining with hunger. (I don't know if you have ever seen hunger, but I have seen it very often.) And the mother of the family took the rice I gave her.

"Where did you go? What did you do?" And she gave me a very simple answer: "They are hungry also." What struck me was that she knew. And who were "they"? A Muslim family. And she knew. I didn't bring any more rice that evening. I wanted them—Hindus and Muslims—to enjoy the joy of sharing.

Because I talk so much of giving with a smile, once a professor from the United States asked me, "Are you married?" And I said, "Yes, and I find it sometimes very difficult to smile at my spouse—Jesus—because He can be very demanding. Sometimes this is really something true. And there is where love comes in—when it is demanding, and yet we can give it with joy.

If we remember that God loves us, and that we can love others as He loves us, then America can become a sign of peace for the world. From here, a sign of care for the weakest of the weak—the unborn child—must go out to the world. If you become a burning light of justice and peace in the world, then really you will be true to what the founders of this country stood for. God bless you!

DAW AUNG SAN SUU KYI
Opening Keynote Address
("The people of my country want the two freedoms that
spell security: freedom from want and freedom from fear")
Fourth World Conference on Women
Huairou, China
August 31, 1995

*Aung San Suu Kyi (born 1945) has been periodically held under house arrest
in the repressive regime of Myanmar (formerly Burma) since 1990, when she
was elected prime minister. She was awarded the Nobel Peace Prize in 1991
for her political activism in her native country, and delivered this speech via
videotape to the United Nations-sponsored conference of women's interests
groups.*

It is a wonderful but daunting task that has fallen on me to say a few
words by way of opening this Forum, the greatest concourse of
women—joined by a few brave men—that has ever gathered on our
planet. I want to try and voice some of the common hopes which
firmly unite us in our splendid diversity.

But first I would like to explain why I cannot be with you in person today. Last month I was released from almost six years of house
arrest. The regaining of my freedom has in turn imposed a duty on
me to work for the freedom of women and men in my country who
have suffered far more—and who continue to suffer far more—than
I have. It is this duty which prevents me from joining you today.
Even sending this message to you has not been without difficulties.
But the help of those who believe in international cooperation and
freedom of expression has enabled me to overcome the obstacles.
They have made it possible for me to make a small contribution to
this great celebration of the struggle of women to mold their own
destiny and to influence the fate of our global village.

The opening plenary of this Forum will be presenting an overview
of the global forces affecting the quality of life of the human com-

munity and the challenges they pose for the global community as a whole and for women in particular as we approach the twenty-first century. However, with true womanly understanding, the convener of this forum suggested that among these global forces and challenges, I might wish to concentrate on those matters which occupy all my waking thoughts these days: peace, security, human rights and democracy. I would like to discuss these issues particularly in the context of the participation of women in politics and governance.

For millennia women have dedicated themselves almost exclusively to the task of nurturing, protecting and caring for the young and the old, striving for conditions of peace that favor life as a whole. To this can be added the fact that, to the best of my knowledge, no war was ever started by women. But it is women and children who have always suffered most in situations of conflict. Now that we are gaining control of the primary historical role imposed on us of sustaining life in the context of the home and family, it is time to apply in the arena of the world the wisdom and experience thus gained in activities of peace over so many thousands of years. The education and empowerment of women throughout the world cannot fail to result in a more caring, tolerant, just and peaceful life for all.

If to these universal benefits of the growing emancipation of women can be added the "peace dividend" for human development offered by the end of the Cold War, spending less on the war toys of grown men and much more on the urgent needs of humanity as a whole, then truly the next millennia will be an age the like of which has never been seen in human history. But there still remain many obstacles to be overcome before we can achieve this goal. And not least among those obstacles are intolerance and insecurity.

This year is the International Year for Tolerance. The United Nations has recognized that "tolerance, human rights, democracy and peace are closely related. Without tolerance, the foundations that form democracy and respect for human rights cannot be strengthened, and the achievement of peace will remain elusive." My own experience during the years I have been engaged in the democracy movement of Burma has convinced me of the need to emphasize the positive aspect of tolerance. It is not enough simply to "live and let live": genuine tolerance requires an active effort to try to understand the point of view of others; it implies broad-mindedness and vision, as well as confidence in one's own ability to meet new challenges without resorting to intransigence or violence. In societies where men are truly confident, women are not merely tolerated, they are valued. Their opinions are listened to with respect; they are given their rightful place in shaping the society in which they live.

There is an outmoded Burmese proverb still recited by men who wish to deny that women too can play a part in bringing necessary change and progress to their society: "The dawn rises only when the rooster crows." But Burmese people today are well aware of the scientific reasons behind the rising of dawn and the falling of dusk. And the intelligent rooster surely realizes that it is because dawn comes that it crows and not the other way 'round. It crows to welcome the light that has come to relieve the darkness of night. It is not the prerogative of men alone to bring light to this world: women with their capacity for compassion and self-sacrifice, their courage and perseverance, have done much to dissipate the darkness of intolerance and hate, suffering and despair.

Often the other side of the coin of intolerance is insecurity. Insecure people tend to be intolerant, and their intolerance unleashes forces that threaten the security of others. And where there is no security there can be no lasting peace. In its "Human Development Report" for this year the UNDP noted that human security "is not a concern with weapons—it is a concern with human life and dignity." The struggle for democracy and human rights in Burma is a struggle for life and dignity. It is a struggle that encompasses our political, social and economic aspirations. The people of my country want the two freedoms that spell security: freedom from want and freedom from fear. It is want that has driven so many of our young girls across our borders to a life of sexual slavery where they are subject to constant humiliation and ill-treatment. It is fear of persecution for their political beliefs that has made so many of our people feel that even in their own homes they cannot live in dignity and security.

Traditionally the home is the domain of the woman. But there has never been a guarantee that she can live our her life there safe and unmolested. There are countless women who are subjected to severe cruelty within the heart of the family which should be their haven. And in time of crisis when their menfolk are unable to give them protection, women have to face the harsh challenges of the world outside while continuing to discharge their duties within the home.

Many of my male colleagues who have suffered imprisonment for their part in the democracy movement have spoken of the great debt of gratitude they owe to their womenfolk, particularly to their wives who stood by them firmly, tender as mothers nursing their newly born, brave as lionesses defending their young. These magnificent human beings who have done so much to aid their men in the struggle for peace and justice—how much more could they not achieve if given the opportunity to work in their own right for the good of their country and of the world?

Our endeavors have also been sustained by the activities of strong and principled women all over the world who have campaigned not only for my release but, more importantly, for our cause. I cannot let this opportunity pass without speaking of the gratitude we feel towards our sisters everywhere, from heads of government to busy housewives. Their efforts have been a triumphant demonstration of female solidarity and of the power of an ideal to cross all frontiers.

In my country at present, women have no participation in the higher levels of government and none whatsoever in the judiciary. Even within the democratic movement only fourteen out of the 485 MPs elected in 1990 were women—all from my own party, the National League for Democracy. These fourteen women represent less than three percent of the total number of successful candidates. They, like their male colleagues, have not been permitted to take office since the outcome of those elections has been totally ignored. Yet the very high performance of women in our educational system and in the management of commercial enterprises proves their enormous potential to contribute to the betterment of society in general. Meanwhile our women have yet to achieve those fundamental rights of free expression, association and security of life denied also to their menfolk.

The adversities that we have had to face together have taught all of us involved in the struggle to build a truly democratic political system in Burma that there are no gender barriers that cannot be overcome. The relationship between men and women should, and can be, characterized not by patronizing behavior or exploitation, but by metta (that is to say loving kindness), partnership and trust. We need mutual respect and understanding between men and women, instead of patriarchal domination and degradation, which are expressions of violence and engender counter-violence. We can learn from each other and help one another to moderate the "gender weaknesses" imposed on us by traditional or biological factors.

There is an age-old prejudice the world over to the effect that women talk too much. But is this really a weakness? Could it not in fact be a strength? Recent scientific research on the human brain has revealed that women are better at verbal skills while men tend towards physical action. Psychological research has shown on the other hand that disinformation engendered by men has a far more damaging effect on its victims than feminine gossip. Surely these discoveries indicate that women have a most valuable contribution to make in situations of conflict, by leading the way to solutions based on dialogue rather than on viciousness and violence.

The Buddhist *Pavarana* ceremony at the end of the rainy season retreat was instituted by the Lord Buddha, who did not want human beings to live in silence, I quote, "like dumb animals." This ceremony, during which monks ask mutual forgiveness for any offense given during the retreat, can be said to be a council of truth and reconciliation. It might also be considered a forerunner of that most democratic of institutions, the parliament, a meeting of peoples gathered together to talk over their shared problems. All the world's great religions are dedicated to the generation of happiness and harmony. This demonstrates the fact that together with the combative instincts of man there exists a spiritual aspiration for mutual understanding and peace.

This forum of non-governmental organizations represents the belief in the ability of intelligent human beings to resolve conflicting interests through exchange and dialogue. It also represents the conviction that governments alone cannot resolve all the problems of their countries. The watchfulness and active cooperation of organizations outside the spheres of officialdom are necessary to ensure the four essential components of the human development paradigm as identified by the UNDP: productivity, equity, sustainability and empowerment. The last is particularly relevant: it requires that "development must be by people, not only for them. People must participate fully in the decisions and processes that shape their lives." In other words people must be allowed to play a significant role in the governance of their country. And "people" include women, who make up at least half the population of the world.

The last six years afforded me much time and food for thought. I came to the conclusion that the human race is not divided into two opposing camps of good and evil. It is made up of those who are capable of learning and those who are incapable of doing so. Here I am not talking of learning in the narrow sense of acquiring an academic education, but of learning as the process of absorbing those lessons of life that enable us to increase peace and happiness in our world. Women in their role as mothers have traditionally assumed the responsibility of teaching children values that will guide them throughout their lives. It is time we were given the full opportunity to use our natural teaching skills to contribute towards building a modern world that can withstand the tremendous challenges of the technological revolution which has in turn brought revolutionary changes in social values.

As we strive to teach others, we must have the humility to acknowledge that we too still have much to learn. And we must have the flexibility to adapt to the changing needs of the world around us. Women who have been taught that modesty and pliancy are among the prized virtues of our gender are marvelously equipped for the learning process. But they must be given the opportunity to turn these often merely passive virtues into positive assets for the society in which they live.

These, then, are our common hopes that unite us—that as the shackles of prejudice and intolerance fall from our own limbs we can together strive to identify and remove the impediments to human development everywhere. The mechanisms by which this great task is to be achieved provide the proper focus of this forum. I feel sure that women throughout the world who, like me, cannot be with you join me now in sending you all our prayers and good wishes for a joyful and productive meeting.

I thank you.

BENAZIR BHUTTO
Male Domination of Women
("The ethos of Islam is equality,
equality between the sexes")
Fourth World Conference on Women
Beijing, China
September 4, 1995

At the same conference to which San Suu Kyi spoke (see page 212), the prime minister of Pakistan, Benazir Bhutto (1953–2007), addressed issues of Islam and women. Bhutto was the first and only woman ever elected prime minister in Pakistan, serving in that position twice. After returning to Pakistan from exile, she became the leading candidate for prime minister again but was assassinated in late 2007.

As the first woman ever elected to head an Islamic nation, I feel a special responsibility about issues that relate to women. In addressing the new exigencies of the new century, we must translate dynamic religion into a living reality. We must live by the true spirit of Islam, not only by its rituals. And for those of you who may be ignorant of Islam, cast aside your preconceptions about the role of women in our religion.

Contrary to what many of you may have come to believe, Islam embraces a rich variety of political, social and cultural traditions. The fundamental ethos of Islam is tolerance, dialogue, and democracy.

Just as in Christianity and Judaism, we must always be on guard for those who will exploit and manipulate the Holy Book for their own narrow political ends, who will distort the essence of pluralism and tolerance for their own extremist agendas.

To those who claim to speak for Islam but who would deny to women our place in society, I say:

The ethos of Islam is equality, equality between the sexes. There is no religion on earth that, in its writing and teachings, is more respectful of the role of women in society than Islam.

218

My presence here, as the elected woman prime minister of a great Muslim country, is testament to the commitment of Islam to the role of women in society.

It is this tradition of Islam that has empowered me, has strengthened me, has emboldened me.

It was this heritage that sustained me during the most difficult points in my life, for Islam forbids injustice; injustice against people, against nations, against women.

It denounces inequality as the gravest form of injustice.

It enjoins its followers to combat oppression and tyranny.

It enshrines piety as the sole criteria for judging humankind.

It shuns race, colour, and gender as a basis of distinction amongst fellowmen.

When the human spirit was immersed in the darkness of the Middle Ages, Islam proclaimed equality between men and women. When women were viewed as inferior members of the human family, Islam gave them respect and dignity.

When women were treated as chattels, the Prophet of Islam (Peace Be Upon Him) accepted them as equal partners.

Islam codified the rights of women. The Koran elected their status to that of men. It guaranteed their civic, economic, and political rights. It recognized their participative role in nation building.

Sadly, the Islamic tenets regarding women were soon discarded. In Islamic society, as in other parts of the world, their rights were denied. Women were maltreated, discriminated against, and subjected to violence and oppression, their dignity injured and their role denied.

Women became the victims of a culture of exclusion and male dominance. Today more women than men suffer from poverty, deprivation, and discrimination. Half a billion women are illiterate. Seventy percent of the children who are denied elementary education are girls.

The plight of women in the developing countries is unspeakable. Hunger, disease, and unremitting toil is their fate. Weak economic growth and inadequate social support systems affect them most seriously and directly.

They are the primary victims of structural adjustment processes which necessitate reduced state funding for health, education, medical care, and nutrition. Curtailed resource flows to these vital areas impact most severely on the vulnerable groups, particularly women and children.

This, Madam Chairperson, is not acceptable. It offends my religion. It offends my sense of justice and equity. Above all, it offends common sense.

That is why Pakistan, the women of Pakistan, and I personally have been fully engaged in recent international efforts to uphold women's rights. The Universal Declaration of Human Rights enjoins the elimination of discrimination against women.

The Nairobi Forward Looking Strategies provide a solid framework for advancing women's rights around the world. But the goal of equality, development, and peace still eludes us. Sporadic efforts in this direction have failed. We are satisfied that the Beijing Platform of Action encompasses a comprehensive approach toward the empowerment of women. This is the right approach and should be fully supported.

Women cannot be expected to struggle alone against the forces of discrimination and exploitation. I recall the words of Dante, who reminded us that "The hottest place in Hell is reserved for those who remain neutral in times of moral crisis."

Today in this world, in the fight for the liberation of women, there can be no neutrality.

My spirit carries many a scar of a long and lonely battle against dictatorship and tyranny. I witnessed, at a young age, the overthrow of democracy, the assassination of an elected prime minister, and a systematic assault against the very foundations of a free society.

But our faith in democracy was not broken. The great Pakistani poet and philosopher Dr. Allama Iqbal says, "Tyranny cannot endure forever." It did not. The will of our people prevailed against the forces of dictatorship.

But, my dear sisters, we have learned that democracy alone is not enough.

Freedom of choice alone does not guarantee justice.

Equal rights are not defined only by political values.

Social justice is a triad of freedom, an equation of liberty: Justice is political liberty. Justice is economic independence. Justice is social equality.

Delegates, sisters, the child who is starving has no human rights.

The girl who is illiterate has no future.

The woman who cannot plan her life, plan her family, plan a career, is fundamentally not free. . . . I am determined to change the plight of women in my country. More than sixty million of our women are largely sidelined.

It is a personal tragedy for them. It is a national catastrophe for my nation. I am determined to harness their potential to the gigantic task of nation building. . . . I dream of a Pakistan in which women contribute to their full potential. I am conscious of the struggle that lies ahead. But, with your help, we shall persevere. Allah willing, we shall succeed.

ELIE WIESEL
The Perils of Indifference
(". . . indifference is always the friend of the enemy,
for it benefits the aggressor")
Washington, D.C.
April 12, 1999

*Born in 1928 in Romania, the Nobel Peace Prize winner is a prolific author.
In* Night, *he wrote about his and his family's experiences at Auschwitz, the
Nazi concentration camp. A United States citizen since 1955, Wiesel has
taught at universities and lectured on the Holocaust. At the invitation of First
Lady Hillary Clinton, Wiesel spoke at the Millennium Lecture Series at the
White House.*

Mr. President, Mrs. Clinton, members of Congress, Ambassador Hol-
brooke, Excellencies, friends:

Fifty-four years ago to the day, a young Jewish boy from a small
town in the Carpathian Mountains woke up, not far from Goethe's
beloved Weimar, in a place of eternal infamy called Buchenwald. He
was finally free, but there was no joy in his heart. He thought there
never would be again.

Liberated a day earlier by American soldiers, he remembers their
rage at what they saw. And even if he lives to be a very old man, he
will always be grateful to them for that rage, and also for their compassion. Though he did not understand their language, their eyes told
him what he needed to know—that they, too, would remember, and
bear witness.

And now, I stand before you, Mr. President—Commander-in-
Chief of the army that freed me, and tens of thousands of others—and
I am filled with a profound and abiding gratitude to the American
people.

Gratitude is a word that I cherish. Gratitude is what defines the
humanity of the human being. And I am grateful to you, Hillary—or
Mrs. Clinton—for what you said, and for what you are doing for

children in the world, for the homeless, for the victims of injustice, the victims of destiny and society. And I thank all of you for being here.

We are on the threshold of a new century, a new millennium. What will the legacy of this vanishing century be? How will it be remembered in the new millennium? Surely it will be judged, and judged severely, in both moral and metaphysical terms. These failures have cast a dark shadow over humanity: two World Wars, countless civil wars, the senseless chain of assassinations—Gandhi, the Kennedys, Martin Luther King, Sadat, Rabin—bloodbaths in Cambodia and Nigeria, India and Pakistan, Ireland and Rwanda, Eritrea and Ethiopia, Sarajevo and Kosovo; the inhumanity in the gulag and the tragedy of Hiroshima. And, on a different level, of course, Auschwitz and Treblinka. So much violence, so much indifference.

What is indifference? Etymologically, the word means "no difference." A strange and unnatural state in which the lines blur between light and darkness, dusk and dawn, crime and punishment, cruelty and compassion, good and evil.

What are its courses and inescapable consequences? Is it a philosophy? Is there a philosophy of indifference conceivable? Can one possibly view indifference as a virtue? Is it necessary at times to practice it simply to keep one's sanity, live normally, enjoy a fine meal and a glass of wine, as the world around us experiences harrowing upheavals?

Of course, indifference can be tempting—more than that, seductive. It is so much easier to look away from victims. It is so much easier to avoid such rude interruptions to our work, our dreams, our hopes. It is, after all, awkward, troublesome, to be involved in another person's pain and despair. Yet, for the person who is indifferent, his or her neighbors are of no consequence. And, therefore, their lives are meaningless. Their hidden or even visible anguish is of no interest. Indifference reduces the other to an abstraction.

Over there, behind the black gates of Auschwitz, the most tragic of all prisoners were the "Muselmanner," as they were called. Wrapped in their torn blankets, they would sit or lie on the ground, staring vacantly into space, unaware of who or where they were, strangers to their surroundings. They no longer felt pain, hunger, thirst. They feared nothing. They felt nothing. They were dead and did not know it.

Rooted in our tradition, some of us felt that to be abandoned by humanity then was not the ultimate. We felt that to be abandoned by God was worse than to be punished by Him. Better an unjust God than an indifferent one. For us to be ignored by God was a harsher punishment than to be a victim of His anger. Man can live far from God—not outside God. God is wherever we are. Even in suffering? Even in suffering.

In a way, to be indifferent to that suffering is what makes the human being inhuman. Indifference, after all, is more dangerous than anger and hatred. Anger can at times be creative. One writes a great poem, a great symphony, one does something special for the sake of humanity because one is angry at the injustice that one witnesses. But indifference is never creative. Even hatred at times may elicit a response. You fight it. You denounce it. You disarm it. Indifference elicits no response. Indifference is not a response.

Indifference is not a beginning, it is an end. And, therefore, indifference is always the friend of the enemy, for it benefits the aggressor—never his victim, whose pain is magnified when he or she feels forgotten. The political prisoner in his cell, the hungry children, the homeless refugees—not to respond to their plight, not to relieve their solitude by offering them a spark of hope is to exile them from human memory. And in denying their humanity we betray our own.

Indifference, then, is not only a sin, it is a punishment. And this is one of the most important lessons of this outgoing century's wide-ranging experiments in good and evil.

In the place that I come from, society was composed of three simple categories: the killers, the victims, and the bystanders. During the darkest of times, inside the ghettoes and death camps—and I'm glad that Mrs. Clinton mentioned that we are now commemorating that event, that period, that we are now in the Days of Remembrance—but then, we felt abandoned, forgotten. All of us did.

And our only miserable consolation was that we believed that Auschwitz and Treblinka were closely guarded secrets; that the leaders of the free world did not know what was going on behind those black gates and barbed wire; that they had no knowledge of the war against the Jews that Hitler's armies and their accomplices waged as part of the war against the Allies.

If they knew, we thought, surely those leaders would have moved heaven and earth to intervene. They would have spoken out with great outrage and conviction. They would have bombed the railways leading to Birkenau, just the railways, just once.

And now we knew, we learned, we discovered that the Pentagon knew, the State Department knew. And the illustrious occupant of the White House then, who was a great leader—and I say it with some anguish and pain, because, today is exactly 54 years marking his death—Franklin Delano Roosevelt died on April the 12th, 1945, so he is very much present to me and to us.

No doubt, he was a great leader. He mobilized the American people and the world, going into battle, bringing hundreds and thousands of valiant and brave soldiers in America to fight fascism, to fight dictatorship, to fight Hitler. And so many of the young people fell in battle. And, nevertheless, his image in Jewish history—I must say it—his image in Jewish history is flawed.

The depressing tale of the *St. Louis* is a case in point. Sixty years ago, its human cargo—maybe 1,000 Jews—was turned back to Nazi Germany. And that happened after the Kristallnacht, after the first state-sponsored pogrom, with hundreds of Jewish shops destroyed, synagogues burned, thousands of people put in concentration camps. And that ship, which was already on the shores of the United States, was sent back.

I don't understand. Roosevelt was a good man, with a heart. He understood those who needed help. Why didn't he allow these refugees to disembark? A thousand people—in America, a great country, the greatest democracy, the most generous of all new nations in modern history. What happened? I don't understand. Why the indifference, on the highest level, to the suffering of the victims?

But then, there were human beings who were sensitive to our tragedy. Those non-Jews, those Christians, that we called the "Righteous Gentiles," whose selfless acts of heroism saved the honor of their faith. Why were they so few? Why was there a greater effort to save SS murderers after the war than to save their victims during the war?

Why did some of America's largest corporations continue to do business with Hitler's Germany until 1942? It has been suggested, and it was documented, that the Wehrmacht could not have conducted its invasion of France without oil obtained from American sources. How is one to explain their indifference?

And yet, my friends, good things have also happened in this traumatic century: the defeat of Nazism, the collapse of communism, the rebirth of Israel on its ancestral soil, the demise of apartheid, Israel's peace treaty with Egypt, the peace accord in Ireland. And let us remember the meeting, filled with drama and emotion, between Rabin and Arafat that you, Mr. President, convened in this very place. I was here and I will never forget it.

And then, of course, the joint decision of the United States and NATO to intervene in Kosovo and save those victims, those refugees, those who were uprooted by a man whom I believe that because of his crimes, should be charged with crimes against humanity. But this time, the world was not silent. This time, we do respond. This time, we intervene.

Does it mean that we have learned from the past? Does it mean that society has changed? Has the human being become less indifferent and more human? Have we really learned from our experiences? Are we less insensitive to the plight of victims of ethnic cleansing and other forms of injustices in places near and far? Is today's justified intervention in Kosovo, led by you, Mr. President, a lasting warning that never again will the deportation, the terrorization of children and their parents be allowed anywhere in the world? Will it discourage other dictators in other lands to do the same?

What about the children? Oh, we see them on television, we read about them in the papers, and we do so with a broken heart. Their fate is always the most tragic, inevitably. When adults wage war, children perish. We see their faces, their eyes. Do we hear their pleas? Do we feel their pain, their agony? Every minute one of them dies of disease, violence, famine. Some of them—so many of them—could be saved.

And so, once again, I think of the young Jewish boy from the Carpathian Mountains. He has accompanied the old man I have become throughout these years of quest and struggle. And together we walk towards the new millennium, carried by profound fear and extraordinary hope.

APPENDIX
GREAT SPEECHES OF THE 21ST CENTURY

RUDOLPH GIULIANI
9/11
("... the City of New York and the United States
of America is much stronger than any
group of barbaric terrorists")
New York City
September 11, 2001

*On September 11, 2001, a coordinated plot by the terrorist group Al-Qaeda
destroyed the World Trade Center in downtown New York City and attacked
the Pentagon in Washington, D.C.; a fourth aircraft, headed toward the nation's capital, crashed near Shanksville, Pennsylvania. The mayor of New
York City, Rudolph Giuliani (born in 1944), addressed his city and country
that day.*

The tragedy that we're all undergoing right now is something that
we've had nightmares about, probably thought wouldn't happen. My
heart goes out to all of the innocent victims of this horrible and vicious act of terrorism, acts of terrorism. And our focus now has to be
on saving as many lives as possible. We have hundreds of police officers and fire fighters who are engaging in rescue efforts in lower
Manhattan. I want to thank Governor Pataki for the incredible cooperation and coordination, including deploying the National Guard
that will be available to relieve our police officers and fire fighters and
emergency workers in the next couple of hours.

The governor and I just spoke to the President of the United
States. The coordination with the federal government from the time
of the first attack has been excellent, including closing off the air space
around Manhattan and doing everything that can possibly be done in
the face of this barbaric act to make the city secure.

And we will strive now very hard to save as many people as possible and to send a message that the City of New York and the United States of America is much stronger than any group of barbaric terrorists, that our democracy, that our rule of law, that our strength and our willingness to defend ourselves will ultimately prevail.

And I'd ask the people of New York City to do everything that they can to cooperate, not to be frightened, to go about their lives as normal. Everything is safe right now in the city. And the people who are doing the relief effort need all of the help they can get.

And then governor, thank you very, very much for your assistance and your help and your support. Thank you.

BARACK OBAMA
Presidential Election-Night Speech
(". . . the true strength of our nation comes not from the
might of our arms or the scale of our wealth, but from the
enduring power of our ideals: democracy, liberty,
opportunity and unyielding hope")
Chicago, Illinois
November 5, 2008

*The 2008 presidential election ended, on November 4, with the Democratic
senator of Illinois, Barack Obama (born 1961), defeating Republican John
McCain, senator from Arizona. Obama's father, from Kenya, and mother,
from Kansas, did not live to see their son become the first African-American
president. Just after midnight, Obama made his acceptance speech to a jubilant
crowd.*

Hello, Chicago. (Applause)

If there is anyone out there who still doubts that America is a place
where all things are possible, who still wonders if the dream of our
founders is alive in our time, who still questions the power of our
democracy, tonight is your answer. (Applause)

It's the answer told by lines that stretched around schools and
churches in numbers this nation has never seen, by people who
waited three hours and four hours, many for the first time in their
lives, because they believed that this time must be different, that their
voices could be that difference.

It's the answer spoken by young and old, rich and poor, Democrat
and Republican, black, white, Hispanic, Asian, Native American,
gay, straight, disabled and not disabled. Americans who sent a message
to the world that we have never been just a collection of individuals
or a collection of red states and blue states.

We are, and always will be, the United States of America. (Applause)

It's the answer that led those who've been told for so long by so
many to be cynical and fearful and doubtful about what we can

achieve to put their hands on the arc of history and bend it once more toward the hope of a better day.

It's been a long time coming, but tonight, because of what we did on this date in this election at this defining moment change has come to America. (Applause)

It's the answer that led those who've been told for so long by so many to be cynical and fearful and doubtful about what we can achieve to put their hands on the arc of history and bend it once more toward the hope of a better day.

It's been a long time coming, but tonight, because of what we did on this date in this election at this defining moment change has come to America. (Applause)

A little bit earlier this evening, I received an extraordinarily gracious call from Senator McCain. (Applause)

Senator McCain fought long and hard in this campaign. And he's fought even longer and harder for the country that he loves. He has endured sacrifices for America that most of us cannot begin to imagine. We are better off for the service rendered by this brave and selfless leader.

I congratulate him; I congratulate Governor Palin for all that they've achieved. And I look forward to working with them to renew this nation's promise in the months ahead. (Applause)

I want to thank my partner in this journey, a man who campaigned from his heart, and spoke for the men and women he grew up with on the streets of Scranton . . . (Applause) . . . and rode with on the train home to Delaware, the vice president-elect of the United States, Joe Biden. (Applause)

And I would not be standing here tonight without the unyielding support of my best friend for the last sixteen years . . . (Applause) . . . the rock of our family, the love of my life, the nation's next first lady . . . (Applause) . . . Michelle Obama. (Applause) Sasha and Malia . . . (Applause) . . . I love you both more than you can imagine. And you have earned the new puppy that's coming with us . . . (Laughter) . . . to the new White House. (Applause)

And while she's no longer with us, I know my grandmother's watching, along with the family that made me who I am. I miss them tonight. I know that my debt to them is beyond measure.

To my sister Maya, my sister Alma, all my other brothers and sisters, thank you so much for all the support that you've given me. I am grateful to them. (Applause) And to my campaign manager, David Plouffe . . . (Applause) the unsung hero of this campaign, who built the best—the best political campaign, I think, in the history of the United States of America. (Applause)

To my chief strategist David Axelrod . . . (Applause) . . . who's been a partner with me every step of the way. To the best campaign team ever assembled in the history of politics . . . (Applause) . . . you made this happen, and I am forever grateful for what you've sacrificed to get it done.

But above all, I will never forget who this victory truly belongs to. It belongs to you. It belongs to you.

I was never the likeliest candidate for this office. We didn't start with much money or many endorsements. Our campaign was not hatched in the halls of Washington. It began in the backyards of Des Moines and the living rooms of Concord and the front porches of Charleston. It was built by working men and women who dug into what little savings they had to give $5 and $10 and $20 to the cause.

It grew strength from the young people who rejected the myth of their generation's apathy . . . (Applause) . . . who left their homes and their families for jobs that offered little pay and less sleep.

It drew strength from the not-so-young people who braved the bitter cold and scorching heat to knock on doors of perfect strangers, and from the millions of Americans who volunteered and organized and proved that more than two centuries later a government of the people, by the people, and for the people has not perished from the Earth.

This is your victory. (Applause)

And I know you didn't do this just to win an election. And I know you didn't do it for me.

You did it because you understand the enormity of the task that lies ahead. For even as we celebrate tonight, we know the challenges that tomorrow will bring are the greatest of our lifetime—two wars, a planet in peril, the worst financial crisis in a century.

Even as we stand here tonight, we know there are brave Americans waking up in the deserts of Iraq and the mountains of Afghanistan to risk their lives for us.

There are mothers and fathers who will lie awake after the children fall asleep and wonder how they'll make the mortgage or pay their doctors' bills or save enough for their child's college education.

There's new energy to harness, new jobs to be created, new schools to build, and threats to meet, alliances to repair.

The road ahead will be long. Our climb will be steep. We may not get there in one year or even in one term. But, America, I have never been more hopeful than I am tonight that we will get there.

I promise you, we as a people will get there. (Applause)

AUDIENCE: Yes we can! Yes we can! Yes we can!

OBAMA: There will be setbacks and false starts. There are many who won't agree with every decision or policy I make as president. And we know the government can't solve every problem.

But I will always be honest with you about the challenges we face. I will listen to you, especially when we disagree. And, above all, I will ask you to join in the work of remaking this nation, the only way it's been done in America for 221 years—block by block, brick by brick, calloused hand by calloused hand.

What began 21 months ago in the depths of winter cannot end on this autumn night.

This victory alone is not the change we seek. It is only the chance for us to make that change. And that cannot happen if we go back to the way things were.

It can't happen without you, without a new spirit of service, a new spirit of sacrifice.

So let us summon a new spirit of patriotism, of responsibility, where each of us resolves to pitch in and work harder and look after not only ourselves but each other.

Let us remember that, if this financial crisis taught us anything, it's that we cannot have a thriving Wall Street while Main Street suffers.

In this country, we rise or fall as one nation, as one people. Let's resist the temptation to fall back on the same partisanship and pettiness and immaturity that has poisoned our politics for so long.

Let's remember that it was a man from this state who first carried the banner of the Republican Party to the White House, a party founded on the values of self-reliance and individual liberty and national unity.

Those are values that we all share. And while the Democratic Party has won a great victory tonight, we do so with a measure of humility and determination to heal the divides that have held back our progress. (Applause)

As Lincoln said to a nation far more divided than ours, we are not enemies but friends. Though passion may have strained, it must not break our bonds of affection.

And to those Americans whose support I have yet to earn, I may not have won your vote tonight, but I hear your voices. I need your help. And I will be your president, too. (Applause)

And to all those watching tonight from beyond our shores, from parliaments and palaces, to those who are huddled around radios in the forgotten corners of the world, our stories are singular, but our destiny is shared, and a new dawn of American leadership is at hand. (Applause)

To those—to those who would tear the world down: We will defeat you. To those who seek peace and security: We support you. And to all those who have wondered if America's beacon still burns as bright: Tonight we proved once more that the true strength of our nation comes not from the might of our arms or the scale of our wealth, but from the enduring power of our ideals: democracy, liberty, opportunity and unyielding hope. (Applause)

That's the true genius of America: that America can change. Our union can be perfected. What we've already achieved gives us hope for what we can and must achieve tomorrow.

This election had many firsts and many stories that will be told for generations. But one that's on my mind tonight's about a woman who cast her ballot in Atlanta. She's a lot like the millions of others who stood in line to make their voice heard in this election except for one thing: Ann Nixon Cooper is 106 years old. (Applause)

She was born just a generation past slavery; a time when there were no cars on the road or planes in the sky; when someone like her couldn't vote for two reasons—because she was a woman and because of the color of her skin. And tonight, I think about all that she's seen throughout her century in America—the heartache and the hope; the struggle and the progress; the times we were told that we can't, and the people who pressed on with that American creed: Yes we can. At a time when women's voices were silenced and their hopes dismissed, she lived to see them stand up and speak out and reach for the ballot. Yes we can. When there was despair in the dust bowl and depression across the land, she saw a nation conquer fear itself with a New Deal, new jobs, a new sense of common purpose. Yes we can.

AUDIENCE: Yes we can.

OBAMA: When the bombs fell on our harbor and tyranny threatened the world, she was there to witness a generation rise to greatness and a democracy was saved. Yes we can.

AUDIENCE: Yes we can.

OBAMA: She was there for the buses in Montgomery, the hoses in Birmingham, a bridge in Selma, and a preacher from Atlanta who told a people that "We Shall Overcome." Yes we can.

AUDIENCE: Yes we can.

OBAMA: A man touched down on the moon, a wall came down in Berlin, a world was connected by our own science and imagination.

And this year, in this election, she touched her finger to a screen, and cast her vote, because after 106 years in America, through the best of times and the darkest of hours, she knows how America can change.

Yes we can.

AUDIENCE: Yes we can.

OBAMA: America, we have come so far. We have seen so much. But there is so much more to do. So tonight, let us ask ourselves—if our children should live to see the next century; if my daughters should be so lucky to live as long as Ann Nixon Cooper, what change will they see? What progress will we have made?

This is our chance to answer that call. This is our moment.

This is our time, to put our people back to work and open doors of opportunity for our kids; to restore prosperity and promote the cause of peace; to reclaim the American dream and reaffirm that fundamental truth, that, out of many, we are one; that while we breathe, we hope. And where we are met with cynicism and doubts and those who tell us that we can't, we will respond with that timeless creed that sums up the spirit of a people: Yes, we can. (Applause)

Thank you. God bless you. And may God bless the United States of America. (Applause)

DOVER · THRIFT · EDITIONS

POETRY

LA VITA NUOVA, Dante Alighieri. 56pp. 0-486-41915-0

101 GREAT AMERICAN POEMS, The American Poetry & Literacy Project (ed.). (Available in U.S. only.) 96pp. 0-486-40158-8

ENGLISH ROMANTIC POETRY: An Anthology, Stanley Appelbaum (ed.). 256pp. 0-486-29282-7

BHAGAVADGITA, Bhagavadgita. 112pp. 0-486-27782-8

THE BOOK OF PSALMS, King James Bible. 128pp. 0-486-27541-8

IMAGIST POETRY: AN ANTHOLOGY, Bob Blaisdell (ed.). 176pp. (Available in U.S. only.) 0-486-40875-2

BLAKE'S SELECTED POEMS, William Blake. 96pp. 0-486-28517-0

SONGS OF INNOCENCE AND SONGS OF EXPERIENCE, William Blake. 64pp. 0-486-27051-3

THE CLASSIC TRADITION OF HAIKU: An Anthology, Faubion Bowers (ed.). 96pp. 0-486-29274-6

TO MY HUSBAND AND OTHER POEMS, Anne Bradstreet (Robert Hutchinson, ed.). 80pp. 0-486-41408-6

BEST POEMS OF THE BRONTË SISTERS (ed. by Candace Ward), Emily, Anne, and Charlotte Brontë. 64pp. 0-486-29529-X

SONNETS FROM THE PORTUGUESE AND OTHER POEMS, Elizabeth Barrett Browning. 64pp. 0-486-27052-1

MY LAST DUCHESS AND OTHER POEMS, Robert Browning. 128pp. 0-486-27783-6

POEMS AND SONGS, Robert Burns. 96pp. 0-486-26863-2

SELECTED POEMS, George Gordon, Lord Byron. 112pp. 0-486-27784-4

JABBERWOCKY AND OTHER POEMS, Lewis Carroll. 64pp. 0-486-41582-1

SELECTED CANTERBURY TALES, Geoffrey Chaucer. 144pp. 0-486-28241-4

THE RIME OF THE ANCIENT MARINER AND OTHER POEMS, Samuel Taylor Coleridge. 80pp. 0-486-27266-4

THE CAVALIER POETS: An Anthology, Thomas Crofts (ed.). 80pp. 0-486-28766-1

SELECTED POEMS, Emily Dickinson. 64pp. 0-486-26466-1

SELECTED POEMS, John Donne. 96pp. 0-486-27788-7

SELECTED POEMS, Paul Laurence Dunbar. 80pp. 0-486-29980-5

"THE WASTE LAND" AND OTHER POEMS, T. S. Eliot. 64pp. (Available in U.S. only.) 0-486-40061-1

THE RUBÁIYÁT OF OMAR KHAYYÁM: FIRST AND FIFTH EDITIONS, Edward FitzGerald. 64pp. 0-486-26467-X

A BOY'S WILL AND NORTH OF BOSTON, Robert Frost. 112pp. (Available in U.S. only.) 0-486-26866-7

THE ROAD NOT TAKEN AND OTHER POEMS, Robert Frost. 64pp. (Available in U.S. only.) 0-486-27550-7

THE GARDEN OF HEAVEN: POEMS OF HAFIZ, Hafiz. 112pp. 0-486-43161-4

HARDY'S SELECTED POEMS, Thomas Hardy. 80pp. 0-486-28753-X

A SHROPSHIRE LAD, A. E. Housman. 64pp. 0-486-26468-8

LYRIC POEMS, John Keats. 80pp. 0-486-26871-3

GUNGA DIN AND OTHER FAVORITE POEMS, Rudyard Kipling. 80pp. 0-486-26471-8

SNAKE AND OTHER POEMS, D. H. Lawrence. 64pp. 0-486-40647-4

DOVER · THRIFT · EDITIONS

POETRY

THE CONGO AND OTHER POEMS, Vachel Lindsay. 96pp. 0-486-27272-9

EVANGELINE AND OTHER POEMS, Henry Wadsworth Longfellow. 64pp. 0-486-28255-4

FAVORITE POEMS, Henry Wadsworth Longfellow. 96pp. 0-486-27273-7

"TO HIS COY MISTRESS" AND OTHER POEMS, Andrew Marvell. 64pp. 0-486-29544-3

SPOON RIVER ANTHOLOGY, Edgar Lee Masters. 144pp. 0-486-27275-3

SELECTED POEMS, Claude McKay. 80pp. 0-486-40876-0

RENASCENCE AND OTHER POEMS, Edna St. Vincent Millay. 64pp. (Not available in Europe or the United Kingdom) 0-486-26873-X

SELECTED POEMS, John Milton. 128pp. 0-486-27554-X

CIVIL WAR POETRY: An Anthology, Paul Negri (ed.). 128pp. 0-486-29883-3

ENGLISH VICTORIAN POETRY: AN ANTHOLOGY, Paul Negri (ed.). 256pp. 0-486-40425-0

GREAT SONNETS, Paul Negri (ed.). 96pp. 0-486-28052-7

THE RAVEN AND OTHER FAVORITE POEMS, Edgar Allan Poe. 64pp. 0-486-26685-0

ESSAY ON MAN AND OTHER POEMS, Alexander Pope. 128pp. 0-486-28053-5

EARLY POEMS, Ezra Pound. 80pp. (Available in U.S. only.) 0-486-28745-9

GREAT POEMS BY AMERICAN WOMEN: An Anthology, Susan L. Rattiner (ed.). 224pp. (Available in U.S. only.) 0-486-40164-2

GOBLIN MARKET AND OTHER POEMS, Christina Rossetti. 64pp. 0-486-28055-1

CHICAGO POEMS, Carl Sandburg. 80pp. 0-486-28057-8

CORNHUSKERS, Carl Sandburg. 157pp. 0-486-41409-4

COMPLETE SONNETS, William Shakespeare. 80pp. 0-486-26686-9

SELECTED POEMS, Percy Bysshe Shelley. 128pp. 0-486-27558-2

AFRICAN-AMERICAN POETRY: An Anthology, 1773–1930, Joan R. Sherman (ed.). 96pp. 0-486-29604-0

100 BEST-LOVED POEMS, Philip Smith (ed.). 96pp. 0-486-28553-7

NATIVE AMERICAN SONGS AND POEMS: An Anthology, Brian Swann (ed.). 64pp. 0-486-29450-1

SELECTED POEMS, Alfred Lord Tennyson. 112pp. 0-486-27282-6

AENEID, Vergil (Publius Vergilius Maro). 256pp. 0-486-28749-1

CHRISTMAS CAROLS: COMPLETE VERSES, Shane Weller (ed.). 64pp. 0-486-27397-0

GREAT LOVE POEMS, Shane Weller (ed.). 128pp. 0-486-27284-2

CIVIL WAR POETRY AND PROSE, Walt Whitman. 96pp. 0-486-28507-3

SELECTED POEMS, Walt Whitman. 128pp. 0-486-26878-0

THE BALLAD OF READING GAOL AND OTHER POEMS, Oscar Wilde. 64pp. 0-486-27072-6

EARLY POEMS, William Carlos Williams. 64pp. (Available in U.S. only.) 0-486-29294-0

FAVORITE POEMS, William Wordsworth. 80pp. 0-486-27073-4

WORLD WAR ONE BRITISH POETS: Brooke, Owen, Sassoon, Rosenberg, and Others, Candace Ward (ed.). (Available in U.S. only.) 0-486-29568-0

EARLY POEMS, William Butler Yeats. 128pp. 0-486-27808-5

"EASTER, 1916" AND OTHER POEMS, William Butler Yeats. 80pp. (Not available in Europe or United Kingdom.) 0-486-29771-3

DOVER · THRIFT · EDITIONS

FICTION

FLATLAND: A ROMANCE OF MANY DIMENSIONS, Edwin A. Abbott. 96pp. 0-486-27263-X

SHORT STORIES, Louisa May Alcott. 64pp. 0-486-29063-8

WINESBURG, OHIO, Sherwood Anderson. 160pp. 0-486-28269-4

PERSUASION, Jane Austen. 224pp. 0-486-29555-9

PRIDE AND PREJUDICE, Jane Austen. 272pp. 0-486-28473-5

SENSE AND SENSIBILITY, Jane Austen. 272pp. 0-486-29049-2

LOOKING BACKWARD, Edward Bellamy. 160pp. 0-486-29038-7

BEOWULF, Beowulf (trans. by R. K. Gordon). 64pp. 0-486-27264-8

CIVIL WAR STORIES, Ambrose Bierce. 128pp. 0-486-28038-1

WUTHERING HEIGHTS, Emily Brontë. 256pp. 0-486-29256-8

THE THIRTY-NINE STEPS, John Buchan. 96pp. 0-486-28201-5

TARZAN OF THE APES, Edgar Rice Burroughs. 224pp. (Not available in Europe or United Kingdom.) 0-486-29570-2

ALICE'S ADVENTURES IN WONDERLAND, Lewis Carroll. 96pp. 0-486-27543-4

THROUGH THE LOOKING-GLASS, Lewis Carroll. 128pp. 0-486-40878-7

MY ÁNTONIA, Willa Cather. 176pp. 0-486-28240-6

O PIONEERS!, Willa Cather. 128pp. 0-486-27785-2

FIVE GREAT SHORT STORIES, Anton Chekhov. 96pp. 0-486-26463-7

TALES OF CONJURE AND THE COLOR LINE, Charles Waddell Chesnutt. 128pp. 0-486-40426-9

FAVORITE FATHER BROWN STORIES, G. K. Chesterton. 96pp. 0-486-27545-0

THE AWAKENING, Kate Chopin. 128pp. 0-486-27786-0

A PAIR OF SILK STOCKINGS AND OTHER STORIES, Kate Chopin. 64pp. 0-486-29264-9

HEART OF DARKNESS, Joseph Conrad. 80pp. 0-486-26464-5

LORD JIM, Joseph Conrad. 256pp. 0-486-40650-4

THE SECRET SHARER AND OTHER STORIES, Joseph Conrad. 128pp. 0-486-27546-9

THE "LITTLE REGIMENT" AND OTHER CIVIL WAR STORIES, Stephen Crane. 80pp. 0-486-29557-5

THE OPEN BOAT AND OTHER STORIES, Stephen Crane. 128pp. 0-486-27547-7

THE RED BADGE OF COURAGE, Stephen Crane. 112pp. 0-486-26465-3

MOLL FLANDERS, Daniel Defoe. 256pp. 0-486-29093-X

ROBINSON CRUSOE, Daniel Defoe. 288pp. 0-486-40427-7

A CHRISTMAS CAROL, Charles Dickens. 80pp. 0-486-26865-9

THE CRICKET ON THE HEARTH AND OTHER CHRISTMAS STORIES, Charles Dickens. 128pp. 0-486-28039-X

A TALE OF TWO CITIES, Charles Dickens. 304pp. 0-486-40651-2

THE DOUBLE, Fyodor Dostoyevsky. 128pp. 0-486-29572-9

THE GAMBLER, Fyodor Dostoyevsky. 112pp. 0-486-29081-6

NOTES FROM THE UNDERGROUND, Fyodor Dostoyevsky. 96pp. 0-486-27053-X

THE ADVENTURE OF THE DANCING MEN AND OTHER STORIES, Sir Arthur Conan Doyle. 80pp. 0-486-29558-3

THE HOUND OF THE BASKERVILLES, Arthur Conan Doyle. 128pp. 0-486-28214-7

THE LOST WORLD, Arthur Conan Doyle. 176pp. 0-486-40060-3

DOVER · THRIFT · EDITIONS

FICTION

A JOURNAL OF THE PLAGUE YEAR, Daniel Defoe. 192pp. 0-486-41919-3

SIX GREAT SHERLOCK HOLMES STORIES, Sir Arthur Conan Doyle. 112pp. 0-486-27055-6

SHORT STORIES, Theodore Dreiser. 112pp. 0-486-28215-5

SILAS MARNER, George Eliot. 160pp. 0-486-29246-0

JOSEPH ANDREWS, Henry Fielding. 288pp. 0-486-41588-0

THIS SIDE OF PARADISE, F. Scott Fitzgerald. 208pp. 0-486-28999-0

"THE DIAMOND AS BIG AS THE RITZ" AND OTHER STORIES, F. Scott Fitzgerald. 0-486-29991-0

MADAME BOVARY, Gustave Flaubert. 256pp. 0-486-29257-6

THE REVOLT OF "MOTHER" AND OTHER STORIES, Mary E. Wilkins Freeman. 128pp. 0-486-40428-5

A ROOM WITH A VIEW, E. M. Forster. 176pp. (Available in U.S. only.) 0-486-28467-0

WHERE ANGELS FEAR TO TREAD, E. M. Forster. 128pp. (Available in U.S. only.) 0-486-27791-7

THE IMMORALIST, André Gide. 112pp. (Available in U.S. only.) 0-486-29237-1

HERLAND, Charlotte Perkins Gilman. 128pp. 0-486-40429-3

"THE YELLOW WALLPAPER" AND OTHER STORIES, Charlotte Perkins Gilman. 80pp. 0-486-29857-4

THE OVERCOAT AND OTHER STORIES, Nikolai Gogol. 112pp. 0-486-27057-2

CHELKASH AND OTHER STORIES, Maxim Gorky. 64pp. 0-486-40652-0

GREAT GHOST STORIES, John Grafton (ed.). 112pp. 0-486-27270-2

DETECTION BY GASLIGHT, Douglas G. Greene (ed.). 272pp. 0-486-29928-7

THE MABINOGION, Lady Charlotte E. Guest. 192pp. 0-486-29541-9

"THE FIDDLER OF THE REELS" AND OTHER SHORT STORIES, Thomas Hardy. 80pp. 0-486-29960-0

THE LUCK OF ROARING CAMP AND OTHER STORIES, Bret Harte. 96pp. 0-486-27271-0

THE HOUSE OF THE SEVEN GABLES, Nathaniel Hawthorne. 272pp. 0-486-40882-5

THE SCARLET LETTER, Nathaniel Hawthorne. 192pp. 0-486-28048-9

YOUNG GOODMAN BROWN AND OTHER STORIES, Nathaniel Hawthorne. 128pp. 0-486-27060-2

THE GIFT OF THE MAGI AND OTHER SHORT STORIES, O. Henry. 96pp. 0-486-27061-0

THE ASPERN PAPERS, Henry James. 112pp. 0-486-41922-3

THE BEAST IN THE JUNGLE AND OTHER STORIES, Henry James. 128pp. 0-486-27552-3

DAISY MILLER, Henry James. 64pp. 0-486-28773-4

THE TURN OF THE SCREW, Henry James. 96pp. 0-486-26684-2

WASHINGTON SQUARE, Henry James. 176pp. 0-486-40431-5

THE COUNTRY OF THE POINTED FIRS, Sarah Orne Jewett. 96pp. 0-486-28196-5

THE AUTOBIOGRAPHY OF AN EX-COLORED MAN, James Weldon Johnson. 112pp. 0-486-28512-X

DUBLINERS, James Joyce. 160pp. 0-486-26870-5

A PORTRAIT OF THE ARTIST AS A YOUNG MAN, James Joyce. 192pp. 0-486-28050-0

THE METAMORPHOSIS AND OTHER STORIES, Franz Kafka. 96pp. 0-486-29030-1

THE MAN WHO WOULD BE KING AND OTHER STORIES, Rudyard Kipling. 128pp. 0-486-28051-9

YOU KNOW ME AL, Ring Lardner. 128pp. 0-486-28513-8

SELECTED SHORT STORIES, D. H. Lawrence. 128pp. 0-486-27794-1

THE CALL OF THE WILD, Jack London. 64pp. 0-486-26472-6

FIVE GREAT SHORT STORIES, Jack London. 96pp. 0-486-27063-7

THE SEA-WOLF, Jack London. 248pp. 0-486-41108-7

WHITE FANG, Jack London. 160pp. 0-486-26968-X

DEATH IN VENICE, Thomas Mann. 96pp. (Available in U.S. only.) 0-486-28714-9

THE NECKLACE AND OTHER SHORT STORIES, Guy de Maupassant. 128pp. 0-486-27064-5